*Studies of the New Testament and Its World*

EDITED BY JOHN RICHES

# THE END OF THE AGES
# HAS COME

TO MY PARENTS

'Words, after speech,
reach into the silence.'

T. S. Eliot, *Burnt Norton*

# The End of the Ages Has Come

An Early Interpretation of the Passion
and Resurrection of Jesus

*by*
DALE C. ALLISON, JR.

T. & T. CLARK
59 GEORGE STREET
EDINBURGH

Biblical quotations, unless otherwise noted, are from the Revised
Standard Version of the Bible, copyright 1946, 1952, © 1971, 1973 by
the Division of Christian Education of the National Council of the
Churches of Christ in the U.S.A. and are used by permission.

Printed in the U.K. by Billing & Sons, Worcester,
bound by Hunter & Foulis Ltd., Edinburgh,

for

T. & T. CLARK LTD., EDINBURGH.

First printed in the U.K. 1987.

British Library Cataloguing in Publication Data
Allison, Dale C.
The End of the ages has come: an early
interpretation of the Passion and
Resurrection of Jesus.—(Studies in the
New Testament and its world)
1. Jesus Christ—Crucifixion—Biblical teaching.
2. Jesus Christ—Resurrection—Biblical teaching.
I. Title  II. Series
232.9'6    BT450
ISBN 0-567-09447-2

# CONTENTS

# PREFACE

This book is based upon my Ph.D. Thesis, which was accepted by Duke University in the summer of 1982. For the purposes of this publication, I have abbreviated portions of the text, omitted or shortened many of the footnotes, and eliminated a lengthy bibliography. I trust that the result is not excessive laconism but easier reading and a concentration upon the truly pertinent issues.

I must thank those who served on my doctoral committee at Duke: James H. Charlesworth, James L. Price, D. Moody Smith, and Franklin W. Young. This book bears the marks of their insightful criticisms. Above all, I am grateful for having had the opportunity to study under W. D. Davies, now of Texas Christian University. He directed my efforts to produce a dissertation, and his generosity, wise counsels, and interest in me and my work I shall never forget. My debt to David Winston Suter, my undergraduate instructor at Wichita State University, must also be recorded. He first introduced me to the world of the apocalypses, and the seed for this book was planted in an essay I wrote for him my senior year. To my ever-supportive wife, Kristine, I am especially beholden. In addition to all her other duties, she has, over the past few years, unselfishly offered her secretarial skills for my disposal. At Fortress Press, Norman A. Hjelm and John A. Hollar proved a pleasure to work with. Lastly, I dedicate this book to my parents.

# ABBREVIATIONS

| | |
|---|---|
| AB | Anchor Bible |
| *Adv. haer.* | Irenaeus, *Adversus haereses* [*Against Heresies*] |
| AGJU | Arbeiten zur Geschichte des antiken Judentums und des Urchristentums |
| *ANF* | Alexander Roberts and James Donaldson, eds., *The Ante-Nicene Fathers: Translations of the Writings of the Fathers down to* A.D. *325* (reprint, Grand Rapids: Wm. B. Eerdmans, 1978) |
| ANTJ | Arbeiten zum Neuen Testament und Judentum |
| *Apoc.* | *Apocalypse of* (*Moses, Zephaniah,* etc.) |
| *Apoc. Ab.* | *Apocalypse of Abraham,* trans. G. H. Box (London: SPCK, 1918) |
| *APOT* | R. H. Charles, ed., *The Apocrypha and Pseudepigrapha of the Old Testament* (Oxford: At the Clarendon Press, 1913) |
| *As. Mos.* | *Assumption* (or *Testament*) *of Moses* |
| *b.* | Tractates in the Babylonian Talmud (*Baba Meṣiʿa, Baba Batra, Ketubot, Megilla, Šabbat, Sanhedrin, Sukka, Yoma, Zebaḥim,* etc.) |
| BETL | Bibliotheca ephemeridum theologicarum lovaniensium |
| *Bib* | *Biblica* |
| *Bib. Ant.* | Ps.-Philo. *Biblical Antiquities* |
| *BJRL* | *Bulletin of the John Rylands Library* |
| *BR* | *Biblical Research* |
| BU | Biblische Untersuchungen |
| *BZ* | *Biblische Zeitschrift* |
| *CBQ* | *Catholic Biblical Quarterly* |
| CBQMS | Catholic Biblical Quarterly Monograph Series |
| CD | Cairo (Genizah text of the) Damascus (Document) |
| *CTM* | *Concordia Theological Monthly* |
| EKKNT | Evangelisch-katholischer Kommentar zum Neuen Testament |

| Ep. Arist. | *Epistle of Aristeas* |
| ETL | *Ephemerides theologicae lovanienses* |
| EvT | *Evangelische Theologie* |
| FRLANT | Forschungen zur Religion und Literatur des Alten und Neuen Testaments |
| Gos. | *Gospel of (Peter, Thomas,* etc.) |
| HNT | Handbuch zum Neuen Testament |
| HNTC | Harper's New Testament Commentaries |
| HSM | Harvard Semitic Monographs |
| HTKNT | Herders Theologischer Kommentar zum Neuen Testament |
| HTR | *Harvard Theological Review* |
| HTS | Harvard Theological Studies |
| HUCA | *Hebrew Union College Annual* |
| IBS | *Irish Biblical Studies* |
| Ign. Magn. | Ignatius, *Letter to the Magnesians* |
| JAAR | *Journal of the American Academy of Religion* |
| JBL | *Journal of Biblical Literature* |
| JBLMS | Journal of Biblical Literature Monograph Series |
| JJS | *Journal of Jewish Studies* |
| Jos. Ant. | Josephus' *Antiquities* |
| JSNT | *Journal for the Study of the New Testament* |
| JTS | *Journal of Theological Studies* |
| LD | Lectio divina |
| Liv. Pro. | *Lives of the Prophets* (Daniel, Habakkuk, etc.) |
| LXX | Septuagint |
| m. | Tractates in the Mishna (*Soṭa, Sukka,* etc.) |
| Mek. | *Mekilta* |
| MeyerK | H. A. W. Meyer, Kritisch-exegetischer Kommentar über das Neue Testament |
| Midr. | *Midraš* (Psalms, Genesis, etc.) |
| MT | Masoretic Text |
| NCB | New Century Bible |
| NIGTC | New International Greek Testament Commentary |
| NovT | *Novum Testamentum* |
| NovTSup | Novum Testamentum, Supplements |
| NTS | *New Testament Studies* |
| OBO | Orbis biblicus et orientalis |
| Pss.-Clem. Rec. | *Pseudo-Clementine Recognitions* |
| Pss. Sol. | *Psalms of Solomon* |

| | |
|---|---|
| Q | Qumran texts (numbered by cave) |
| 1QH | *Hôdāyôt* (*Thanksgiving Hymns*) |
| 1QM | *Milhāmāh* (*War Scroll*) |
| 1QS | *Serek hayyahad* (*Rule of the Community, Manual of Discipline*) |
| 1QSa | Appendix A to 1QS (*Rule of the Congregation*) |
| 1QSb | Appendix B to 1QS (*Blessings*) |
| 4QFlor | *Florilegium* (or *Eschatological Midrashim*) |
| RelSRev | *Religious Studies Review* |
| RevThom | *Revue thomiste* |
| RNT | Regensburger Neues Testament |
| SB | H. Strack and P. Billerbeck, *Kommentar zum Neuen Testament aus Talmud und Midrash* (Munich: C. H. Beck, 1926–63) |
| SBLDS | Society of Biblical Literature Dissertation Series |
| SBS | Stuttgarter Bibelstudien |
| SBT | Studies in Biblical Theology |
| SCS | Septuagint and Cognate Studies |
| Sib. Or. | *Sibylline Oracles* |
| SJT | *Scottish Journal of Theology* |
| SNTSMS | Society for New Testament Studies Monograph Series |
| SPB | Studia postbiblica |
| Spec. Leg. | Philo, *De specialibus legibus* [*On the Special Laws*] |
| SUNT | Studien zur Umwelt des Neuen Testament |
| T. | *Testament of* (*Adam, Daniel, Job, Levi,* etc.) |
| TDNT | G. Kittel and G. Friedrich, eds., *Theological Dictionary of the New Testament,* trans. G. W. Bromiley (Grand Rapids: Wm. B. Eerdmans, 1964–74) |
| TDOT | G. J. Botterweck and H. Ginggren, eds., *Theological Dictionary of the Old Testament,* trans. J. T. Willis (Grand Rapids: Wm. B. Eerdmans, 1974–78) |
| TEH | Theologische Existenz heute |
| TF | *Theologische Forschung* |
| Tg. | Targumic materials (Isaiah, Zechariah, Obadiah, etc.) |
| TLZ | *Theologische Literaturzeitung* |
| TS | *Theological Studies* |
| TZ | *Theologische Zeitschrift* |
| UUA | Uppsala universitetsårsskrift |
| y. | Tractates in the Jerusalem Talmud (*Ta'anit,* etc.) |
| ZNW | *Zeitschrift für die neutestamentliche Wissenschaft* |

# One

# INTRODUCTION

In his book on *The Apostolic Preaching and Its Developments*, C. H. Dodd sought to lay bare the contours of the oldest kerygma, the proclamation of the primitive church.[1] By means of a comparison of the Pauline epistles and the Acts of the Apostles, he concluded that the primitive preaching was characterized above all by what he called "realized eschatology." The Pauline kerygma and the pre-Lukan kerygma of Acts have in common this announcement: "The great divine event, the eschaton, has already entered history." That is, "the decisive thing has already happened. The prophecies are fulfilled; God has shown his 'mighty works'; the Messiah has come; he has been exalted to the right hand of God; he has given the Spirit which according to the prophets should come 'in the last days.' . . . The unprecedented has happened: God has visited and redeemed his people. . . . The Day of the Lord has dawned: the age to come has begun."[2]

If one be asked to account for the content of the primitive preaching, for the genesis of "realized eschatology," Jewish precedent—according to Dodd—offers little aid, for the kerygma "differed from all earlier prophecy and apocalypse in declaring that the eschatological process was already in being." An answer does, however, arise in the Gospels, according to which Jesus announced that "the kingdom of God has come upon you" (Luke 11:20). On Dodd's reading of the evidence, "the primitive *kerygma* arises directly out of the teaching of Jesus about the kingdom of God and all that hangs upon it." If the story of Jesus was told as a "realized apocalypse," this is because Jesus himself so interpreted his own ministry. The "realized eschatology" of the post-Easter period thus marks a line of continuity with the "realized eschatology" of the pre-Easter period.[3]

Since its publication in 1937, *The Apostolic Preaching* has been widely read.

1. C. H. Dodd, *The Apostolic Preaching and Its Developments: Three Lectures,* intro. by Ernest F. Scott (Chicago: Willet, Clark & Co., 1937).
2. Ibid., 44, 45, 47, and 11, respectively.
3. Ibid., 53, 125, and 148, respectively.

1

Notwithstanding heavy criticism, it has proven to be of far-reaching influence. Yet, oddly enough, the book has stimulated little inquiry into the difficult question, How does one account for the "realized eschatology" of the post-Easter period? Discussion has usually focused upon the question of whether the newly born faith evolved toward or away from a "realized eschatology." Some, most notably T. Francis Glasson and John A. T. Robinson, have argued that the expectation of a second advent was a secondary development.[4] Others have argued just the opposite: the prospect of an impending Parousia was pivotal for the earliest church.[5] It is our opinion, and one for which we shall argue later, that the presupposition of a one-directional development is simplistic. We concur with Werner Georg Kümmel:

> The oldest recognizable tradition of the preaching of Jesus and of the earliest Christian community, and the concept of faith that Paul took over and thought through theologically, all point in the same way to a combination of beliefs: on the one hand, the expectation of the imminent coming of the eschatological fulfilment of salvation and, on the other hand, the beginning of this fulfilment in God's action in Jesus Christ. . . . For this reason there is no sense in claiming that in the very beginning of primitive Christianity in the period between Jesus and Paul . . . there arose a development from a purely present-realized eschatology to a futuristic eschatology which was an extension of Jewish apocalyptic. It is equally impossible to substantiate the assumption that the earliest Christianity looked only to the near future, and that only gradually and as a parallel development there came about a consciousness of the presence of the eschaton.[6]

Assuming for the moment the correctness of this conclusion, we are still confronted by the question, How does one explain the texts that seemingly announce or presuppose the arrival of the long-awaited Day of the Lord? Does it suffice to draw a line between the pre- and post-Easter periods and contend that at this point the preaching of the church simply continued the preaching of Jesus? Was Dodd right in thinking that there was no precedent in Judaism for the New Testament's proclamation of fulfillment?

This book attempts to answer these questions. Its thesis is that Dodd was correct to relate the church's announcement of fulfillment to the pre-Paschal period but wrong in thinking that its impulse came from Jesus' announcement

---

4. T. Francis Glasson, *The Second Advent: The Origin of a New Testament Doctrine*, 3d ed. (London: Epworth Press, 1963); and John A. T. Robinson, *Jesus and His Coming*, 2d ed. (Philadelphia: Westminster Press, 1979).

5. Thus, Ferdinand Hahn, *The Titles of Jesus in Christology: Their History in Early Christianity*, trans. Harold Knight and George Ogg (Cleveland: World Pub. Co., 1969); and Heinz Eduard Tödt, *The Son of Man in the Synoptic Tradition*, New Testament Library, trans. Dorothea M. Barton (Philadelphia: Westminster Press, 1965).

6. Werner Georg Kümmel, "Futuristic and Realized Eschatology in the Earliest Stages of Christianity," *Journal of Religion* 43 (1963): 311.

that the kingdom of God had come. On the contrary, the "realized eschatology" of the early communities was parented first by Jesus' words about outstanding eschatological events. Jesus hoped that the great denouement might be near and interpreted his prospective fate as part of the approaching eschatological transition. He announced that the tribulation of the last days had set in, that the resurrection of the dead was just around the corner, and that he himself would meet his end in the one and know vindication in the other. When, therefore, he suffered and died and was seen again alive, his disciples naturally interpreted his fate in the categories at hand: Jesus had suffered and died in the great tribulation, and his resurrection betokened the onset of the general resurrection of the dead. The eschatological process was believed to have begun because certain eschatological promises had seemingly been fulfilled.

The argument, reduced to its bare minimum, will move as follows. First, it will be shown that the New Testament contains texts in which the death of Jesus is interpreted as belonging to the great tribulation and in which his resurrection is set forth as marking the onset of the general resurrection of the dead. Second, it will be argued that previous discussions of "realized eschatology" do not satisfactorily account for these texts. For one reason or another, the phenomenon under review has not yet received satisfactory treatment. Third, it will be established that Jesus anticipated for himself both death and resurrection and understood these two prospects to be defined by the eschatological sequence of tribulation—vindication. Fourth, it will be urged that the church's interpretation of Jesus' fate as inaugurating the eschatological turning point was almost inevitable, given the pre-Easter eschatological expectations of Jesus and his disciples. The fate of the master was such that it could be seen to mark the beginning of the fulfillment of his prophecies concerning the future. In arguing this last point, we will direct attention toward messianic movements in which promise has dictated fulfillment, that is, in which eschatological prophecies, even if unrealized, have continued to supply the categories for interpreting history. This book thus concerns a point of continuity between the pre- and post-Easter periods and attempts evaluation by reference to the problem of promise and fulfillment in messianic movements in general.

Before proceeding to the New Testament, however, an examination of certain aspects of Jewish eschatology is requisite. Of particular importance for our purposes is the expectation of a great tribulation, for our work centers around two themes of eschatology: the trials of the latter days and the general resurrection of the dead. The former, unlike the latter, has rarely received more than passing treatment. Moreover, and as we shall show, the closest parallels in Jewish sources to the New Testament's "realized eschatology" only come to light when one understands the various uses made of the idea of an eschatological tribulation.

# *Two*

# THE GREAT TRIBULATION
# IN JEWISH LITERATURE

Many of the ancient Jewish texts that foretell the end of the present world order also announce the coming of a great tribulation, a final time of trouble that is to mark the transition between this age and the messianic age or the age to come. The stereotyped descriptions of this catastrophic period which culminates in the final judgment are well known. Before the redemption there will be earthquakes.[1] Famine will ravage the land.[2] Wars will wage.[3] Friends will turn against one another.[4] There will be signs in the heavens.[5] The regular recurrence of these and similar portents in the literature is striking: the many descriptions of the final terror and tribulation are very close indeed. Yet this must not lead one to suppose that the expectation of a final catastrophe was strictly well defined. On the contrary, a critical review of the relevant materials reveals a variety of interpretations. In some documents, for example, the woes encompass the sufferings of an author's own time, while in others they are yet to come. And while in some documents the righteous are not spared the pains of the end, in others they are miraculously preserved, and it is the wicked alone who suffer affliction. Again, while in some documents the time of trouble is dwelt upon and described at length, in others it is an acknowledged yet subsidiary doctrine drawing only brief notice, or even conspicuously absent altogether. Thus, the idea of a great tribulation heralding the eschatological age was flexible, and different writers have bent it in their own interests. It would seem, then, that careful attention to treatment of this expectation in Jewish literature might lead to certain insights concerning the

---

1. *As. Mos.* 10:4; *T. Levi* 4:1; *4 Ezra* 9:3; *2 Apoc. Bar.* 27:7; *Apoc. Ab.* 30. Cf. Mark 13:8.

2. *4 Ezra* 6:22; *2 Apoc. Bar.* 27:6; 70:8; *Apoc. Ab.* 30; *b. Sanh.* 97a. Cf. Mark 13:8; also Rev. 6:8 and 18:8.

3. *1 Enoch* 90; *4 Ezra* 9:3; *2 Apoc. Bar.* 27:4; 48:32, 37; 70:3, 6, 8; *b. Sanh.* 97a, b; *b Meg.* 17b. Cf. Mark 13:8 and Rev 6:4.

4. *Jub.* 23:16; *1 Enoch* 100:1-2; 56:7; *4 Ezra* 6:24; *2 Apoc. Bar.* 70:3-7; *m. Soṭa* 9:15; *b. Sanh.* 97a.

5. *Sib. Or.* III, 796-808; *1 Enoch* 80:4-6; *As. Mos.* 10:5-6; *4 Ezra* 5:4, 5; *b. Sanh.* 99a.

particular situations that lie behind various documents. Such attention will in any case supply the necessary background against which to understand the early church's use of the doctrine of the "messianic woes" (*ḥeblô šel māšîḥa*).[6] We begin with a question:

## When Will the Great Tribulation Come?

According to John J. Collins, the great tribulation is usually, in the Pseudepigrapha, an impending but still future affair. He writes:

> [An] accurate generalization of apocalyptic patterns might say that the final judgment is preceded by a time of great distress, which may on occasion contain a historical description of the time of the author, but most often is future prediction, either entirely or in part.[7]

H. H. Rowley, on the other hand, was of the opinion that

> more often it would seem that . . . [an author] was living in an evil age, and believed it to be the final fling of evil. He depicted the conditions he saw around him, but in a cosmic setting, viewed not merely as a local affair, but as something of universal significance, and accompanied by supernatural signs as the fitting expression of his sense of its importance. . . . [The writers of the apocalypses] believed that they were engaged in a final struggle, that they were suffering the last great persecution, that never before had evil been so evil, and never again could it so raise its head, for its final destruction was nigh.[8]

The difference of viewpoint between Collins and Rowley is illuminating. It arises first from the ambiguity of the data. Descriptions of the great tribulation are sometimes so brief or so thoroughly stereotyped that one cannot determine whether the picture painted is an exaggerated representation of the evil pres-

---

6. According to J. Christiaan Beker, *Paul the Apostle: The Triumph of God in Life and Thought* (Philadelphia: Fortress Press, 1980), 146, "the Jewish doctrine of the messianic woes" is a "concept not documented in Jewish literature until A.D. 135." This statement, asserted without primary or secondary documentation, is rather baffling. The technical term, *ḥeblô šel māšîḥa*, does not certainly occur until the second century (although in *b. Sanh.* 98b and *Mek.* on Exod. 16:25 the term is found on the lips of Eliezer, perhaps ben Hyrcanus [ca. 90]). But, as the sources cited in this chapter attest, the concept of a time of trouble that would precede the decisive coming of God or the advent of the Messiah was firmly established long before the second century A.D. Further, as Mark 13:8 probably shows, *ōdin* with reference to the great tribulation was already a technical term in the first century—even though *ōdinōn* (Mark 13:8) is plural, *ḥeblô* (Hebrew) and *ḥeblêh* (Aramaic) singular. Note also *1 Enoch* 62:4; 1 Thess. 5:3; and Rev. 12:2–5. In the Old Testament the coming of "the Day of the Lord" is already associated with the pangs of birth; see Isa. 13:8; 25:17–18; 66:7–8; Jer. 22:23; 30:5–6; 48:41; Hos. 13:13; Mic. 4:9–10; 5:1(2).

7. John J. Collins, "The Date and Provenance of the Testament of Moses," in *Studies on the Testament of Moses: Seminar Papers*, ed. G. W. E. Nickelsburg, SCS 4 (Cambridge, Mass.: Society of Biblical Literature, 1973), 20.

8. H. H. Rowley, *The Relevance of Apocalyptic: A Study of Jewish and Christian Apocalypses from Daniel to the Revelation*, new and rev. ed. (London: Lutterworth Press, 1963), 172.

ent or a depiction of the dreaded future. The point at which history ends and prophecy begins eludes the interpreter, and the question of whether or not a particular writer equated current events with the time of trouble remains unsolved. The second cause for diverse evaluation emerges from documents in which matters are clearer, documents demonstrating that the eschatological woes were sometimes thought of as present, sometimes as future. Thus, both Collins and Rowley may rightfully refer to texts in support of their respective positions. There is, moreover, even one text that seemingly locates the great tribulation in the past.

*The great tribulation is present.* For a long time there was all but universal agreement that the *Assumption* or *Testament of Moses* reflects Herodian times and was probably written ca. 7–30 A.D. Jacob Licht, however, in an article on the enigmatic figure of Taxo, suggested that the *Testament* was originally composed ca. 165 B.C. (a bit before Daniel) and subsequently assumed its present form at the hands of a redactor in the first century A.D.[9] The primary impetus for this proposal is clear. Although chapters 8—9 seem to envision the persecution under Antiochus IV Epiphanes (see esp. 8:1–5), they also clearly describe the final time of trouble; and yet chapters 6—7 describe Herodian times. How can chapters 8—9 set forth the time of Antiochus as the eschatological turning point if earlier sections (chaps. 6—7) recount events of the Herodian period? R. H. Charles solved this problem in the *APOT* by moving chapters 8—9 and arguing for an original order: 8—9, 6—7. But, as Licht has observed, chapter 9 cannot be separated from chapter 10, for the death of Taxo in the former is the event which directly calls for the climax in the latter.[10] Hence, the solution of Charles is inadequate. Two alternatives remain. Either chapters 6—7 are an insertion updating an earlier apocalypse to later times (so Licht), or chapter 8 was not really intended to describe the persecution under Antiochus Epiphanes.

It is beyond the scope of this work to enumerate the arguments that might be marshaled for these last two alternatives. Fortunately, therefore, reference may be made to a recent debate between John J. Collins and G. W. E. Nickelsburg on this very issue. Nickelsburg sided with Licht: chapters 6—7 belong to a second edition of the *Testament.*[11] Collins, conversely, argued that the document is coherent in its present form and that chapters 8—9 provide a stereo-

---

9. Jacob Licht, "Taxo, or the Apocalyptic Doctrine of Vengeance," *JJS* 12 (1961): 95–103.

10. See also now David C. Carlson, "Vengeance and Angelic Mediation in the Testament of Moses 9 and 10," *JBL* 101 (1982): 85–92.

11. G. W. E. Nickelsburg, *Resurrection, Immortality, and Eternal Life in Intertestamental Judaism*, HTS 26 (Cambridge: Harvard Univ. Press, 1972), 43–45.

typed description of the coming tribulation; the parallels between *Assumption of Moses* 8—9 and the persecution under Antiochus no more indicate an original composition ca. 165 B.C. than does the reference to the "abomination of desolation" in Mark 13:14.[12] But Nickelsburg's rejoinder[13] has since converted Collins, who now concedes the probability of two compositional stages for the *Testament of Moses*.[14] Two points, among others, induced this change of mind. First, the parallels between the time of Antiochus and *As. Mos.* 8—9 are extensive and specific. This suggests that *As. Mos.* 8—9, although a description of the end, must also have a concrete history in view. Its specificity requires this. The history in view is the devastation wrought by Antiochus. Second, the dream visions of Daniel, which on Licht's view come from approximately the same time as the *Testament of Moses*, plainly interpret the persecution under Antiochus as though it were the last great persecution; see Dan. 12:1, which refers to the author's own time. This text, therefore, offers a parallel to Licht's reading of *As. Mos.* 8—9. Both books identify contemporary events—namely, those involving Antiochus and the early Maccabees—with the arrival of the eschatological tribulation. There are, consequently, sound reasons for concurring with Licht, Nickelsburg, and Collins. The *Testament of Moses* was probably composed ca. 165 B.C. and later redacted, as chapters 6—7 attest, in Herodian times.[15]

If the view just outlined is correct, the original *Testament of Moses*, like the dream visions of Daniel, identified current events with the eschatological affliction. The author of the book thought that his time, the time of Antiochus (chap. 8), the time of Taxo (chap. 9), stood immediately before the appearance of God's kingdom throughout all creation, when there would be no more Satan (10:1). The woes presently experienced were thought to be *the* woes, the last woes, and soon to be followed by the renewal.

One finds a similar interpretation of contemporary events in the sectarian literature discovered in the caves near Khirbet Qumran. 1QH III, 7–10 reads as follows:

> I was in distress as a woman in travail with her first child, when her pains come upon her (8) and a grievous travail upon her womb, causing writhing in the crucible of the pregnant woman. When children come to the waves of death; (9)

---

12. Collins, "Date and Provenance," 15–32.
13. Nickelsburg, "An Antiochian Date for the Testament of Moses," in *Studies on the Testament of Moses,* 38–43.
14. Collins, "Some Remaining Traditio-Historical Problems in the Testament of Moses," in *Studies on the Testament of Moses,* 38–43.
15. So also Jonathan A. Goldstein, "The Testament of Moses: Its Content, Its Origin, and Its Attestation in Josephus," in *Studies on the Testament of Moses,* 44–52; and A. Yarbro Collins, "Composition and Redaction in the Testament of Moses 10," *HTR* 69 (1976): 179–86.

and the one bearing a man suffers in her travail, because in the waves of death she gives birth to a man-child; and in deadly travail he breaks forth (10) from the crucible of the pregnant woman, The Wonderful One takes counsel in his might and a man comes forth safely from the throes of birth in her who is pregnant with him [au. trans.].

Although this passage has received much discussion, little consensus has been reached. Some have thought that 1QH III, 7–10 foretells the advent of the Messiah in the period of eschatological distress; the mother in the hymn is the community at Qumran, the child is the Messiah, and the latter will come forth from the former. Most scholars have rejected this messianic interpretation. It is problematic, among other reasons, because (1) the "I" of line 7 seemingly indicates that the psalmist is describing his own troubles, not those of a group; (2) the plurals in lines 8 and 11 ostensibly exclude reference to an individual (the Messiah); and (3) the birth-pangs are clearly a simile (line 7: "as"), not a reference to the birth of a historical person. Elaborating on the second point, the use of "children" in line 8 especially indicates that the hymnist probably has a collectivity in view. If so, then presumably this collectivity should be identified with the community of Qumran. On this reading, in line 9 both "man-child" and "man" stand for a group (cf. Isa. 66:7; 1QS III, 20–23). On the other hand, the one who labors to bring forth the group must be an individual, and probably none other than the so-called Teacher of Righteousness, whom many hold to be the author of much of the *Hôdāyôt*, including 1QH III, 3–18. So just as Paul likened his relationship with the Thessalonians to that between a nurse and a child (1 Thess. 2:7; cf. 2:11), and just as he thought of himself as in "travail" with the Galatians, his "children," until Christ be formed in them (Gal. 4:19), so the Teacher of Righteousness evidently could declare that he had given birth to a community (cf. CD I, 11 and 4QpPsᵃ III, 15–16). 1QH VII, 20–22 offers a parallel. Here the hymnist— again, probably the Teacher—cries out to God, "Thou hast made me a father to the sons of grace, and as a foster-father to marvellous men. They have opened their mouths like little infants . . . like a child playing in the lap of its nurse" ( au. trans.).

1QH III, 7–10 is striking because the text focuses first upon the pangs attending the birth of the community. A possible precedent for the use of such imagery appears in Isa. 26:16–18:

O Lord, in distress they sought thee,
  they poured out a prayer
  when thy chastening was upon them.
Like a woman with child,
  who writhes and cries out in her pangs,

when she is near her time,
so were we because of thee, O Lord;
we were with child, we writhed,
we have as it were brought forth wind.
We have wrought no deliverance in the earth,
and the inhabitants of the world have not fallen.

But it would be unsatisfactory to leave matters without further comment, for the sect at Qumran believed that the Teacher of Righteousness had come "at the end of days" (CD VI, 11). Further, in 1QH III the image of the pangs of birth is joined to motifs drawn from the eschatological tradition of Judaism— an earthquake (12—13), a flood (14), and a disturbance in the heavens (13). The eschatological orientation of 1QH III, 3–18 becomes particularly evident in III, 14–18, a prophecy of the fall of the wicked into the pit of hell at the judgment. Given its context, then, and the widespread use of imagery connected with labor to depict transition to the new age, 1QH III, 7–10 likely recounts the birth of the community in the eschatological travail. As Matthew Black has written, "The eschatological setting of the hymn suggests that its subject is the 'birth-pangs of the Messiah' in the sense of the emergence through trial and suffering of the redeemed Israel."[16] Others concur.[17]

CD I, 5–11 states that 390 years passed between the captivity under Nebuchadnezzar and the emergence of a remnant. This remnant, the precursors of the sectaries at Qumran, wandered and groped in the wilderness for twenty years. Then God raised up for them a guide, the Teacher of Righteousness. CD XX, 13–15 states that forty years must elapse between his death and the dawn of the messianic epoch, "until the annihilation of all the men of war who returned with the Man of Falsehood." If the duration of the Teacher's ministry be estimated at forty years, and if this figure be added to those just given, the result is 490, the classic seventy times seven prophesied by Daniel (9:24) in his reinterpretation of Jer. 25:11 and 29:10. This may be a coincidence. But it is consistent with the sectarians' belief that they were living in the last generation, just prior to or at the beginning of the great messianic war (1QM). In this connection the account of the Kittim in 1QpHab notably recalls the stereotyped prophecies of the messianic woes in much of the apocalyptic literature. The Kittim (= the Romans) come "in the last days" (IX, 9). Wars

16. Matthew Black, *The Scrolls and Christian Origins: Studies in the Jewish Background of the New Testament* (New York: Charles Scribner's Sons, 1961), 150.
17. Thus, M. de Jonge, "The Role of Intermediaries in God's Final Intervention in the Future According to the Qumran Scrolls," in *Studies on the Jewish Background of the New Testament*, ed. M de Jonge, et al. (Assen, Neth.: Van Gorcum, 1969), 58–59; A. S. van der Woude, *Die messianische Vorstellung der Gemeinde von Qumran*, Studia Semitica Neerlandica (Assen, Neth.: Van Gorcum, 1957), 155–56; and Georg Bertram, "ōdin, ōdinō," *TDNT* 9 (1974): 671.

rage and many perish (II, 12–14). The law of God is not believed (II, 14–15; cf. *2 Apoc. Bar.* 48:38; *m. Soṭa* 9:15; *b. Sanh.* 97a). The cities of the earth are plundered (III, 1). Men, women, and children perish by the sword (IV, 10–12). The eschatological presuppositions of 1QpHab. are clear. The Essenes believed not only that a new era was near but that the time of trouble and travail that would herald its coming had already arrived. They lived in fear and terror and affliction in the dominion of Satan (1QS I, 17–19) and hoped that the turning point was near. They labeled the present "the end period of wickedness" (CD VI, 10, 14; XV, 7–10).[18] Herbert Braun and others have even proposed that the retreat of the Essenes into the desert was construed in terms of the *topos* of eschatological flight.[19] However that may be, certainly the conviction that a return to the wilderness would herald the redemption is well attested,[20] and we have already seen that the authors of Dan. 8:1—12:13 and of the *Testament of Moses* identified the Hellenistic crisis of the second century B.C. with the onset of the great tribulation. The Essenes at about the same time made the same identification. They understood their own sufferings to signal the advent of the tribulation attendant upon the new age.

*Fourth Ezra* provides one more witness—this from a later time, the end of the first century A.D.—for the equation of contemporary events with the messianic travail. The relevant texts are *4 Ezra* 5:1–13, 50–55; 6:21–24; and 9:3. The first is particularly illuminating and should be quoted in full (RSV):

Now concerning the signs: behold, the days are coming when those who dwell on earth shall be seized with great terror, and the way of truth shall be hidden, and the land shall be barren of faith. (2) And unrighteousness shall be increased beyond what you yourself see, and beyond what you heard of formerly. (3) And the land which you now see ruling shall see it desolate. (4) But if the Most High grants that you live, you shall see it thrown into confusion after the third period; and the sun shall suddenly shine forth at night, and the moon during the day. (5) Blood shall drip from wood, and the stone shall utter its voice; the peoples shall be troubled, and the stars shall fall. (6) And one shall reign whom those who dwell on earth do not expect, and the birds shall fly away together; (7) and the sea of Sodom shall cast up fish; and one whom the many do not know shall make his voice heard by night, and all shall hear his voice. (8) There shall be chaos also in many places, and fire shall often break out, and the wild beasts shall roam beyond their haunts, and menstruous women shall bring forth monsters. (9) And salt waters shall be found in the sweet; and all friends shall conquer one another; then shall reason hide itself, and wisdom shall withdraw into its chamber, (10) and it shall be sought

18. On the expression quoted, see Hans Kosmala, "'At the End of Days,'" in *Messianism in the Talmudic Era*, ed. L. Landman (New York: Ktav, 1979), 308–9.

19. Herbert Braun, *Qumran und das Neue Testament* 2 (Tübingen: J. C. B. Mohr [Paul Siebeck], 1966), 268–69.

20. W. D. Davies, *The Gospel and the Land: Early Christianity and Jewish Territorial Doctrine* (Berkeley and Los Angeles: Univ. of California Press, 1974), 76–77, 83–85.

by many but shall not be found. And one country shall ask its neighbor, "Has righteousness, or any one who does right, passed through you?" And it will answer, "No." (12) And at that time men shall not prosper. (13) These are the signs which I am permitted to tell you, and if you pray again, and weep as you do now, and fast for seven days, you shall hear greater things than these.

This passage divides itself into two sections, 5:1–3 and 5:4–13. The signs announced in 5:4–12 occur only "after the third period," those in 5:2–3 before. The reference to "the third period" is obscure, and the textual tradition is confused.[21] But in 14:11–12 one reads that "the age is divided into twelve parts, and nine of its parts remain, besides half of the tenth part."[22] From the standpoint of the historical Ezra (but not the readers of *4 Ezra*; the book is a pseudepigraphon and antedated several centuries), three more historical periods must be completed before the end of the age. That is, if Ezra were to live to see the completion of the remaining three periods of history, he would see the prophecies of 5:4–12 fulfilled. This makes perfect sense,[23] for the great tribulation, the subject of 5:4–12, comes when the old age has run its course. But why are the woes in 5:2–3 not also placed after the third period? The signs in 5:2–3 are more mundane than those in 5:4–12, and the first section could easily reflect historical occurrences. Thus, 5:3 could refer to Roman occupation, and 5:2 might be somebody's estimation of contemporary religiosity. But the signs in 5:4–12—including blood dripping from wood, a stone speaking, and menstruous women bearing monsters—are predominately preternatural. They could scarcely be taken as *vaticinia ex eventu*. *Fourth Ezra* 5:1–13 is, accordingly, divided into two parts, not only by the explicit statement in 5:4 but also by the dissimilarity of content between 5:2–3 and 5:4–12. The reason for this is probably the author's endeavor to locate his own time within the final tribulation. He sees around himself fear, apostasy, and occupying forces, and he views these as the beginning of the eschatological woes (5:2–3). But the seer also expects evils to increase even more, and this accounts for verses 4–13. The scheme reminds one of Mark 13. In the synoptic apocalypse, certain events are only "the beginning of the birth pangs" (13:8), and the woes become more terrible as the chapter moves forward.

*Fourth Ezra* 9:1–4 tells the same story. It reads:

He answered me and said, "Measure carefully in your mind, and when you see that a certain part of the predicted signs are past, (2) then you will know that it is

21. Latin: after the third; Ethiopic: after three months; Armenian: after the third vision; Georgian: after the third day.
22. Contrary to some, there is nothing to compel the conclusion that chap. 14 is a secondary expansion.
23. Thus, *APOT* 2:569.

the very time when the Most High is about to visit the world which he has made. (3) So when there shall appear in the world earthquakes, tumult of peoples, intrigues of nations, wavering of leaders, confusion of princes, (4) then you will know that it was of these that the Most High spoke from the days that were of old, from the beginning."

Verse 3, which rehearses the woes that will precede the end, probably concerns the present. First, the signs are sufficiently indefinite to tempt a Jewish community living in a time of trouble to see itself and its time therein. Second, verse 1 encourages the reader to believe that "predicted signs are past." Thus, the time for divine visitation has come; the seer and his readers know themselves to be suffering the tribulation that must come before the Messiah's advent.

Our last example of the conviction that the great tribulation was present is from *m. Soṭa* 9:15.

> With the footprints of the Messiah presumption shall increase and dearth reach its height; the vine shall yield its fruit but the vine shall be costly; and the empire shall fall into heresy and there shall be none to utter reproof. The council-chamber shall be given to fornication. Galilee shall be laid waste and Gablan shall be made desolate; and the people of the frontier shall go about from city to city with none to show pity on them. The wisdom of the Scribes shall become insipid and they that shun sin shall be deemed contemptible, and truth shall nowhere be found. Children shall shame the elders, and the elders shall rise up before the children, for the son dishonoureth the father, the daughter riseth up against her mother, the daughter-in-law against her mother-in-law; a man's enemies are the men of his own house. The face of this generation is as the face of a dog, and the son will be put to shame by his father. On whom can we stay ourselves?—on our Father in heaven.[24]

The tradition history of this passage is unclear. In *b. Sanh.* 97a, parts of it are assigned to R. Nehemiah, R. Judah, and R. Nahorai. But regardless of the problem of authenticity, the important point for our investigation is this: the text, in its present form, is "without doubt written under the impression of very concrete political events."[25] "The empire shall fall into heresy" probably envisions the rise of Christianity in the second half of the second century.[26] "Gablan shall be made desolate," although obscure, is unusually specific and thus presumably alludes to something that actually happened. "The wisdom of

---

24. Herbert Danby, *The Mishnah* (London: Oxford Univ. Press, 1933), 306.

25. Thus, Peter Schäfer, "Die messianischen Hoffnungen des rabbinischen Judentums zwischen Naherwartung und religiösem Pragmatismus," in *Studien zur Geschichte und Theologie des rabbinischen Judentums*, AGJU 15 (Leiden: E. J. Brill, 1978), 222.

26. So ibid., 222-23; and Joseph Klausner, *The Messianic Idea in Israel from Its Beginnings to the Completion of the Mishnah*, trans. W. F. Stinespring (New York: Macmillan & Co., 1955), 445-46.

the Scribes shall be made insipid and they that shun sin shall be deemed contemptible" likely adverts to the dreadful circumstances that arose first during the Hadrianic persecution and continued thereafter. Perhaps also "one can detect here [in *m. Soṭa* 9:15] the frustration of rabbinic thought concerning its own failures in the province" of Galilee.[27] In any event, without question the closing line—"The face of this generation is as the face of a dog, and the son will be put to shame by his father. On whom can we stay ourselves? —on our Father in heaven"—makes plain that *m. Soṭa* 9:15 treats not solely of the future but also of the present. So the pangs of the Messiah are here more than a prospect; they have revealed themselves in contemporary circumstances. At this point there is agreement with Daniel, the *Testament of Moses*, the Dead Sea Scrolls, and *4 Ezra*.

Before leaving this section, it will prove profitable to reproduce a paragraph from a late Christian text, Eusebius's *Ecclesiastical History:*

> At the same period Jude, another author, wrote a treatise on Daniel's seventy weeks, bringing his account to an end in the tenth year of Severus [A.D. 202–203]. He believed that the much-talked-of advent of antichrist would take place at any moment—so completely had the persecution set in motion against us at that time thrown many off their balance.[28]

The historian Jude (about whom nothing more is known than what is preserved in this paragraph) evidently identified his own time with the final time of trouble and taught the advent of antichrist to be imminent. A calculation based upon Dan. 9:24–27 undergirded his opinion. The concluding remark of Eusebius is perceptive. It reveals the real cause for the belief that the end was at hand: persecution and pessimism were so intense that many supposed themselves to be suffering the messianic affliction. One assumes that matters were much the same for the several Jewish writers who, as we have seen, characterized their own tribulation as the great tribulation. Life had become so terrible that only language drawn from eschatological teaching could do it justice.[29]

---

27. Sean Freyne, *Galilee from Alexander the Great to Hadrian, 323 B. C. E. to 135 C. E.* (Wilmington, Del.: Michael Glazier; Notre Dame, Ind.: Univ. of Notre Dame Press, 1980), 328.

28. *Ecclesiastical History* 6.6; G. A. Williamson, trans., *Eusebius: The History of the Church from Christ to Constantine* (Minneapolis: Augsburg Pub. House, 1975), 246–47.

29. It is worth noting that the equation of contemporary evils with the final tribulation has occurred again and again. On the massacres of Jews in Poland in 1648 see Gershom Scholem, *Sabbatai Ṣevi: The Mystical Messiah*, trans. R. J. Zwi Werblowsky, Bollinger Series XCIII (Princeton, N.J.: Princeton Univ. Press, 1973), 91–93. On the expulsion of Jews from Spain in 1492 see idem, "The Messianic Idea in Kabbalism," in *The Messianic Idea in Judaism and Other Essays on Jewish Spirituality*, trans. M. A. Meyer and H. Halkin (New York: Schocken Books, 1971), 41–42.

*The great tribulation is yet to come. 1 Enoch* 91—105 (200-100 B.C.) divides history into ten periods.[30] The first six of these—from Adam to some time after the temple's destruction—have passed, and the author and his community find themselves in the seventh week, a period of great wickedness, full of apostate deeds (93:3-9). In it the wicked prosper and their sins go unpunished (94:6-7; 96:5-6; 97:8-9; 98:1-3; 99:13) while the righteous have grief and darkness (102:4-11), shame and affliction (104:2), toil and tribulation (103:9-15), being oppressed and persecuted by their rulers and the rich and powerful (95:7; 96:5, 8; 99:13; 103:9-15; 104:3). But circumstances will soon be otherwise, for the eighth week is near, and it will turn fortunes around.

> And after that there shall be another, the eighth week, that of righteousness,
> And a sword shall be given to it that a righteous judgement may be executed on
>     the oppressors,
> And sinners shall be delivered into the hands of the righteous.
>
> (91:12)
>
> Fear not the sinners, ye righteous;
> For again will the Lord deliver them into your hands,
> That ye may execute judgement upon them according to your desires.
>
> (95:3)
>
> Be hopeful, ye righteous; for suddenly shall the sinners perish before you,
> And ye shall have lordship over them according to your desires.
>
> (96:1)
>
> Woe to you that love the deeds of unrighteousness: wherefore do ye hope for good
>     hap unto yourselves? know that ye shall be delivered into the hands of the
>     righteous, and they shall cut off your necks and slay you, and have no mercy
>     upon you.
>
> (98:12; *APOT*)

The lot of the sinners is also described in *1 Enoch* 100:1-4 (*APOT*):

> And in those days in one place the fathers together with their sons shall be smitten
> And brothers one with another shall fall in death
> Till the streams flow with their blood.
> For a man shall not withhold his hand from slaying his sons and his sons' sons,
> And the sinner shall not withhold his hand from his honoured brother:
> From dawn till sunset they shall slay one another.
> And the horse shall walk up to the breast in the blood of sinners,
> And the chariot shall be submerged to its height.
> In those days the angels shall descend into the secret places

---

30. The Apocalypse of Weeks (*1 Enoch* 93 and 91:12-17) was, in all probability, originally an isolated piece; but it was later incorporated into its present context by the author of *1 Enoch* 91—105, and it is with his work (with its title in 92:1) that we are concerned.

And gather together into one place all those who brought down sin,
And the Most High will arise on that day of judgement
To execute great judgement amongst the sinners.

The texts we have cited treat of the time of trouble before the new heaven
appears (93:16) and present it as one when the righteous will wreak vengeance
upon the sinners. That is, the eschatological tribulation is, in *1 Enoch* 91—
105, not a period of distress or testing for God's people but the season when
the wicked receive their merited judgment. The righteous, who are already
being renewed (93:10), will be spared at the end (100:5) and find in their hands
the instruments with which to inflict reprisal upon their enemies. So although
the present (the seventh week, by the author's reckoning) may be miserable for
those who fear God, it is in truth the wicked who should wail and weep, for the
days of the eighth week are coming when sinners will suffer God's judgment
in the great tribulation.

In *Syriac Baruch* (ca. 100 A.D.), the messianic woes are also future yet
imminent. Reference should be made especially to *2 Apoc. Bar.* 25—29; 32;
48:31-41; and 70—72. While the problem of suffering and evil is bound up
with eschatology in this apocalypse, the concern with theodicy is evidently not
determined by a community that sees itself in the great tribulation but rather
by the fall of Jerusalem in 70 A.D. Despite the concentration on eschatology
and the nearness of the end (20:1-2; 85:10), the present itself is not properly
eschatological time. The book addresses itself, to be sure, to a situation of
acute suffering. But the author, in an attempt to encourage his readers, dis-
tinguishes the sufferings of his own time from those of the future. He writes,
"We should not be distressed so much over the evil which has now come as
over that which is still to be. For there will be a great trial . . . when the Mighty
One will renew His creation" (32:5-6; *APOT*). In other words, one may take
heart because the trials of the present are not as frightful as those that are yet to
come. It is consistent with this that Baruch tells his readers that when the
tribulation does finally come, the righteous will be protected (see 20-21
herein). The woes will not touch the keepers of the law in the land (29:2; 32:1).
Rather, they will fall upon the wicked. Therefore, the present tribulation of
the righteous cannot be part of the great tribulation.

Matters are pretty much the same in the *Apocalypse of Abraham* (later first or
early second century A.D.?).[31] According to the author of this book, the present
age has been divided into twelve "years" (29); and "at the passing over of the
twelfth hour of the earth," the eternal will let loose on the earth ten plagues

---

31. We are dependent upon the edition of G. H. Box, *The Apocalypse of Abraham* (London:
SPCK, 1918).

(30; cf. 29). Just as he punished the Egyptians with ten plagues in the days of Moses because they scorned the descendants of Abraham, so will God, in the end, punish the lawless heathen for their provocation and corruption. The elect righteous, on the other hand, having already been punished for their sins at the hands of the Romans, will survive the tribulation to enter a new age (29).

In the *Apocalypse of Abraham*, then, as in *1 Enoch* 91—105 and *Syriac Baruch*, the woes preceding the age of the righteous are part of the eschatological reversal and are conceived of as divine judgment within history, the recompense which the ungodly richly deserve.[32] If Israel has suffered and still suffers, and if the heathen are now in command, the end, which is fastly approaching, will see the heavy hand of divine chastisement pass from the people of God to the nations.

Before proceeding to the next section, account should be taken of texts that locate the great tribulation in the future but, unlike those just discussed, do not necessarily regard it as near. *T. Levi* 4:1 (ca. 100 B.C.?) and *Adam and Eve* 29:7 (first century A.D.) may be cited, and from the rabbinic texts see the statements attributed to various rabbis in *b. Sanh.* 98b and *b. Šabb.* 118a. In these passages we run across instances where the prospect of a great tribulation is not a prominent tenet or conspicuous belief that draws much attention but, rather, something taken over from tradition and mentioned only in passing.

*The great tribulation is past.* The eschatology of the book of *Jubilees* is difficult to unravel, and the various problems cannot be entered into here. But one point has seemed evident to more than one exegete, and it is of special importance for this investigation. In the words of R. H. Charles, "The author of Jubilees, we can hardly doubt, thought that the era of the Messianic Kingdom had already set in."[33] This has also been the opinion of quite a few other scholars.[34] The principal evidence for it is *Jub.* 23:1-31. This chapter has as its center a description of the Maccabean revolt. But according to Charles and most critics, the last few verses move beyond the revolt and reflect the Maccabean hegemony, under either Simon (143/2-135/4) or John Hyr-

---

32. Also, as in *1 Enoch* 91—105, the righteous will execute judgment on the wicked: *Apoc. Ab.* 29.

33. *APOT,* 2:9.

34. So G. H. Box, in R. H. Charles and G. H. Box, *The Book of Jubilees or the Little Genesis* (London: SPCK, 1917), xxviii; Paul Volz, *Die Eschatologie der jüdischen Gemeinde im neutestamentlichen Zeitalter,* 2d ed. (Tübingen: J. C. B. Mohr [Paul Siebeck, 1934], 29; M.-J. Lagrange, *Le Judaïsme avant Jésus Christ* (Paris: J. Gabalda et Cⁱᵉ, 1931), 118-19; Rowley, *Relevance of Apocalyptic,* 65; David S. Russell, *The Method and Message of Jewish Apocalyptic 200 BC—AD 100,* Old Testament Library (Philadelphia: Westminster Press, 1964), 292; and G. L. Davenport, *The Eschatology of the Book of Jubilees,* SPB 20 (Leiden: E. J. Brill, 1971), 45 (although Davenport finds this true only for one stage in his hypothetical literary history of *Jubilees*).

canus I (135/4–104). Specifically, verses 11–25 describe the wars with Syria, and 23:36 introduces the Hasmonean state. Moreover, the concluding verses of chapter 23 describe the final salvation. No clear line, however, is drawn between the Hasmonean state and the eschatological redemption. The one seems to evolve into the other, and the kingdom emerges gradually: "And the days shall begin to grow" (23:37; *APOT*). Thus, Charles and others have plausibly claimed that the final transformation has already begun.[35]

Remark must be made here of the function, on this reading, of verses 11–25 within chapter 23. *Jubilees* 23:11–25 does not simply recount a past history. Not only is the language eschatological[36] but 23:11–25 leads immediately to the "messianic" kingdom; 23:11–25 thus describes the great tribulation, the season of trouble which must come before the new age. But as the passage describes the Maccabean wars and as the kingdom has already set in, the tradition of the eschatological woes is here used to interpret a past conflict.

Before moving on, it is necessary to recognize that Charles's interpretation of *Jubilees* has not gone unchallenged. Most important, James C. VanderKam has maintained that *Jubilees* contains no certain reference to any event after 161 B.C. and was thus probably written between 161 and 152 B.C.[37] He contends (1) that 23:14–23 represents a chronological sequence that culminates in a reference to Alcimus and his party and (2) that 23:24–31 basically represents a poetical version or doublet of 23:14–23.[38] If VanderKam is correct, there can be no thought of a "messianic" kingdom emerging out of the reign of either Simon or John Hyrcanus I. Yet it still seems that, on his reading, the great tribulation should be equated with a past series of events. *Jubilees* 23:24–25 must, if a poetic doublet of preceding verses, recount the early Maccabean conflict, for they reproduce, on VanderKam's view, part of the prosaic depiction of past events in 23:14–23. Further, 23:26–30, which immediately follows verses 24–25, clearly depicts the eschatological transformation. This implies that no further distress is envisioned and that verses 24–25, which describe the last woes, relate what is already past. Accordingly, the author of *Jubilees* thinks himself to stand at the inception of a new day. The great tribulation (identified with the early Maccabean wars: 14–23 plus 24–25) is past. The kingdom of God is now coming into the world.

35. Note the glowing, messianic terms with which the reign of Simon is described in 1 Maccabees 14.
36. The signs include pain and sorrow and tribulation and no peace (12, 16); calamity following upon calamity (13); famine, death, sword, and captivity (13, 22); an evil generation (14); the forgetting of the commandment (19); war (21); and the defilement of the Holy of Holies (21; cf. Dan 9:24).
37. James C. VanderKam, *Textual and Historical Studies on the Book of Jubilees*, HSM 14 (Missoula, Mont.: Scholars Press, 1977), 214–85.
38. Ibid., 253–54, in agreement with Davenport, *Eschatology of Jubilees*, 32–46.

Such an interpretation fits with what we otherwise know of the years between 160 and 150 B.C. Although 1 Maccabees says comparatively little about much of this period, we do know that in 158 Bacchides and the Syrian forces, after an unsuccessful military campaign against the Maccabean party, made peace with Jonathan (1 Macc. 9:58–73; Jos. *Ant.* 13.1.5–6); that, ca. 152, Jonathan not only drove out the pro-Greek faction from Judea but also received concessions from Demetrius, including the withdrawal of many Syrian garrisons (1 Macc. 10:1–14; Jos. *Ant.* 13.2.1); and that, both before and after Alexander's defeat of Demetrius in 150, Palestine had several years of peace (1 Macc. 10:22–26; Jos. *Ant.* 13.2.3–4.2). "And the sword ceased from Israel ... and Jonathan began to judge the people, and he removed the impious ones from Israel" (1 Macc. 9:73). The author of *Jubilees,* then, encouraged in his optimism by good turns of fortune, could well have hoped that tribulation belonged to the past and that God was ushering in a new time.

*Summary.* The pertinent results of this section may be summarized quite succinctly. In ancient Jewish literature, the final, great tribulation is sometimes present, sometimes pending, and sometimes yet to come at an unspecified, possibly distant time; and in one instance (*Jubilees*) it seems to be entirely past. The import of this conclusion and its relation to other facts will be considered below.[39]

### Who Will Suffer?

It is extremely interesting to discover that our documents do not agree concerning the fate of God's people in the eschatological tribulation. In perhaps most books the righteous must pass through the woes and are not spared affliction. But in more than one text they are protected by divine intervention.

*The saints suffer.* To illustrate the first prospect: in Daniel the unprecedented time of trouble means affliction for the people of God until Michael the prince delivers them. "This horn made war with the saints, and prevailed over them, until the Ancient of Days came" (Dan. 7:21–22; cf. 12:1). In *Jub.* 23:1–31 all Israel is caught up in the tribulation: the Gentiles "shall use violence against Israel and transgression against Jacob" (*Jub.* 23:23; *APOT*). In *As. Mos.* 9:1–7, Taxo and his sons meet death immediately before the end, and their blood is

---

39. Heinrich Schlier, "Thlibō, thlipsis," *TDNT* 3 (1964): 146, is incorrect when he writes, "The basic distinction between the Jewish and the Christian understanding of the eschatological *thlipsis* is to be found, of course, in the fact that this tribulation, which is still future in Judaism, has already begun according to the early Christian view."

innocent: "Let us fast for the span of three days and on the fourth let us go into a cave which is in the field, and let us die rather than transgress the commands of the Lord of Lords" (9:6–7; *APOT*). In *Liv. Pro. Hab.* 14 (first century A.D.) the end occasions the persecution of the righteous: the veils and pillars of the first temple, carried off by angels into the wilderness, "will give light to those being pursued by the serpent in darkness as from the beginning." In *Liv. Pro. Jer.* 12 (first century A.D.) the faithful flee from their enemy into the desert: on Mount Sinai "all the holy ones will be assembled to it [the ark] there, expecting the Lord and fleeing from the enemy who wishes to undo them." In *b. Sanh.* 98b, Rab and Ulla do not wish to live to see the Messiah because the attending woes will be too painful, even for the godly: "Let him come but let me not see him." In the *Apocalypse of Elijah,* which perhaps incorporates a Jewish apocalypse of the first or second century A.D., the antichrist unleashes a great persecution: "He will pursue all the saints" (4:21). The trend of these texts, from various times and places, is clear. The righteous will be tested and suffer affliction at the end. The Most High will not spare the faithful until the very turning point.

The Dead Sea Scrolls also deserve mention here. In 1QH III, 3–18 the past and present are, as we have seen, understood in terms of the final travail, and in 1QM the men of the covenant with the aid of angels fight the final battle of destruction of the sons of darkness. Thus, the sons of light must struggle with the angel of darkness until the very end (1QS III, 13—IV, 26).[40]

*The wicked suffer. Syriac Baruch* has another view of things. The eschatological woes will not envelop the righteous. Rather, the land (Eretz Israel) "shall have mercy on its own and it shall protect its inhabitants at that time" (*2 Bar* 71:1; *APOT*). Verse 2 in chapter 9 is similar: "At that time I will protect only those who are found in those self-same days in this land" (*APOT*). Compare also 32:1 and 40:2. The troubles depicted so vividly throughout this book apparently fall only upon the ungodly who dwell outside the land. Such an expectation may also be present in portions of *4 Ezra. Fourth Ezra* 9:7–8 tells of those who, on account of faith or works, will be able to escape the dangers predicted and find salvation in the land. According to 13:48–50, those left within the "holy borders" will be saved.[41]

40. Richard J. Bauckham, "The Great Tribulation in the Shepherd of Hermas," *JTS* 25 (1974): 27–40, errs in affirming that, in contrast to Christian teaching, the sufferings of the people of God were no prominent part of Jewish eschatological expectation.

41. It is difficult to reconcile this with the author's conviction that he and his community already suffer the pains of the end (see 11–13). But it is possible that the author of *4 Ezra* believed that the saints would suffer only at the beginning of the great tribulation, not at its end.

In the *Apocalypse of Abraham* the terrors of the latter days are thought of as God's punishment of the Gentiles, particularly those who have oppressed the offspring of Abraham. The eternal declares in chapter 29, "Before the Age of the righteous beginneth to grow, my judgment shall come upon the lawless heathen. . . . In those days I will bring upon all creatures of the earth ten plagues, through misfortune and disease and sighing of the grief of their soul" (*Apoc. Ab.* 29). In chapter 30, the eschatological woes are introduced as "the plagues which I [God] have prepared for the heathen." The elect in Israel, because they have already suffered their punishment in the events of 70 A.D. and thereafter, will evidently not suffer God's wrath in the great tribulation which is about to come.

*First Enoch* 91—105 and perhaps the *Sibylline Oracles* III (second century B.C.) should be mentioned at this juncture. In the former, the last times will witness father slaying son, brother slaying brother, blood flowing unto the horse's bridle, and a gathering of the wicked into one place for judgment (100:1-4). But amid all this the righteous will be guarded; tribulation will not touch them. "And over all the righteous and holy He will appoint guardians from amongst the holy angels, to guard them as the apple of an eye, until He makes an end of all wickedness and all sin" (100:5; *APOT*). The same picture emerges in chapter 99. *1 Enoch* 99:1-9 recounts the evil plight of sinners in the latter days, but in verse 10 those who observe the paths of the Most High are called blessed, for "they shall be saved" from the woes enumerated. As for *Sib. Or.* III, mention is nowhere made of judgment or affliction coming upon the people of God. Woes are always and exclusively directed against the nations that sin against God; the calamities that God will send immediately before ushering in an everlasting kingdom (601—15) will come as retribution "because they would not honour in holiness the eternal Father of all men" (604; *APOT*).

*The saints may suffer.* If in most of the literature the woes either overtake the wicked or the righteous, there are instances (in addition to texts from which no conclusion can be extracted, such as *Adam and Eve* 29:7 and *T. Levi* 4:1) in which matters are not so clear cut. In *Liv. Pro. Dan.* 21 we read that when the end is at hand, "If the mountain in the south flows with water, the people will return to its land, and if blood runs there will be a slaughter by Beliar in all the earth." Here the character of the end is not predetermined. It may mean salvation for Israel, or it may mean a slaughter upon *all* the earth. The question of whether God's people will be spared seems to be deliberately left open. Perhaps the prediction is contingent upon the faithfulness of Israel.

A similar conviction seems to lie behind several rabbinic passages. Thus, in

*Mekilta* on Exod. 16:25 (Vayassa' 5.74–75), the following is attributed to R. Eliezer (b. Hyrcanus? ca. 100 A.D.): "If you will succeed in keeping the Sabbath you will escape the three visitations: The day of God, the suffering preceding the advent of the Messiah, and the Great Judgment Day."[42] In *b. Sanh.* 98b, the disciples of R. Eliezer (b. Hyrcanus?) ask the master, "What should a man do to be spared the pangs of the Messiah?" The rabbi responds, "Let him engage in study and good deeds." According to *b. Šabb.* 118a, R. Simeon b. Pazzi in the name of R. Joshua b. Levi in Bar Kappara's name (ca. 200) said that the one who observes the three meals on the Sabbath will be saved from the woes of the Messiah.

Notice might also be taken of *b. Ketub.* 111a. R. Abaye (d. 338) reportedly knew a tradition according to which Babel will not witness the sufferings of the Messiah. He explained that Babel might be Huẓal in Benjamin, called "corner of safety." There, apparently, one could be spared from the final travail.

*Summary.* Our review has led to the conclusion that there were mutually exclusive views as to who would suffer in the great tribulation. Some texts present the messianic travail as a time when God will chasten or test his own people. Others foretell a period in which woes will be the means by which the Almighty punishes not the faithful but the wicked. Finally, there are some passages in which the godly may or may not suffer. In these, repentance and piety have the power to deliver one from the coming evils.

## How Long Will the Great Tribulation Last?

In the canonical book of Daniel, the final time of trouble evidently spans seven years. The period of destruction, war, and desolation that culminates in the unprecedented affliction (Dan. 12:1) is a week (= seven years), the last of the seventy weeks of years decreed concerning Israel. Surprisingly, few subsequent seers took up this reckoning. It probably does lie behind a Baraita in *b. Sanh.* 97a, according to which the Son of David will come at the end of a calamitous seven-year cycle: "Our rabbis taught: In the seven year cycle at whose end the Son of David will come, in the first year . . . at the conclusion of the septennate the Son of David will come." Dan. 9:24–27 must also be the inspiration for *2 Apoc. Bar.* 82:2 ("the measure and reckoning of that time are two parts a week of seven years"; *APOT*), an obscure verse whose meaning

---

42. *Mekilta de-Rabbi Ishmael,* ed. J. Lauterbach (Philadelphia: Jewish Publication Society, 1933) 2:119–20.

eludes the interpreter. But one is pressed to find other examples of the belief that the great tribulation will cover a period of seven years.

The rabbinic sources display no unanimity with regard to the question under review. Neither the phrase "the generation in which the Son of David will come," which recurs in the Talmud, nor the use of "generation" in other contexts depends upon a chronological conception. The statement attributed to Rab in *b. Sanh.* 98b ("The Son of David will not come until the [Roman] power enfolds Israel for nine months") probably marks an inference drawn from the technical term, *heblô šel māšîha*: as the travail of a woman is nine months, so will be the travail of the Messiah. But this inference stands alone. Although the rabbis discussed when the Messiah might come (*b. Sanh.* 97a–99a), they did not much concern themselves to estimate the duration of the messianic birth pangs.

Like the later rabbinic texts, most of the Jewish documents composed between 200 B.C. and 200 A.D. and treating of eschatology do not explicitly consider the duration of the coming tribulation. This includes *1 Enoch* 91—105; *Sib. Or.* III, 532–51, 796–806; *Liv. Pro. Hab.* 14; *Liv. Pro. Jer.* 12; *Liv. Pro. Dan.* 21; *4 Ezra* 5:1–13, 50–56; 6:21–24; 9:3; and *Apoc. Ab.* 29—30. One might also include in this list *As. Mos.* 8—9 and *Jubilees* 23. But conclusions drawn above allow us to offer remarks on these chapters. In *As. Mos.* 8—9 the final period of distress is identified with events preceding and following 164 B.C.; it therefore ostensibly covers a period of a couple of years or more. In *Jubilees* 23 the days of duress are identified with the trouble under one or more of the early Hasmoneans. Here, too, a period of at least several years, maybe even a decade or more, is involved. The texts from Qumran likewise envision the prospective evil season as relatively long. In 1QM the eschatological conflict rages for forty years (= the years of a generation; see column II). Moreover, we have already observed that the Essenes located their birth and subsequent history within the eschatological time of distress. Thus, as both the forty years of 1QM and the span between the founding of the community and the redemption belong to "the end period of wickedness," the documents from Qumran preserve the conviction that the years of tribulation might be even more than those of a generation. One may account for this by observing that the early Dead Sea community interpreted its experience in terms of the "messianic woes" and expected God's decisive intervention in the near future; therefore, as the redemption delayed (cf. 1QpHab I and VIII), the time allotted to the period of distress necessarily increased.

*Summary.* Our survey uncovers no agreement. The length of the great tribulation was variously estimated—from a few years to more than forty; and most texts simply do not broach the subject.

## The Relative Importance of the Great Tribulation

The great tribulation is, in several texts, a central or controlling idea; in others it is only of marginal import and in still others strikingly absent.

*A central theme.* The fundamental significance of the great tribulation is perhaps most conspicuous in *Syriac Baruch.* Almost ten chapters of this book are devoted to depicting the final affliction (*2 Apoc. Bar.* 25—29; 32; 48:31-41; 70—72). The author is as much concerned to predict the coming woes that will strike down the sinners as to predict the coming salvation. It would, of course, be an exaggeration to declare that the thought of an impending tribulation is the overriding theme of *2 Apoc. Bar.* But the expectation of a coming time of trouble is central to this book. The coming crisis is viewed with utter seriousness; it is a genuine and dreaded prospect. The same may be said of *1 Enoch* 91—105 (see especially 92:5-7; 99—100); *Sib. Or.* III (see, for instance, 532-51, 796-806); and *4 Ezra* (see 5:1-12; 6:21-23; 9:3). The writers of these works offer detailed pictures of the coming distress and return to it again and again.

*An apparently marginal conviction.* There are a number of pseudepigrapha that refer to the great tribulation only in passing. Examples include *T. Dan.* 6:6; *T. Levi* 4:1; *Adam and Eve* 29:7; *Liv. Pro. Jer.* 12; and *Liv. Pro. Hab.* 14. Here there are no extended descriptions and no constant recall of the theme as in *2 Apoc. Bar.* An eschatological expectation has been taken over from the tradition but appears to be of minor consequence. The books cited would not be appreciably different if the tenet were absent.

*A conspicuously absent belief.* As their authors are not concerned with the end of the present age, many Jewish texts give no occasion for alluding to a coming time of trouble—for example, the *Testament of Job* and *Liber Antiquitatum Biblicarum.* But there are other books—books concerned with eschatology— that do have the occasion and yet do not exploit it. In this connection we may mention *1 Enoch* 1—36; the first and third Similitudes of Enoch (*1 Enoch* 38— 44; 58—71); the *Psalms of Solomon;* and *2 Enoch.* Even though judgment is a prominent theme in each of these writings, the eschatological tribulation is absent.

*Summary.* An examination of the relative significance of the expectation of a great tribulation in Jewish texts both before and after the birth of Christianity strikes a note of diversity: there are great differences from book to book. While the expectation receives considerable attention in a number of sources, it gains only passing notice in others, and it is surprisingly not present in several books that treat of eschatological matters.

## Conclusions

(1) The results of this chapter serve to accent the variegated nature of Jewish eschatological expectation as it is attested in the ancient literature. Not only is the idea of a final tribulation not always present in documents heavily informed by eschatological teaching, but when it does appear it receives no standard interpretation: there was no fixed eschatological doctrine. Scholarly treatments of the great tribulation in Jewish literature have not always made this sufficiently clear.

(2) Such diversity, if explored from a sociological perspective, would no doubt prove to be of valuable service in gaining a picture of the various situations from which different documents emerged. Certain questions suggest themselves. What are the differences between a group that expects the future to bring suffering and affliction and one that believes it will be spared tribulation? What is the distinction between an eschatological perspective born of a present so terrible it becomes the great tribulation and a perspective arising primarily from a past catastrophe, such as the fall of Jerusalem? What are the differences between a document written for people compelled to interpret their present existence as the great time of trouble and a document directed toward those who yet await the eschatological woes? The task indicated by these questions demands separate, lengthy treatment. The present chapter has only introduced the data requisite for answering these and other queries.

(3) Our results bear on New Testament exegesis. More than one scholar has suggested that in Mark's Gospel the tribulation in chapter 13 actually reflects the present experience of the community and that the time of trouble, identified with the time of the church, extends from the passion of Jesus to the Parousia. Further, some have urged that Paul understood his apostolic sufferings in terms of the "messianic woes" and that even Jesus interpreted his ministry or immediate future in these terms. Although usually offered without adequate reflection on the possible Jewish background, these proposals have plausible precedent. The notion of a final, great tribulation was sufficiently pliant to interpret present experience and even past events; and the belief that the time of trouble might extend over a period of many years is also attested. With this in mind, we now turn to the New Testament.

*Three*

# THE GOSPEL OF MARK

The synoptic passion narratives probably contain the most persuasive evidences for Dodd's claim that the story of Jesus was reckoned to have fulfilled certain eschatological expectations. One would not, however, draw this conclusion from a reading of the *The Apostolic Preaching*. In fact, Dodd's work neglects almost entirely the many passion traditions that seemingly set the crucifixion and resurrection of Jesus within an eschatological context. The fact of this omission should be underlined, and for two reasons. First, several significant German studies have made much of those traditions that appear to surround the passion of Jesus with eschatological signs,[1] but the connection between these traditions and the problems signified by the term "realized eschatology" have hardly been clarified or even addressed. Second, the key to early Christianity's proclamation of fulfillment can, we suggest, be most readily discovered through an examination of the passion narratives, for it is in these that the correspondence between the eschatological expectations of Jesus and post-Easter interpretations of the passion and resurrection is most clear. But before we can persuasively establish this second point and explore the first, it is necessary to review those texts that interpret the end of Jesus in eschatological categories. We turn first to the Markan materials.

## Mark 15:33: Darkness at Noon

*Tradition and redaction.* Mark 15:33 reads as follows: "And when the sixth hour had come, there was darkness over the whole land until the ninth hour" (*kai genomenēs hōras hektēs skotos egeneto eph holēn tēn gēn heōs hōras enatēs*). Even though this verse contains possible signs of Markan redaction (the use of *holos*, the multiplication of cognate verbs, the genitive absolute), these scarcely suffice to establish the redactional origin of Mark 15:33. The most they

---

1. See, e.g., the studies of Hans-Werner Bartsch (see 93–97 herein); also Ludgar Schenke, *Der gekreuzigte Christus*, SBS 69 (Stuttgart: Katholisches Bibelwerk, 1974); and Johannes Schreiber, *Theologie des Vertrauens* (Hamburg: Furche, 1967).

indicate is that any tradition preserved in 15:33 has been recast—like all tradition taken up into the second Gospel—by Mark's hand, and this claim is supported by observations that render the pre-Markan genesis of 15:33 highly probable. *Skotos, hektēs,* and *enatēs* are *hapax legomena* for Mark. In addition, Mark 15:33 is to be read in conjunction with 15:25 and 15:34, which matters because the chronological notes in these three verses set the crucifixion within a six-hour span marked by events at the third, sixth, and ninth hours. This scheme cannot readily be assigned to the redactor. As Johannes Schreiber remarks, "The rest of the chronological notices in the gospel which come from Mark do not have the precision of the hour notices in Mark 15:25, 33. Thus these notices by their singularity point to tradition being preserved in Mark 15."[2] Also relevant is the presumption that the pre-Markan passion narrative was characterized by triadic patterns: three denials of Peter (Mark 15:68, 70), three scenes of mockery (14:65; 15:16–20, 29–32), three questions of Pilate (15:9–14), three utterances of the High Priest (15:60, 61, 63), three pericopes concerned with the activity of Judas (14:10–11, 17–21, 43–47), and perhaps three times of prayer in Gethsemane (14:35, 36, 39) and three lists of female witnesses (15:40–41, 47; 16:1). One also, admittedly, finds incidents of triadic structure outside the Markan passion,[3] but their frequency in Mark 14:1—16:8 allows the plausible inference that sets of three characterized the pre-Markan passion narrative. So Mark 15:33, belonging as it does to a triadic scheme, may be from Mark's passion source. Finally, Mark 15:33 exhibits no traits obviously peculiar to Markan theology. Indeed, as will be maintained below, the darkness over the earth derives from the teachings of Jewish eschatology, and eschatological motifs were associated with the passion of Jesus long before Mark took up his pen. It appears, therefore, that Mark 15:33 should be assigned to tradition, not to redaction.

*Interpretation.* As to the darkness, Rudolf Pesch has noted: "Because an eclipse with a full moon at the time of Passover is astronomically impossible, an atmospheric darkening, such as through black, gathering, low hanging clouds (so already Origen) cannot be excluded; an understanding of v. 33 as an historical-meteorological notice is possible."[4] But many would agree with Vincent Taylor: Mark's text represents "a legendary development of the kind commonly associated with the death of great men."[5] Philo (according to

---

2. Schreiber, *Theologie des Vertrauens,* 24.
3. See Frans Neirynck, "L'Évangile de Marc (II). À propos de R. Pesch, *Das Markusevangelium,* 2 Teil," *ETL* 55 (1979): 35–42.
4. Rudolf Pesch, *Das Markusevangelium II. Teil,* HTKNT II/2 (Freiburg: Herder, 1977), 494.
5. Vincent Taylor, *The Gospel According to St. Mark,* 2d ed. (New York: St. Martin's Press,

Eusebius, *Praeparatio Evangelica* 8. 14. 50) declared that an eclipse of the sun or of the moon signifies the death of a king or the destruction of a great city. In *2 Enoch* 67 (of disputed origin) a darkness or murk is said to have covered the earth when Enoch was taken up into the highest heaven. Notice might also be taken of *T. Adam* 3:6. This text, of perhaps the fourth or sixth century A.D., and Christian in its present form, affirms that, when Adam passed away, the sun and moon were darkened and there was a thick darkness for seven days. The same tradition appears in the earlier *Adam and Eve* 46 (first century A.D.; cf. *Apoc. Mos.* 36), where there is little reason to suspect Christian influence. Outside the Jewish tradition, Virgil (*Georgics* 1.466–67) writes that when Julius Caesar was murdered on the ides of March, from the sixth hour until night the sun was in eclipse.[6] It was also reported that a supernatural darkness coincided with the death of Theodosius I (Ambrose, *De Obitu Theodosii Oration* 1).[7]

The simple alternative, historical reminiscence or legendary development, does not exhaust the interpretive possibilities. Numerous passages in the Old Testament speak of darkness in connection with God's judgment. In Isa. 13:9–16 the prophet introduces his announcement of the coming judgment of God by proclaiming that the stars "and their constellations will not give their light," that "the sun will be dark at its rising," and that the moon will hide its face. In Amos 5:18 and 20, because the Day of the Lord is a day of judgment, it is darkness, not light. In Jer. 13:16 those addressed are implored to give glory to God before he brings darkness, before he renders fitting judgment. Given this scriptural background, the proposition that Mark 15:33 signals the advent of divine judgment is sensible. Also sensible, however, is the proposal that the darkness at noon conveys the thought of mourning. Certainly mourning is sometimes conjoined with darkness in Jewish texts. See, for example, Jer. 4:27–28: "For thus says the Lord, 'The whole land shall be a desolation; yet I will not make a full end. For this the earth shall mourn, and the heavens above be black; for I have spoken, I have purposed; I have not relented nor will I turn back.'" Darkness seems to function similarly in *2 Apoc. Bar.* 10:12: "And do thou, O sun, withhold the light of thy rays. And do thou, O man, extinguish the multitude of thy light; for why should light rise again where the light of Zion is darkened?" (*APOT*). In *b. Sukk.* 29a we read that on account of four things is the sun in eclipse, the first being the *Ab Beth din* who died and was

1966), 593.

6. Cf. Diogenes Laertius 4.64 and Plutarch, *Pelopidas* 295A. For Romulus, see Cicero, *Republic* 2.10; 6.21 and Livy 1.16.

7. For wonders associated with the deaths of rabbis, see Paul Fiebig, *Jüdische Wunder-geschichten des neutestamentlichen Zeitalters* (Tübingen: J. C. B. Mohr [Paul Siebeck], 1911), 38–49, 57–61.

not properly mourned. The thought seems to be that the sun mourns for the man if men do not. Perhaps, then, one should understand the darkness of Mark 15:33 to signify that the death of Jesus brought the sun to lamentation. Compare *Ps.-Clem. Rec.* 1.41: "While He [Jesus] was suffering, all the world suffered with Him; for the sun was darkened. . . ."[8] Still another reading of the Markan text holds that the darkness primarily denotes the cosmic dimensions of the crucifixion or simply its signal consequences. Exodus 20:21 (the giving of the Torah on Sinai) and 2 Sam. 22:10 (the descent of Yahweh for battle) emphasize the importance or cosmic significance of some particular matter by making reference to an unnatural darkness (cf. *Herod.* 7. 37).

Despite the plausibility of the several interpretations just cataloged (not all of which are mutually exclusive), perhaps most recent scholars have turned to the eschatological traditions of Judaism for an explanation of Mark 15:33. The expectation of an obscuration of heavenly lights in connection with the consummation is found in many texts, such as *As. Mos.* 10:5; *Sib. Or.* III, 801–802; V, 344–50; *T. Levi* 4:1; *2 Apoc. Bar.* 10:12; 18:2; 46:2; 77:14; *Liv. Pro. Hab.* 14; *2 Enoch* 34:3; *b. Sanh.* 99a. It is also met with in the synoptic tradition itself: Mark 13:23 = Matt. 24:29. On this reading the crucifixion in the second Gospel is in some sense an event of the end time or compared to such an event.

The apparent link between Amos 8:9–10 and Mark 15:33 justifies this last solution. According to the prophetic passage, God will, on the Day of the Lord, make the sun go down at noon, and there will be mourning as for an only son. In Mark, the Son of God (see 15:39) is crucified, and darkness covers all the land,[9] beginning with the sixth hour—that is, at noon. It is understandable that Irenaeus (*Adv. haer.* 4.33.12) brought the two texts together, and the author of the *Gospel of Peter* also evidently made the connection,[10] as have many since. Hence, it seems that Mark 15:33 originally registered the fulfillment of the prophecy in Amos—which fact indicates that the eschatological interpretation is vindicated, for Amos 8:9–10 pertains to the Day of the Lord, and in the early church, "the Day of the Lord" was a technical term for the passage to and the period of the messianic age or the age to come (cf. 1 Cor. 1:8; 2 Thess. 2:2; 2 Pet. 3:10). Further, Amos 8:2 asserts that "the end (*hqṣ*) has come upon my people Israel"; and 8:8–10 prophesies earthquakes, darkness, and judgment—things regularly associated with the dawning of the

---

8. *ANF*, 8:88.

9. Commentators have debated whether *eph holēn tēn gēn* should be translated, "all the earth" or "all the land" (the land being Judea). The question is not easily answered. It is, however, worth noting that in Amos 8:8 MT there is a reference to "the land . . . all of it" (diff. LXX).

10. He uses "midday" (*mesēmbria*), which is found in Amos 9:8 LXX but not in the Synoptics, and "sun" (*hēlios*), which appears in Amos but not in Matthew or Mark. See 5(15).

new age in intertestamental and later Judaism. One concludes, therefore, that Mark 15:33, drawn up as it is in dependence upon Amos 8:9, sees in the historical crucifixion of Jesus the fulfillment of a prophesy concerned with the great Day of the Lord.

## Mark 15:38: The Rending of the Veil

*Tradition and redaction.* In Mark, after Jesus breathes his last (15:37), a strange event occurs: "And the curtain of the temple was torn in two, from top to bottom" (*kai to katapetasma tou naou eschisthē eis duo ap anōthen heōs katō*). This sentence should not be attributed to the redactor's hand. Although the use of *-then* with *ek* or *apo* is sometimes Markan,[11] *katapetasma* and *anōthen* are *hapax legomena* for Mark, and the only other occurrence of *schizō* is in 1:10. *Naos* is used in 14:58 and 15:29, but the latter two verses are probably from the tradition; contrast the favoring of *hieron* elsewhere (nine times). As nothing marks *eis duo* or *heōs katō* as redactional, 15:38 is relatively free of characteristic Markan vocabulary. Further, as the judgment that Mark 15:33 and 38 belong to the same stage of the tradition is close to unanimous, and as there is some reason to suspect that 15:33 derives from a pre-Markan passion complex (as argued above), there is justification for the prevalent verdict that Mark 15:38 also derives from a pre-Markan passion complex.

*Interpretation.* Assuming the correctness of this conclusion, the problem of interpretation arises. Commentators have long debated the significance of *to katapetasma tou naou*, "the veil of the temple." Is the *katapetasma* the inner veil that covered the entrance to the Holy of Holies (cf. Exod. 26:31–35; Lev. 21:23; Philo, *Spec. Leg.* 1.270; Jos. *Ant.* 8.3.3) or the outer curtain that separated the sanctuary from the forecourt (Exod. 26:37; Num. 3:26; *Ep. Arist.* 86)? The word *katapetasma* is ambiguous. In the LXX it designates both veils (note Exod. 26:31–37 and 27:16). Further, the meaning of *naos* is uncertain. Although some scholars have affirmed that *naos* designated the inner shrine as opposed to *to hieron*—that is, the entire temple—such a distinction cannot constantly be maintained. Josephus seemingly does not always differentiate between *ho naos, to hieron,* and *ho oikos tou theou.*[12] In the New Testament, while *naos* must be the temple proper in several places (Luke 1:8–11 and Rev. 11:1 being examples), in Matt. 27:5 and John 2:20 the word cannot refer to the

---

11. See Frans Neirynck, *Duality in Mark,* BETL 31 (Louvain: Louvain Univ. Press, 1972), 75–76, 190.

12. See, e.g., Jos. *Ant.* 15.11.1–7. Cf. *Herod.* 2.155, 156, 170. On terminology for the temple in Josephus, see Gottlob Schrenk, "Hieros ktl.," *TDNT* 3 (1965): 232–34.

temple in the narrow sense. Linguistic considerations, then, do not resolve the issue: what is the *katapetasma*?

The question is the more difficult as a fitting interpretation of Mark 15:38 can be offered for either reading of *katapetasma*. Assuming that the sign is more than a simple *teras*, if the veil is the outer veil, its rending may foreshadow or symbolize the end of the temple. This view is already found in *Ps.-Clem. Rec.* 1.41: "The veil of the temple was rent, as in lamentation for the destruction impending over the place."[13] Such an interpretation is especially attractive as similar portents announcing the doom of the temple are recorded by both Josephus (*Jewish War* 6.5.3) and the Talmud (*b. Yoma* 39b). One should also observe that in *Liv. Pro. Hab.* 12 (late first century A.D.?) the following prophecy is attributed to the prophet Habakkuk:

> Concerning the end of the temple [*tou naou*] he foretold that it would be accomplished by a western nation. Then, he said, the veil of the sanctuary [*haplōma tou dabeir* (= *dbyr*)] will be torn to pieces, and the capitals of the pillars will be removed and no one will know where they are.[14]

A reference to the destruction of 70 A.D. seems likely (cf. *2 Baruch* 6). The text does not appear to suffer from Christian influence.

If the wonder in Mark 15:38, like the wonders recorded by Josephus, the Talmud, and *Liv. Pro. Hab.* 12, foretells or means the end of the temple, it also vindicates Jesus' warnings against the place (13:1-2; 14:58; 15:29). Therefore, even as Jesus dies upon the cross, his words are vindicated, and the judgment of his adversaries, the Jewish leaders, is sealed, or a warning to them given (cf. *T. Levi* 10).

The other major line of interpretation understands *katapetasma* to be the inner veil in the Holy of Holies and concludes that Mark 15:38, in the words of Vincent Taylor, "symbolizes the opening of the way to God effected by the death of Christ, or alternatively, and perhaps at the same time, the end of the Temple system."[15] The barrier heretofore existing between God and man has been broken through—an idea paralleled in Hebrews (6:9; 9:1-28; 10:19-22).

It is important to note that the two standard interpretations of Mark 15:38 have this in common: both understand the rending of the veil to mark or symbolize the end of the temple or the end of that for which it stands. That is, both involve an end. The point of agreement is inevitable, for the rending of the veil can only be interpreted as a destructive act ("torn in two, from top to bottom"). The significance of this for our purposes becomes manifest in the

13. *ANF*, 8:88.
14. Au. trans., based upon the Greek text of C. C. Torrey, *The Lives of the Prophets*, JBLMS (Lancaster, Pa.: Society of Biblical Literature, 1949), 29.
15. Taylor, *Gospel According to St. Mark*, 596.

light of Jewish speculation concerning the fate of the temple in Jerusalem.[16] Several Jewish texts composed before 70 A.D. announce that the old temple will not continue into the new age. God will instead build a new temple. *1 Enoch* 90:28-29 is typical:

> And I [Enoch] stood up to see till they folded up that old house; and carried off all the pillars, and all the beams and ornaments of the house were at the same time folded up with it. ... And I saw till the Lord of the sheep brought a new house greater and loftier than that first, and set it up in the place of the first which had been folded up: all its pillars were new, and its ornaments were new and larger than those of the first, the old one which He had taken away, and all the sheep were within it. (*APOT*)[17]

Other pertinent passages include *Jub.* 1:27; Tob. 13:16-18; 14:5; *11QTemple* XXIX, 8-10; 4QFlor I, 1-3; *Sib. Or.* V, 414-33; *Tg. Isa* on 53:5; *Midr. Ps.* on 90:17; and perhaps *Mek.* on Exod. 15:17.

The texts just cited should not be left out of account in the attempt to explicate Mark 15:38. Whatever the precise meaning of *to katapetasma* and *ho naos*, the verse surely signifies an end of the temple: in some sense the old house has or soon will pass away. With the death of Jesus, "the temple is symbolically destroyed."[18] Now, given that the present temple in Jerusalem was, at least in some Jewish circles, expected to pass away with the coming of the final redemption, Mark 15:38 apparently associates an eschatological theme with the passion of Jesus. It was anticipated that, at the consummation, the old temple would come to its end. According to Mark 15:38, this has, with the death of Jesus, already happened. Such a reading is supported by the eschatological character of the other *teras* in Mark 15, the darkening of the sun; for here, too, an eschatological event is moved into the passion narrative.

Our interpretation, which does not require resolution over the precise meaning of *to katapetasma*, is further bolstered by the sayings, found in all four Gospels and in Acts, that prophesy the end of the temple. A dominical word almost certainly underlies the various texts, and the original prophecy was likely tied to eschatological expectations. Further, Mark 13:1-2 preserves the eschatological dimension of the saying, for here the prophecy of the temple's ruin serves to introduce a discourse about the end of the age. Hence, it is clear that the Jewish expectation concerning the end of the old temple found its way

16. See recently Ferdinand Dexinger, "Ein 'messianisches Szenarium' als Gemeingut des Judentums in nachherodianischer Zeit," *Kairos* 17 (1975): 249-78.
17. "All the pillars, and all the beams and ornaments" seems more fitting if the reference is to the temple, not the entire city of Jerusalem—although in Jewish sources the city and its temple are often identified; cf. W. D. Davies, *Gospel and the Land,* 143-44.
18. Paul J. Achtemeier, *Mark,* Proclamation Commentaries (Philadelphia: Fortress Press, 1975), 25.

into at least some quarters of the early church. This encourages one to interpret Mark 15:38 against that expectation. Before passing on to the next topic, it is worth noting that Jos. *Ant.* 5.5.5 may bear on Mark 15:38. According to this text, a Babylonian curtain, embroidered with blue, scarlet, linen thread, and purple hung before the main entrance of the sanctuary, at the back of the vestibule, and "worked into the tapestry was the whole vista of the heavens (excepting the signs of the Zodiac)." Now *if* Mark 15:38 pertains to this particular curtain (an unresolved problem), then the picture conjured up by the verse is of a panorama of the heavens splitting. (Note that Ps. 104:2; Isa. 40:22; and *b. B. Meṣ* 59a liken the sky to a curtain or tent.) It may not be coincidence that the rending or dissolution of the heavenly firmament occurs in the Old Testament and later came to be a fixed item of the eschatological scenario. See Job 14:12 LXX; Ps. 102:26; Isa. 34:4; 63:19 (64:1); Hag. 2:6, 21; *Sib. Or.* III, 82; Matt. 24:29; Rev. 6:14; 2 Pet. 3:10; and *Sib. Or.* VIII, 233, 413.

## Zechariah 9—14 and the Passion of Jesus

The scriptural background of Mark 11:1—16:8 (excluding chap. 13) consists primarily of three blocks of material: the Psalms (especially 22, 41—43, 61, 69, 109, 118); Deutero-Isaiah; and Zechariah 9—14. The impetus for drawing upon the Psalms and Deutero-Isaiah is immediately evident. These texts incorporate the theme of the suffering righteous one and are employed to interpret Jesus' sufferings and death as *passio iusti*. Further, Psalms 22, 41, 69, 71, and Isaiah 53 refer to the vindication or exaltation of the suffering righteous one. Thus, as Pesch affirms, "The OT substructure of the Passion history serves the interpretation of the suffering *and* resurrection of the Son of Man."[19] But what of Deutero-Zechariah? In Dodd's words, "The second half of the Book of Zechariah, chs. ix–xiv, has the character of an apocalypse, and while its component visions (like those of many apocalypses) are not easy to bring into a consistent scheme, it can be understood as setting forth a whole eschatological programme."[20] Given the repeated employment and thematic significance of particular psalms and Deutero-Isaiah in the Markan narrative, one should not lightly pass over the general character of Zechariah 9—14. On the contrary, the systematic use made of Zechariah 9—14 is evidence that the section as a whole was meaningful—the more so as passion traditions preserved in Matthew and John likewise cite or allude to passages from Zechariah 9—14. The following quotations and allusions may be observed:

19. Pesch, *Markusevangelium*, 2:14.
20. C. H. Dodd, *According to the Scriptures: The Sub-structure of New Testament Theology* (London: William Collins Sons, 1965), 64.

|                    | *Quotation*     | *Allusion*           |
|--------------------|-----------------|----------------------|
| Mark 11:1-2, 7     |                 | Zech. 9:9; 14:4      |
| Mark 11:15-19      |                 | Zech. 14:16, 20-21[21] |
| Mark 14:11         |                 | Zech. 11:12          |
| Mark 14:22-25      |                 | Zech. 9:11           |
| Mark 14:26-31      | Zech. 13:7      |                      |
| Mark 14:50-52      |                 | Zech. 13:7(?); 14:5(?) |
| *From Matthew add:* |                |                      |
| Matt. 21:4-5       | Zech. 9:9       |                      |
| Matt. 26:15        |                 | Zech. 11:12          |
| Matt. 27:3-10      | Zech. 11:12-13  |                      |
| Matt. 27:51b-53[22] |                | Zech. 14:4-5         |
| *From John add:*   |                 |                      |
| John 19:37         | Zech. 12:10     |                      |
| John 2:16[23]      |                 | Zech. 14:21          |

It may also be noted that when Jesus enters Jerusalem the crowd that greets him cuts branches and sings, "'Hosanna! Blessed be he who comes in the name of the Lord!'" (Mark 11:8-9). At the Feast of Booths it was customary to cut branches, and the hallel cited in Mark 11:9 (from Psalm 118) was sung at the same feast (see *m. Sukk.* 3)—a fact significant for our purposes because Zech. 14:16-19 is an account of Sukkoth, on the first day of which Zech. 14:1-21 was read as the haptarah.[24] Further, Mark 11:23 (on faith moving "*this* mountain" [italics added]; cf. 11:1: "And when they drew near to Jerusalem, to Bethphage and Bethany, at the Mount of Olives. . . .") has been thought to allude to Zech. 14:4-5, which foretells the cleavage of the Mount of Olives on the Day of the Lord.[25]

An examination of the contacts observed between Zechariah 9—14 and Mark 11—16 indicates that Mark recounts the passion of Jesus as though it were the fulfillment of certain eschatological scriptures: the peaceful king enters the holy city (cf. Zech. 9:9), cleanses his temple (cf. Zech. 14:16, 21), establishes the new covenant in blood (cf. Zech. 9:11), experiences a time of

---

21. See Cecil Roth, "The Cleansing of the Temple and Zechariah xiv 21," *NovT* 4 (1960): 174–81; and C. K. Barrett, "The House of Prayer and the Den of Thieves," in *Jesus und Paulus: Festschrift für Werner Georg Kümmel zum 70. Geburtstag*, ed. E. E. Ellis and E. Grässer (Göttingen: Vandenhoeck & Ruprecht, 1975), 19–20.

22. See 42–44 herein.

23. John 2:14–22 is probably displaced; it presumably belonged at one stage to a passion narrative; see Barnabas Lindars, *The Gospel of John*, NCB (Grand Rapids: Wm. B. Eerdmans, 1972), 135.

24. See Charles W. F. Smith, "No Time for Figs," *JBL* 79 (1960): 315–27. Cf. *b. Meg.* 31a.

25. See Pesch, *Markusevangelium*, II:204.

trial and affliction (cf. Zech. 13:7—14:3), and is raised from the dead (cf. Zech. 14:4–5).[26] Detailed attention to Mark 14:(26)27–29 will clarify matters further.

The quotation in Mark 14:27b ("'I will strike the shepherd, and the sheep will be scattered'") interprets the prediction in 27a ("'You will all fall away'") and is from Zech. 13:7. Now, Zech. 13:7 belongs to a portion of Scripture— Zech. 13:7—14:5—which is primarily a prophecy of the tribulations that are to precede the Day of the Lord. The verse in fact heads the section, and it has been suggested that, as an interpretative addition in Mark 14, its function is to recollect all of Zech. 13:7—14:5. According to Max Wilcox, with the striking of the shepherd and the scattering of his flock, "the hour has dawned for the time of desolation and testing described in Zech. XIII 7—XIV 4."[27] Of course, on the assumption that "atomistic exegesis" of the Tanach was then the rule, it is nowadays fashionable to prohibit taking account of the original contexts of verses cited in the New Testament. But such an evaluation of first-century hermeneutics is not entirely satisfactory,[28] and here in particular there are indications that the quotation from Zech. 13:7 is intended to alert the reader to an extended portion of the Bible, Zech. 13:7—14:5, and mark its fulfillment.

Zechariah 9—14 was an early source of testimonia.[29] It is thus at least plausible that a quotation from those chapters would recall neighboring verses. With this in mind, it may be remarked that the parallels between Zech. 13:7—14:5 and Mark 14—16 are quite striking. The prophet writes of a smiting of the shepherd (13:7) and of a scattering of sheep (13:7), of a time of testing (13:9) and of fleeing (14:5), of the Lord's coming to the Mount of Olives (14:4) and, according to an old interpretation,[30] of a resurrection (14:4–5). Corresponding to all this, in the passion traditions now collected in Mark 14—16, the Lord comes to the Mount of Olives (14:26; cf. 11:1 and 13:3); he is struck (14:27); his sheep are scattered (14:27, 50); a time of testing comes upon all (14:34–41, 54, 66–72); men flee (14:50–52); there is a resurrection (14:28; 16:1-8). Thus, an extensive correlation obtains between Zech. 13:7—14:5 and Mark 14—16. It should not be credited to chance. Rather, Zech. 13:7, cited as a fulfilled text within the context of Christian passion traditions, would surely have recalled all of Zech. 13:7—14:5. Evidently, the passage from Zechariah, which describes the final catastrophe and the coming of the Lord, was at one

---

26. On Zech. 14:4–5 as a prophecy of the resurrection, see 42–44 herein.
27. Max Wilcox, "The Denial Sequence in Mark XIV. 26–31, 66–72," *NTS* 17 (1971): 426–36.
28. Note in this connection C. J. A. Hickling, "Paul's Reading of Isaiah," in *Studia Biblica 1978 III: Papers on Paul and Other New Testament Authors,* ed. E. A. Livingstone (Sheffield: JSOT Press, 1980), 215–23.
29. See Dodd, *According to the Scriptures,* 64–67.
30. See n. 26.

time used to interpret the final events of the life of Jesus as the fulfillment of certain prophetic expectations: Jesus has passed through the eschatological time of trouble, and the Day of the Lord has dawned. Such a proposal is strongly buttressed by our earlier analysis of the signs and wonders joined to the crucifixion; for the use of Deutero-Zechariah in the story of the passion functions as do the signs and wonders—namely, to portray the end of Jesus as the realization of particular eschatological hopes.[31]

## Mark 13 and the Markan
## Passion Narrative

Zechariah 9—14 is not the only apocalypse to which the passion story of Mark exhibits interesting parallels. The second Gospel contains its own apocalypse (the discourse in chapter 13) and, as R. H. Lightfoot observed, several passages in Mark 14—15 recall the predictions of Mark 13.[32] Thus, notice may be taken of the fact that *paradidōmi*, "to hand over," used in connection with the death of Jesus (seven times in Mark 14), is also used in connection with the fate of the disciples in the coming time of trouble (13:9, 11-12). Especially interesting, in the light of Jesus' fate, is 13:9: "'They will deliver you up to councils; and you will be beaten in synagogues; and you will stand before governors and kings. ... '" Just as the master is handed over to the authorities, treated with contempt, scourged, and put to death, so will it be with his followers at the end.

Mark 13:32-33 reads as follows: "'But of that day or that hour no one knows, not even the angels in heaven, nor the Son, but only the Father. Take heed, watch; for you do not know when the time will come.'" An interesting correspondence exists between this passage and the scene in Gethsemane. In Mark 14:32-42, Jesus prays concerning the hour, that it might pass from him, but he submits himself to the Father. "Clearly the hour has not yet arrived in all its fulness; and there is a possibility that it may pass."[33] Meantime, the disciples are exhorted to watch and pray so that they might endure the coming hours of trial—precisely what they are exhorted to do in Mark 13:32-33; see 14:34 and 37-38.

Mark 13:26—"'And then they will see the Son of man coming in clouds with great power and glory'"—immediately recalls 14:62: "'You will see the

---

31. Notably, Mark in his passion narrative "clearly prefers prophetic and eschatologically interpreted passages of scripture. ..." So Howard C. Kee, "The Function of Scriptural Quotations and Allusions in Mark 11—16," in *Jesus und Paulus*, 173; see 166–73 for the evidence.

32. R. H. Lightfoot, *The Gospel Message of St. Mark* (Cambridge: Cambridge Univ. Press, 1950), 48–59.

33. Ibid., 53.

Son of man seated at the right hand of the Power, and coming with the clouds of heaven.'" The coming of the Son of man signals, in the Markan apocalypse, the consummation: after the tribulation of the latter days, he will come in the clouds. In Mark 14:62 Jesus affirms that, after and despite condemnation and death, he will be seen by his enemies and thence vindicated. Both the passion narrative and Mark 13 accordingly announce that the present and coming tribulation will eventuate in the advent of the Son of man.

The statement of Mark 13:35—"'You do not know when the master of the house will come, in the evening, or at midnight, or at cockcrow, or in the morning'"—may also be illuminated by the passion narrative; for the evangelist employs these very times to order the material in 14:17—15:1; see 14:17, 72; and 15:1.[34]

Finally, Lightfoot quotes Mark 13:30 ("'Truly, I say to you, this generation will not pass away before all these things take place'") and asserts, "A first fulfilment at any rate was not far off, which was itself recognized as a sign, a seal of assurance, and a sacrament of the ultimate fulfilment."[35]

Lightfoot's work does not exhaust the significant parallels between Mark 13 and Mark 14—15. (1) In Mark 15:33 a darkness lies upon the land as Jesus hangs upon the cross. According to Mark 13:24, the final tribulation will witness the darkening of the sun. (2) In Mark 15:38, the veil of the temple is rent, signifying that in some sense, the holy place has passed away or will pass away. According to Mark 13:2, before the end comes, the temple will be wrecked. (3) In the passion narrative of Mark, stress is laid on Judas being "one of the twelve" (14:10, 20, 43) and a member of the group closest to Jesus (cf. 14:18-20), and it is he who betrays the master. According to Mark 13:12-13, in the last times, those who should be closest will betray one another: "'Brother will deliver up brother to death.'" (4) In Mark 14:50-52 the disciples of Jesus and an unnamed naked young man flee when Jesus is arrested. According to Mark 13:14-16, the time of the end will be a time of flight: after the desolating sacrilege is set up, "'then let those who are in Judea flee to the mountains . . . and let him who is in the field not turn back to take his mantle.'" (5) In Mark 14:40 Jesus comes (*elthōn*) to his disciples and finds (*heuren*) them sleeping (*katheudontas*). The same construction occurs in 14:37: *erchetai—heuriskei—katheudontas*. According to Mark 13:36, true servants should be on guard, lest, at the end, their master come (*elthōn*) and find (*heurē*) them sleeping (*katheudontas*).

The meaning of the parallelism between Mark 13—which, it should be

---

34. If the three prayer watches of Jesus (14:32-42) are calculated to be of one hour's duration (14:37), then Judas's arrival in Gethsemane occurs at midnight (14:42-43).

35. Lightfoot, *Gospel Message*, 54.

remembered, prefaces the account of the last three days of Jesus' life—and Mark 14—15 becomes evident when one considers the movement of the eschatological discourse, which can be set forth thus:

|       |         |                                                  |
|-------|---------|--------------------------------------------------|
| I.    | 13:1-2: | prophecy against the temple                      |
| II.   | 13:3-4: | introduction to main discourse                   |
| III.  | 13:5-8: | beginning of the birth pangs                     |
| IV.   | 13:9-13: | persecution                                      |
| V.    | 13:14-23: | desolating sacrilege, flight, and false Christs |
| VI.   | 13:24-27: | coming of the Son of man                        |
| VII.  | 13:28-36: | call to watch                                   |

Sections III and IV (13:5-13) clearly refer to the reader's present (see especially 13:10) and no doubt mirror the difficult experiences of the Markan church. Only in 13:14 ("'But when you see'") does the discourse move into the future. Hence, Norman Perrin can analyze Mark 13:5-37 as follows:[36]

|      |        |                              |
|------|--------|------------------------------|
| Vv.  | 5-13:  | the reader's present         |
| Vv.  | 14-23: | the reader's future, epoch 1 |
| Vv.  | 24-37: | the reader's future, epoch 2 |

For Mark, the time of the end has begun. The church is already suffering the tribulation attendant upon the turning of the ages. The events of the present time are the begining of the birth pangs (13:8).

If the Markan church suffers the "messianic woes," then it may be proposed that the time of eschatological tribulation extends from the time of Jesus to the consummation, for the parallels between Mark 13 and the passion narrative suggest that the sufferings of Jesus himself belong to the great tribulation. Robert H. Smith has written, "Jesus' suffering is not just the suffering of one more martyr in a long history of martyrdom. Mark 13 indicates that His death has universal significance, ultimate power, cosmic sweep. His death is itself precisely that event which ushers in the last times, inaugurating eschatology."[37] Certainly, such an interpretation helps to explain the presence of eschatological motifs in the story of the passion. For Mark, then, the denouement has commenced with the passion of Jesus, which is thus "the first act of the end of the world."[38] Jesus has passed through the time of crisis, and the disciples must follow after their Lord, his way being their way (Mark 8:34-38). The sufferings of Jesus and of his church together constitute the labor pains after which the new world comes.

---

36. Norman Perrin, "Towards an Interpretation of the Gospel of Mark," in *Christology and a Modern Pilgrimage*, rev. ed., H. D. Betz, ed. (Missoula, Mont.: Scholars Press, 1974), 24.
37. Robert H. Smith, "Darkness at Noon: Mark's Passion Narrative," *CTM* 49 (1973): 333.
38. Martin Dibelius, *From Tradition to Gospel*, trans. B. L. Woolf (New York: Charles Scribner's Sons, 1966), 22.

## Conclusion

The link between Mark 15:33 and Amos 8:9, the background of Mark 15:38 in Jewish eschatological expectation, the parallels between Zechariah 9—14 and Mark 11—16, and the extensive links between Mark 13 and Mark 14—16 all lead to the same conclusion: Mark and his tradition portray the death of Jesus as though it had coincided with the eschatological transition, with the dreaded tribulation that would herald the Day of the Lord. Now, in view of the fact that the death of Jesus did not coincide with the world's renewal, this is an intriguing result that should immediately give rise to numerous questions. But before we can consider the origin of this interpretation of the end of Jesus and its possible relation to the so-called "realized eschatology" of which Dodd spoke, we must first determine to what extent the interpretation is shared by other books in the New Testament. We turn next to Matthew.

# Four

# THE GOSPEL OF MATTHEW

The association of eschatological motifs with the death and resurrection of Jesus is not confined to Mark or to traditions behind Mark. The association is also found in special Matthean materials. These must now receive attention.

## Matthew 27:51b–53: A Resurrection of Holy Ones

In the passion narrative of Mark, only two miraculous signs accompany the crucifixion of Jesus: the darkness at noon and the rending of the veil. Matthew's Gospel, however, records several other wonders: "And the earth shook [*eseisthē*], and the rocks [*petrai*] were split [*eschisthēsan*]; (52) the tombs also were opened [*aneōchēsan*], and many bodies [*sōmata*] of the saints who had fallen asleep [*tōn kekoimēnenōn hagiōn*] were raised, (53) and coming out of the tombs after his resurrection they went into the holy city and appeared to many" (Matt. 27:51b–53).

*Tradition and redaction.* The preredactional origin of Matt. 27:51b–53 is not easily established. Although perhaps most authorities have claimed that the passage owes something to tradition, the advent of redaction criticism has encouraged several critics to posit an editorial genesis. Most important in this connection has been the work of Donald P. Senior. In three separate studies he has presented the case for interpreting Matt. 27:51b–53 as a free editorial composition, arguing the following points.[1] First, an examination of vocabulary and syntax allows the conclusion that Matt. 27:51b–53 is a redactional product: the language is typically Matthean. Second, the motifs clustered in the passage have their background in the Tanach and do not demand a tradi-

---

1. Donald P. Senior, *The Passion According to Matthew: A Redactional Study,* BETL 29 (Louvain: Louvain Univ. Press, 1975), 207–23; "The Death of Jesus and the Resurrection of the Holy Ones (MT 27:51–53)," *CBQ* 38 (1976): 312–29; "The Death of God's Son and the Beginning of the New Age," in *The Language of the Cross,* ed. A. Lacomara (Chicago: Franciscan Herald Press, 1977), 31–59.

tion history within the church. Third, properly interpreted within the Matthean passion, the resurrection of the holy ones and the accompanying signs highlight the redactor's theology, for Matthew thought of the end of Jesus as an "eschatological" event. Senior understands the confluence of these three points to indicate the redactional nature of Matt. 27:51b–53. There is cause, however, to differ.

The language of Matt. 27:51b–53 does not unambiguously testify to Matthean creativity. It is, for example, impossible to conclude anything about Matthew's editorial activity from the vocabulary and syntax of v. 51b. To be sure, *eseisthē* (Matthew three times, Mark and Luke each zero times) and *petrai* (Matthew five times, Mark one, Luke three) could be regarded as Matthean, and the "divine passive" (also used in v. 52) is frequent in the first Gospel; but then each of these items might just as well come from the tradition. Apart from the observation that the statistics do not demand a redactional derivation for either *eseisthē* or *petrai*, if Matthew inherited a tradition about a resurrection, one can account for all the elements in v. 51b without recourse to the redactional level. The eschatological events, including the resurrection, were traditionally linked with earthquakes, as in Joel 2:10; Ezek. 37:7 LXX; Hag. 2:6; Zech 14:5; *1 Enoch* 1:3–9; *As. Mos.* 10:4; *4 Ezra* 6:13–16; 9:3; and *2 Apoc. Bar.* 70:8. Further, *petrai* is bound to *eschisthēsan* (compare only 27:51a in Matthew [from Mark 15:38]), a verb which is used in Zech. 14:4 LXX in connection with the splitting of the Mount of Olives on the last day. *T. Levi* 4:1 also provides a close parallel: in the end time, *(tōn) petrōn schizomenōn kai tou hēliou sbennymenou* (or: *skotizomenou*).[2] Thus, although one is initially inclined to attribute the use of *schizō* (in the passive) in v. 51b to the influence of v. 51a, the extra-Matthean parallels call for caution. The splitting of rocks or mountains at the end time appears to have been a traditional motif and could have been tied, along with notice of an earthquake, to a story of resurrection before Matthew. Concerning the divine passive in v. 51b, while the device may sometimes be redactional in the first Gospel, it is so frequent in all the Synoptics and in Jewish apocalyptic literature in general as to be no fine index of redactional activity. In sum, then, nothing in 27:51b clearly betrays the hand of Matthew.

Matt. 27:52 is, despite Senior, scarcely more helpful than v. 51b in defining the extent of the Matthean contribution. A case can, admittedly, be made for

---

2. Anticipating the results of this study, it is more likely that Matt. 27:51b–53 represents the Christian adoption of an eschatological tradition than that the Christian redactor of a Jewish pseudepigraphon used Matt. 27:51b–53 to describe the coming end of the world. There are, to be sure, interpolations throughout the *Testaments of the Twelve Patriarchs*, but nothing demands a Christian hand for *T. Levi* 4:1.

regarding *aneōchthēsan* as redactional. The verb shows up several times in verses peculiar to Matthew, only once in Mark (Matthew eleven times, Mark one, Luke seven). But this consideration is offset by a close review of the rest of the verse. The recurrence of *kai* (twice each in vv. 52, 51b, 53) is much more typical of Mark than Matthew; and in a passage treating of resurrection, *sōmta* could well be traditional. More important, *tōn kekoimēmenōn hagiōn* is perhaps unusual. Nowhere else does the first evangelist use *hagios* as a substantive, and throughout the New Testament *hoi hagioi* has reference to the New Testament saints or angels (here the saints of old are meant; compare Dan. 7:18, 21). In addition, Matthew's own preferred usage for the saints is *hoi dikaioi*. Indeed, in 23:29 he writes of *ta mnēmeia tōn dikaiōn*, "the monuments of the righteous." If Matthew were entirely responsible for the formulation of 27:52, it is somewhat surprising that it is *hoi hagioi*, not *hoi dikaioi*, who are raised.

In Matt. 27:53, "holy city" can with relative assurance be ascribed to the redactor (compare 4:5). Further, *meta tēn egersin* may be Matthean. The temporal use of *meta* plus an accusative is found several times in Matthean formulations (for example, 1:12; 25:19; 27:62–63), and while *tēn egersin* is a *hapax legomenon* in the New Testament, Matthew employs *egeirō* more often than either Mark or Luke (Matthew thirty-six times, Mark nineteen, Luke eighteen). Yet it should be underlined that if "after the resurrection" is Matthean, that is reason for concluding that a traditional story has been taken up into the synoptic tradition, for the phrase reads like an insertion correcting a theological inconcinnity (the saints rise before Jesus), and it is unlikely that a redactor would need to emend his own composition.

Regarding the remainder of v. 53, nothing stands out as obviously redactional; and even if it seemed otherwise, that would still be consistent with the supposition that the evangelist is simply relating a tradition in his own words, as he does throughout his Gospel. So we come to the conclusion that a review of the language of Matt. 27:51b–53 neither excludes nor verifies the hypothesis of a redactional origin, although perhaps on balance the use of *hagiōn* and the chronological note, "after the resurrection," remain more problematical on that view. The first link in Senior's chain of argument is not strong.

Senior's evaluation of the background of Matt. 27:51b–53 also invites criticism. His claim that our passage depends primarily upon Ezekiel 37, and that it is therefore probably a product of Matthean reflection on the Scriptures, is questionable. To begin with, the proof that a passage draws upon the Tanach for its inspiration by no means excludes a pre-Matthean origin. It goes without saying that Matthew's special tradition already drew heavily upon the Bible. Moreover, the links between Ezekiel 37 and Matt. 27:51b–53 are not extensive. A close resemblance does obtain between Ezek. 37:12 (*egō anoigō hymōn ta mnēmata*) and Matt. 27:52a (*ta mnēmeia aneōchthēsan*); but beyond this, Ezekiel 37 has little colored Matthew's text. There is, admittedly, an earthquake in Ezekiel 37 LXX; but the return of exiles to Israel (Ezek. 37:12) does not precisely match entrance into Jerusalem (Matt. 27:53). In addition, our evangelist says nothing about bones—surely odd if Ezekiel 37 is so much before his mind's eye. Even less significant is the thematic connection Senior draws between Ezekiel 37 and Matt. 27:51-53 (both have to do with vindication and salvation in the midst of exile or death). Where in Jewish or Christian literature does resurrection *not* carry the thought of vindication and God's saving power?

Despite the parallel between Ezek. 37:12 and Matt. 27:52, there is another Scripture that lays claim to bear directly on our text: Zech. 14:4-5. The affinity between the two passages has probably gone largely unnoticed because, in the Christian tradition, Zech. 14:4-5 has not been interpreted as an account of the resurrection. The north panel of the Dura-Europos synagogue (mid-third century A.D.), however, provides evidence that the passage was so understood within ancient Judaism. Although many scholars have looked primarily to Ezekiel 37 for the interpretation of the panel,[3] there can be little doubt that Zech. 14:4-5 is also reflected.[4] In the section which portrays the resurrection of the dead, the Mount of Olives (indicated by the two olive trees on the top of the mountain) has been split in two—precisely the event prophesied in Zech. 14:4—and the revived dead are emerging from the crack. The fallen building on the slopes of the mountain probably symbolizes an earthquake (Zech. 14:4), and those resurrected are in all likelihood here identified with the "holy ones" of Zech. 14:5. Such an interpretation gains some support by (1) the Targum on Zech. 14:3-5: the passage is introduced with God blowing the trumpet ten times to announce the resurrection of the dead; (2) the Targum on the Song of Songs (8:5): "When the dead rise, the Mount of Olives will be cleft, and all Israel's dead will come up out of it, also the righteous who have died in captivity; they will come by way of a subterranean passage and will emerge from beneath the Mount of Olives"; and (3) later rabbinic uses of Zech. 14:5: the "holy ones" of Zechariah are more than once identified not with the angels but with the ancient saints, specifically the prophets (for example, *Midr. Rabbah* on Song of Songs 4.11.1; on Ruth 2; and on Eccles. 1.11.1; cf. Ign. *Magn.* 9). The passage from the Targum on the Song of Songs (2) clearly represents an

---

3. So, e.g., Erwin R. Goodenough, *Jewish Symbols in the Greco-Roman Period: Symbolism in the Dura Synagogue,* Bollingen Series, vol. X (Princeton, N.J.: Princeton Univ. Press, 1964), 179-96. See vol. XI, plate 21 for the best reproduction of the panel under discussion.
4. Cf. Harald Riesenfeld, *The Resurrection in Ezekiel XXXVIII and in the Dura-Europos Paintings,* UUA 11 (Stockholm: Almqvist & Wiksells, 1948), 27-38; also John B. Curtis, "The Mount of Olives in Tradition," *HUCA* 28 (1957): 170-72.

interpretation of Zech. 14:4–5 and is the perfect literary parallel to the panel at Dura. It appears, therefore, that Zech. 14:4–5 was understood in some Jewish circles to be a prophecy of the resurrection. Once Zech. 14:4–5 LXX is read as a prophecy of the resurrection, its relation to Matt. 27:51b–53 becomes manifest. In both texts (1) a resurrection of the dead takes place immediately outside of Jerusalem (contrast Ezekiel 37, where the resurrection takes places in the Diaspora); (2) there is an earthquake; (3) the verb *schizō* is used in the passive, in connection with a mountain (Zechariah) or rocks (Matthew); and (4) the resurrected ones are called *hoi hagioi*. These parallels are sufficient to permit the conclusion that Matt. 27:51b–53 is based in part upon Zech. 14:4–5 and not, as Senior holds, solely upon Ezekiel 37.[5] The importance of this result for the question of tradition and redaction in our text will soon become evident.

The third pillar of Senior's argument stands no firmer than the first two. That Matt. 27:51b–53 coheres with Matthew's theology may be conceded, for Matthew elsewhere uses eschatological imagery to set forth Jesus' death as a turning point in time (see below). Indeed, Senior's delineation of the lines along which an interpretation should move may very well prove convincing. But the admission that the narrative can be harmonized with Matthean theology does not constitute evidence for a redactional origin. Most of the material in the first Gospel is traditional and at the same time consonant with Matthew's redactional theology. It is a long way from redactional coherence to redactional composition.

If Senior's case for the editorial composition of Matt. 27:51b–53 does not persuade, the question naturally arises, Does anything point in the opposite direction—namely, toward a pre-Matthean origin? An affirmative answer should be given.

(1) The particular application of Zech. 14:4–5 is instructive. One might maintain that, as Matthew alludes to or cites Zechariah more than any other evangelist, a narrative drawn up in dependence upon that minor prophet accords with a redactional origin. The proposal would be uninformed; for the only other allusion to Zech. 14:4–5 in Matthew is probably redactional, and it stands in tension with Matt. 27:51b–53. Matthew has apparently supplied the following introduction to the parable of the sheep and goats in 25:31–46: "'When the Son of man comes in his glory, and all the angels with him [*kai pantes hoi aggeloi met autou*]....'" As others have observed, the Greek [in

5. The north panel of the Dura-Europos synagogue draws upon both Ezekiel 37 and Zech. 14:4–5. It is probably not coincidence that the same is true of Matt. 27:51b–53. There appears to have been a pre-Christian exegetical tradition that brought Zech. 14:4–5 into association with Ezekiel 37.

brackets] strongly recalls Zech. 14:5 LXX: *kai pantes hoi agioi met autou*. Now, if Matt. 25:31 is indeed a redactional composition based on Zech. 14:5, the exegete is faced by two riddles. First, while *hoi hagioi* of Zech. 14:5 are the angels (*hoi aggeloi*) in Matt. 25:31, they are the resurrected saints (*tōn hagiōn*) in Matt. 27:52–53. Second, while Matt. 25:31 sets the fulfillment of Zech. 14:5 in the future ("'When the Son of man comes . . . '"), Matt. 27:53 narrates the realization of Zechariah's vision. One is thus confronted by two rival interpretations of Zech. 14:5. If it is unlikely that both come from the same hand, then since Matt. 25:31 is probably redactional, 27:52–53 probably is not.

(2) It has already been observed that the use of *hoi hagioi* (instead of *hoi dikaioi*) and the phrase "after the resurrection" may favor a pre-Matthean basis for Matt. 27:51b–53. The chronological note calls for further comment here. There is some question as to whether it even originally stood in the first Gospel. The problem is this. While the centurion and those with him at the cross see "the earthquake and what took place" (v. 54), "after the resurrection" (v. 53) seems to locate the events narrated in vv. 51b–53 (or at least the resurrection and witness of the saints) after Easter. But how can those witnessing the crucifixion observe things that did not happen until three days later?

If Matt. 27:51b–53 does not represent purely redactional material, the chronological gap (created by "after the resurrection") between the earthquake and the saints' departure from the tombs can be ascribed to an imperfect conflation of tradition and redaction. Certainly, there are noticeable theological and logical tensions elsewhere in Matthew which can be so explained; the redactional process has not always produced coherence. Matt. 27:51b–53 simply offers one more illustration of the phenomenon. If Matthew inherited the story preserved in 27:51b–53, his joining those verses to the other signs and wonders at the cross resulted in the holy ones rising before Jesus. As can be inferred from Col. 1:18 and Rev. 1:5 (Jesus is the firstborn of the dead; cf. Rom. 8:29; 1 Cor. 15:20, 23; Acts 26:23), such a sequence of events would have troubled certain sectors of the early church. The corrective addition, "after the resurrection," is probable proof that the sequence did in fact trouble Matthew. The phrase marks his interpretation of the tradition. It postpones the resurrection of the saints until after Easter morning. The reader is evidently to understand that, while the rocks split and the graves opened when Jesus died, the holy ones remained in their tombs until Easter. However odd this interpretation may seem (matters would be much plainer if "after the resurrection" introduced Matt. 27:52), it is the only one which makes good sense of the passage. Certainly, nothing is gained by supposing an original "after *their* resurrection" (Greek mss. 30, 220 and Ethiopic mss. have *autōn*): this weakly attested variant is most likely a secondary correction intended to obviate the very difficulty under discussion. The alternative of assigning "after *his* resurrection" to scribal correction is problematical given the unanimous testimony of all extant manuscripts and versions. It thus seems best to take the phrase as a redactional insertion qualifying a traditional story.

(3) The pre-Matthean and indeed primitive character of Matt. 27:51b–53 is suggested by the following consideration: the account falls in with what we otherwise know of primitive Christian eschatology. As the church moved away from its beginnings, Jesus' resurrection came to be viewed as an isolated event in history. There are indications, however, that in the earliest period his resurrection was more closely joined to thought of the general resurrection. For example, on the primitive material embedded in Rom. 1:4, Ernst Käsemann observes that the "hymnic tradition does not isolate Christ's resurrection but rather understands it in its cosmic function as the beginning of the general resurrection."[6] Also to be called upon at this juncture are those elements in earliest Christianity that C. H. Dodd and others have interpreted under the rubric of "realized eschatology." There is much to argue that the primitive Christian community believed that the new age was dawning in their time, that eschatological events had been and were unfolding before their eyes. Matt. 27:51b–53 finds a fitting home within such an environment. So the suggestion that the passage preserves a piece of primitive Christian tradition commends itself.

*Interpretation.* We have already, in our discussion of tradition and redaction, drawn out the point of Matt. 27:51b–53. The passage preserves one more trace of the early church's conviction that the end of Jesus could be depicted as though it marked the eschatological turning point.

### Matthew 27:54: Confession of the Gentiles

Matthew 27:54 is possibly of additional interest for our theme. In Mark, the centurion at the foot of the cross confesses, when Jesus breathes his last, that the crucified is the Son of God (Mark 15:39). Matthew has altered his source—we are not here dealing with pre-Matthean tradition—so that it is the centurion "and those who were with him, keeping watch over Jesus" who make the confession. It is, therefore, a group of Roman soldiers that recognizes Jesus to be the Son of God. Does Matthew see in this confession an anticipation or even the beginning of that salvation which is to come to the Gentiles at the eschatological turning point? Two considerations suggest this. First, if it is

---

6. Ernst Käsemann, *An die Römer,* 3d rev. ed., HNT 81 (Tübingen: J. C. B. Mohr [Paul Siebeck], 1974), 10.

legitimate to harmonize Matt. 10:5-6 (go only to the lost sheep of the house of Israel) and 28:19 (go into all the world), then the first evangelist must have thought the two contradictory commands to be appropriate to different periods of history. That is, before Easter the disciples went to Israel alone; after Easter they must go into all the world. Now, according to Matt. 8:11-12, the Gentiles enter the kingdom of God at the end. Matthew 12:41-42 points in the same direction; and Isa. 2:2-3; 11:9-10; 25:6-7; 45:20-25; Zechariah 8; Tob. 13:11; and *Pss. Sol.* 17:32-35 (30-31) are additional witnesses to their belief that, after the tribulation of the latter days, the Gentiles would turn to God. Matthew's familiarity with this tradition is to be assumed. Second, the confession of the centurion and those with him follows directly upon the ostensibly eschatological events recounted in 27:51b-53. "When the centurion and those who were with him, keeping watch over Jesus, saw the earthquake and what took place, they were filled with awe, and said, 'Truly this was the Son of God!'" The connection between Matt. 27:54 and 27:51b-53 brings the confession of the Gentiles into association with events otherwise eschatological. Is it, then, legitimate to see Matt. 27:54 as the fulfillment of an eschatological expectation? It is difficult to respond to this question without hesitation. But an affirmative answer[7] would harmonize with the tendency (already observed in Mark and elsewhere in Matthew) to portray the end of Jesus as if it were an eschatological event. An affirmative answer would also indicate that Matthew himself took up and furthered this tendency.

## Matthew 28:2-4: At the Tomb of Jesus

"And behold, there was a great earthquake; for an angel of the Lord descended from heaven and came and rolled back the stone, and sat upon it. His appearance was like lightning [*hē eidea autou hōs astrapē*], and his raiment white as snow [*to endyma autou leukon hōs chiōn*]. And for fear of him the guards trembled and became like dead men" (Matt. 28:2-4). This passage is probably not in the first instance a witness to Matthean theology; it presumably derives from Matthew's special tradition. Three times the first evangelist has interpolated into his passion narrative a pericope treating of the military guard for the tomb of Jesus: 27:62-66; 28:2-4; and 28:11-15. These three texts, which together form a coherent, self-contained story, probably constituted a traditional piece—one that is, perhaps, independently attested by *Gos. Pet.* 8—11 (28-49).[8] It related that the Jewish leaders requested and obtained a guard

7. See Rolf Walker, *Die Heilsgeschichte im ersten Evangelium* (Göttingen: Vandenhoeck & Ruprecht, 1967), 72-73.
8. Cf. Nikolaus Walter, "Eine vormatthäische Schilderung der Auferstehung Jesu," *NTS* 19 (1973): 415-29.

for the tomb of Jesus, that an angel descended from heaven and rolled away the great stone at the door of the tomb, and that the soldiers returned to Jerusalem and conspired with the Jewish leaders to hide the truth of what had happened. To judge from Matt. 28:11–15 and *Gos. Pet.* 11(43–49), the story served to meet Jewish polemic.

For our purposes it is the account of the descent of the angel in Matt. 28:2–4 that draws notice, for the language of 28:2–4 is the language of eschatology. The passage is introduced with the notice of an earthquake. Elsewhere in Matthew, earthquakes are associated with eschatological events (24:7 27:51b– 53). Further, the description of the angel's garment recalls the theophany of Dan. 7:9 (*to endyma autou hōsei chiōn leukon*, Theodotian; LXX: *peribolēn hōsei chiona*); and Dan. 10:6b may be the source of the description of the angel's countenance (*to prosōpon autou hōsei horasis astrapēs*). Such imagery is, in any case, a commonplace in ancient apocalyptic literature (cf. *1 Enoch* 71:1– 2; *2 Enoch* 1:3–5; Rev. 1:14–16; 4:5; 10:1). The response of those guarding the tomb of Jesus to the descent of the angel (28:4) also has its counterpart in many apocalypses (for example, Dan. 10:7–9, 16; Rev. 1:17; *2 Enoch* 1:7; *Apoc. Zeph.* 9:12—10:9). Thus, Eduard Schweizer has written: "All the elements [of Matt. 28:2–4] recall the signs expected to accompany the coming of the Lord at the end of the world and the irruption of the Kingdom of God."[9] Matthew 28:2–4 appears to recount the events of Easter morning as though they were events of the last times.

## Matthew 26:64 and 28:16–20:
## Promise and Fulfillment?

In Matt. 26:64, Jesus replies to the High Priest: "'Henceforth (*ap arti*) you will see the Son of man sitting at the right hand of the Power, and coming on the clouds of heaven'" (au. trans.). The "henceforth" immediately gains one's attention. It is not from Mark but does have a parallel in Luke 22:69 (*apo tou nun*) and hence may owe something to tradition. In any case, the qualification seems to suggest that the enthronement and Parousia of the Son of man lie in the near future. It is truly difficult to fathom how Matthew, writing over a generation after the death of Jesus, understood this. But the closing scene of the first Gospel, 28:16–20, may hold an answer. Matt. 28: 18b–19a (*edothē moi pasa exousia en ouranǭ kai epi tēs gēs poreuthentes oun mathēteusate panta ta ethnē*) probably recalls Dan. 7:14a LXX (*edothē autǭ exousia kai panta ta ethnē tēs gēs kata genē kai pasa doxa autǭ latreuousa*), this last verse being from the

---

9. Eduard Schweizer, *The Good News According to Matthew*, trans. David E. Green (Atlanta: John Knox Press, 1975), 524.

classic passage where the future victory of the Son of man is described.[10] Thus
Matt. 28:16–20 has often been represented as setting forth a proleptic Parousia, or the enthronement of the Son of man. The proposal is plausible and
suggests that the promise of Matt. 26:64 finds its partial or initial fulfillment in
the resurrection: Jesus has already received authority in heaven. That is, for
Matthew—and perhaps for the tradition before him—although the Son of
man has not yet come on the clouds of heaven, he has indeed been enthroned.
The Parousia, which will coincide with "the end of the age" (28:20), will only
make manifest on earth a fact already established in heaven.

## Conclusion

Our review of Matt. 27:51b–53, 54; 28:2–4; 26:64; and 28:18b–19a reveals
that, independently of Mark, yet like him, Matthew and his tradition associate
the death and resurrection of Jesus with eschatological motifs; the end of Jesus
is spoken of as though it had concurred with the end of the age. Yet an
interesting difference exists at this point between the first and second Gospels.
Mark is primarily concerned with interpreting the passion of Jesus in terms of
the "messianic woes." Events expected on the far side of tribulation are not
brought into the passion narrative. Accordingly, although the old temple has
passed away, no new temple is said to have come, and the resurrection of Jesus
(assuming that Mark as we know it is complete) is not even recounted. It is as
though the evangelist stands altogether on this side of the age to come. In
Matthew, by way of contrast, this age and the age to come seemingly overlap.
Although the consummation lies ahead, although this age is still full of
tribulation,[11] and although the Christian casts his hope upon the future com-

10. See now Jane Schaberg, *The Father, the Son, and the Holy Spirit: The Triadic Phrase in
Matthew 28:19b*, SBLDS (Chico, Calif.: Scholars Press, 1982), 111–41.
11. According to Douglas R. A. Hare, *The Theme of Jewish Persecution of Christians in the
Gospel According to St. Matthew*, SNTMS 6 (Cambridge: Cambridge Univ. Press, 1967), 99–
100, Matthew, unlike Mark, does not view evangelistic activity and its attendant persecution as
belonging to the trouble of the latter days. In the second Gospel, the missionary preaching of
the church is tied to "the beginning of the birth-pangs" (Mark 13:8–13). But the first evangelist
has radically altered Mark 13:9–13, and most of the material has been moved to chapter 10,
the discourse on mission. Matthew does, to be sure, retain prophecies of persecution in chapter
24, but Mark's words on bearing testimony and preaching the gospel no longer find a place
there. Against Hare, it should be noted that the sayings on mission and persecution, transferred
from Mark 13 to Matthew 10, still retain an eschatological setting, for it is prophesied that the
missionary endeavor (10:5–16) will eventuate in a persecution (10:17–22) that will not end
before the Son of man comes (10:23). Is this not similar to Mark's conception? That is, does
not the structure of Matt. 10:1–23 indicate that 10:17–22 foretells events belonging to the
eschatological transition? Hare argues that 10:23b is not a climax: Matthew wished to use
10:23a, and Matt. 10:23b is where it is because it was already attached to 10:23a. This raises
questions. (1) Why did the first evangelist not simply omit 10:23b? Does Hare attribute too
little freedom to the redactor? (2) Does not Matt. 10:16–23 exhibit an eschatological orientation even without verse 23? Cf., e.g., 10:21 with Micah 7:6 and *m. Soṭa* 9:15, and note the *telos*
in 10:22.

ing of the Son of man, saints have already been raised, the Son of man has already been enthroned in the heavenly places, and the resurrected Jesus is ever present with his followers (28:20). If we may so put it, Matthew's eschatology is, in some ways, more realized than that of Mark.

# Five

# THE GOSPEL OF JOHN[1]

While the Fourth Gospel as it now stands contains references to a coming resurrection and to a yet outstanding "last day" (6:39, 40, 44, 54; 7:37; 11:24; 12:48), the emphasis of Johannine eschatology lies elsewhere, namely, in the claim that certain eschatological expectations have become present realities. C. H. Dodd could write of John: "All that the church hoped for in the second coming of Christ is already given in its present experience of Christ through the Spirit."[2] Thus it is that "eternal life", which in the Synoptics refers strictly to the future (see Mark 10:17, 31; Matt. 25:46; cf. Mark 9:43, 45; Matt. 7:14), is a present possibility for John's readers: "'Truly, truly, I say to you, he who believes has eternal life'" (6:47; cf. 3:15-16, 36; 6:51, 58; 8:51-52; 11:24-26; 10:28). Similarly, while Luke 6:35 and 20:36 (cf. Matt. 5:9) hold forth divine sonship as an eschatological promise, in John it is granted even now to those who believe: "As many as received him, to them he gave authority to become sons of God" (1:12 [au. trans.]; cf. 1:13; 3:3-8; 1 John 3:1, 10; 5:2). Again, the expectation, already met with in the Tanach, that in messianic times living waters would flow out from the temple in Jerusalem (Ezek. 47:1-12; Joel 3:18) or from Jerusalem itself (Zech. 13:1; 14:8), is realized in Jesus, who is himself the living water and its dispenser: "'Whoever drinks of the water that I will give him will no longer thirst forever, but the water that I will give to him will become in him a spring of water welling up to eternal life'" (4:14 [au. trans.]; cf. 7:37-42 and 6:35c). It is the same with the bread from heaven (John 6:25-59): Jesus already gives to his people the manna which the Jews looked forward to receiving again in the latter days (2 Apoc. Bar. 29:8; Sib. Or. frag. iii,

---

1. Our examination of Mark and Matthew has uncovered traditions that (1) portray the passion as though it belonged to the eschatological tribulation and (2) interpret the resurrection of Jesus as though it were part of the general resurrection of Jewish expectation. Because these traditions have left scarcely a trace in Luke-Acts, we put off our examination of that two-volume work; only after looking at John and Paul and the Revelation to John—all three of which take up the traditions we have already studied—will the peculiar position of the third Gospel and its sequel receive scrutiny.

2. Dodd, *Apostolic Preaching*, 121.

49; *Mek.* on Exod. 16:25; Rev. 2:17). Moreover, although the resurrection of the dead is assumed to belong to the future (John 5:28–29; 6:39–40, 44, 54; 11:24), one also reads that "'the hour is coming, *and now is,* when the dead will hear the voice of the Son of God, and those who hear will live'" (John 5:25). And John declares that believers have already received the Spirit and attained to the knowledge or vision of God—things traditionally associated with the eschaton.

Although some scholars have used the term "realized eschatology" with reference to the proclamation of Jesus and the Pauline epistles, the perspective of John is generally held to be unusual and to demand special explanation. For Rudolf Schnackenburg, in John's Gospel "a fundamental rethinking has taken place, connected with a changed intellectual situation, a transformed attitude to the problems of human and Christian existence. It is more than a shift of emphasis; it is a move into different intellectual categories, an intellectual reorientation."[3] In accounting for the apparent shift represented by John, Schnackenburg claims that "the intellectual attitude of the milieu in which the Johannine community lived must be treated as an important element in the assessment."[4] But Schnackenburg lays more stress on Josef Blank's conclusion that in John "the Christology is not a function of the eschatology; rather it is the other way around—the Johannine eschatology is a function of the Christology."[5] Thus, Christology is the basis of the doctrine that salvation is present: "The fulness of salvation is present in Jesus Christ (cf. 1:14, 16), offered to mankind definitively and permanently (cf. 17:3), and accessible in faith (20:31). Because of this the decision made now brings about salvation or judgment, and takes in the whole of the future."[6] Paolo Ricca also grounds the special Johannine eschatology in Christology: "The history of the Son of Man is ... the history of the eschatological Krisis, because the Word of judgment which must be spoken at the last day, is nothing else than the Word become flesh."[7]

Schnackenburg's explanation of the shift in John's eschatology, although not atypical, is probably inadequate, for it pays insufficient attention to certain lines of continuity that run between John and the Synoptics. We have already seen that Mark and Matthew take up traditions that associate the end of Jesus

3. Rudolf Schnackenburg, *The Gospel According to St. John,* vol. 2, trans. C. Hastings, et al. (New York: Seabury Press, 1980), 1:434.
4. Ibid., 436.
5. Josef Blank, *Krisis: Untersuchungen zur johanneischen Christologie und Eschatologie* (Freiburg im Breisgau: Lambertus Verlag, 1964), 38.
6. Thus, Schnackenburg, *Gospel According to St. John,* 2:437.
7. Paolo Ricca, *Die Eschatologie des Vierten Evangeliums* (Zürich: Gotthelf-Verlag, 1966), 98.

with eschatological themes. Events that were expected to mark the transition between this age and the messianic age or the age to come are, in the first two Gospels, moved back to the narratives of the passion and resurrection. As will presently be argued, the same phenomenon is found in the Fourth Gospel, and it is highly pertinent for the discussion concerning the origin of John's notion of eschatological fulfillment.

The coming judgment is one of the most persistent and important themes in Jewish eschatology. Indeed, one may ask whether the ancient Jewish texts treating of eschatology are not concerned above all with God's judgment on the world.[8] Certainly, juridical ideas and images dominate many, if not most, of the relevant texts. The anticipated end evidently gained its meaning in large measure from the sentence that would be spoken over the wicked and the righteous, from the judgment that would grant reward to the latter and bring condemnation to the former. That this prominent expectation was taken over by early Christianity needs no documentation; and although the integrity of the text of John has been held suspect, it is likely that the prospect of a coming judgment originally held a place in Johannine theology. Yet notwithstanding this fact, the fourth evangelist also writes as if the great judgment were past, as if it were coincident with the Christ-event. Jesus the judge has already come among men (3:19; 5:22–24, 27, 30–38; 9:39). The sentences of life and death have already been uttered, and Jesus can announce: "'He who hears my word and believes him who sent me, has eternal life; he does not come into judgment, but has passed from death to life'" (5:24). One also reads that "'whoever believes in him may have eternal life'" (3:15). It is clear, moreover, that a particular hour of judgment has passed, and that this hour is to be identified with the hour when the Son of man was lifted up. When Jesus announces that "now is the judgment of this world" (12:31), it is plain from the context that the crucifixion is in view (see 12:32–33). According to John, then, the judgment of the world has been acted out at the cross. That this represents the transmutation of an eschatological expectation is not missed by the commentators. Rudolf Bultmann can even assert that here John's language "serves to eliminate the traditional eschatology of primitive Christianity. The turn of the ages results now...."[9] Now, while it is not the case that John 12:31 necessarily excludes a yet outstanding judgment, the conception does imply that a particular eschatological expectation has made its appearance in history.[10]

8. Cf. Theo Preiss, *Life in Christ*, SBT 13, trans. H. Knight (London: SCM Press, 1957), 14.

9. Rudolf Bultmann, *The Gospel of John: A Commentary*, trans. G. R. Beasley-Murray, et al. (Philadelphia: Westminster Press, 1971), 437.

10. See further, Blank, *Krisis*, 281–94.

Therefore, as in the other Gospels, an event that, in Judaism, serves to mark the passage between this age and the coming redemption is moved back to the passion of Jesus. The connection with the synoptic tradition is all the closer as the two signs in Mark 15—the darkness at noon and the rending of the veil—are, as we have argued, to be associated with judgment. Hence—and this is to be stressed—John's reinterpretation of the eschatological judgment as proleptically manifest in the death of Jesus may not be as novel as is widely assumed.

The crucifixion for John means not only the judgment of this world but likewise the judgment of the world's ruler, the devil (12:31). This, too, marks a reinterpretation of eschatological expectation. Jewish and Christian teaching anticipated that the eschatological transition would witness an unprecedented unleashing of the powers of evil and that, at the end of a great final conflict, God's chief opponent, Satan, would be condemned. The expectation is conspicuous in the Dead Sea Scrolls. For the present, the angel of darkness leads astray the children of righteousness and rules over the sons of falsehood. But God has appointed an end for falsehood, and at the time of visitation he will destroy it forever (see 1QS III, 13—IV, 26). 1QM is a glorified depiction of the last struggle between good and evil, of the war of the sons of light against the company of the sons of darkness, the army of Belial (see the heading, 1QM I, 1). The Gospel of John offers a stark contrast. In the Fourth Gospel the devil has already met defeat. Consider these declarations: "'Now shall the ruler of this world be cast out'" (12:31); "'I will no longer talk much with you, for the ruler of this world is coming'" (14:30); "'the ruler of this world is judged'" (16:11). When the Son of man is lifted onto the cross, the ruler of this world, Satan, is vanquished. The long-awaited triumph over the evil one has taken place. Unlike the Dead Sea Scrolls, in which Belial and his hosts are defeated only at the final battle, and in which there is an accentuated distinction between the now of a time of war and the then of the time of salvation,[11] John is persuaded that evil has already been judged and cast out. An eschatological hope has been realized.

A reinterpretation of the belief that evil would increase in a great measure only to meet the creator's triumph at the end also lies behind the presentation of Judas in John; for this disciple seems to function in the Johannine passion as the antichrist, a figure expected in other Christian texts to appear immediately before the end of days.[12] Already in 6:70, the disciple who betrayed Jesus is

11. Cf. Heinz-Wolfgang Kuhn, *Enderwartung und gegenwärtiges Heil: Untersuchungen zu den Gemeindeliedern von Qumran mit einen Anhang über Eschatologie und Gegenwart in der Verkündigung Jesu*, SUNT 4 (Göttingen: Vandenhoeck & Ruprecht, 1966), 202.

12. See 2 Thess. 2:9-10; 1 John 2:18, 22; 4:3; 2 John 7; Rev. 13; 17; 19:19-21; and, for discussion, Rudolf Schnackenburg, *Die Johannesbriefe*, 5th ed., HTKNT 13 (Freiburg: Herder, 1975), 145-49. The title "antichrist" seems to be of Christian derivation, but the

labeled "a devil." Later, in 13:2, one reads that it is the devil that has put it into the heart of Judas to betray Jesus, and in 13:27 that, "after the morsel, Satan entered into him." In 14:30 Jesus declares that the ruler of the world now comes, and the title seemingly refers to Judas, or to Judas as the embodiment of the evil archon. Wendy E. Sproston writes:

> There can be little doubt that Jesus is referring at this point to Judas when he uses the devil's title, "the ruler of this world." This is made clear if we compare the Synoptic parallels. The Johannine passage ends with the words, "Rise, let us go hence" (14:31). Where the same exhortation occurs in Mark and Matthew we see that in each case it is accompanied by the remark, "My betrayer is at hand" (Mk. 14:42; Matt. 26:46) and, moreover, that this is immediately before the arrival of Judas. Thus we may conclude that for the fourth evangelist the presence of Judas is synonymous with the presence of the devil.[13]

Even more significantly, in 17:12 Judas is called "the son of perdition," *ho huios tēs apōleias*. This precise phrase is used in 2 Thess. 2:3 to describe the coming man of lawlessness and was, perhaps, a technical term. Paul declares that the Day of the Lord will not come unless "the man of perdition"—who is not Satan himself but Satan's instrument—comes first. According to C. K. Barrett, "It seems probable that John saw in Judas the eschatological character who must appear before the manifestation of the glory of Christ (just as in 1 John 2:18, 22; 4:3 heretical teachers are represented as Antichrist)."[14] This conclusion, if justified, supplies one more example of the transfer to the passion narrative of an eschatological prediction. To quote Sproston once more: "Whereas for Paul the glorious parousia could not take place unless the Satanically inspired 'son of perdition' had first worked the ultimate evil, for the fourth evangelist, to whom the crucifixion of Christ was synonymous with his glorification, it is the figure of Judas which symbolizes the final apostasy."[15]

Also significant for the topic under review is the Johannine use of the title "the Son of man." Its meaning for the evangelist and its background are much disputed, scholars even failing to agree as to whether there is a specific Son of man Christology in John.[16] The various problems cannot be entered into here.

concept has Jewish prototypes; see, for example, Dan. 7:8, 19–25; 2 Apoc. Bar. 40; Sib. Or. V, 28–34, 93–110, 137–61.

13. Wendy E. Sproston, "Satan in the Fourth Gospel," in *Studia Biblica 1978. II. Papers on the Gospels, JSNT* Supplement Series 2, ed. E. A. Livingstone (Sheffield: JSOT Press, 1980), 308–9.

14. C. K. Barrett, *The Gospel According to John*, 2d ed. (Philadelphia: Westminster Press, 1978), 508. Cf. R. H. Lightfoot, *St. John's Gospel*, ed. C. F. Evans (Oxford: Clarendon Press, 1956), 301.

15. Sproston, "Satan," 310.

16. For a survey of critical opinion, see Francis J. Moloney, *The Johannine Son of Man*, Biblioteca di Scienze Religiose 14 (Rome: Las, 1976), 1–22.

For our purposes it need only be asserted that the Johannine Son of man must ultimately rest, at least in part, upon eschatological tradition, and indeed, upon a reinterpretation of such tradition. John 5:27 (*kai exousian edōken autǭ, krisin poiein hoti huois anthrōpou estin*) probably depends upon the Greek text of Dan. 7:13-14 (*hōs huios anthrōpou ercheto . . . kai edothē autǭ, exousia*); and more than once the Son of man is the agent of judgment (5:27; 9:35-39; 12:30-34). Further, several Johannine sayings have points of contact with synoptic logia about the future of the Son of man. For example, John 1:51 ("And he said to him, 'Truly, truly, I say to you, you will see heaven opened, and the angels of God ascending and descending upon the Son of man'"), which uses the verb *horaō* in the future, also mentions angels (cf. Mark 8:38; 13:26-27; 14:62; Matt. 25:31; Luke 17:22); and the use of *hypsoō* and *dei* in connection with the crucifixion in John 3:14, 15; 8:28; and 12:34 links the Johannine Son of man to the synoptic passion predictions[17]—and these, as we shall argue later, originally had an eschatological orientation.

In John, the hour of the Son of man is the hour of the passion. In 12:23 Jesus declares that "'the hour has come for the Son of man to be glorified'" and in 13:31-32, "'Now is the Son of man glorified, and in him God is glorified; if God is glorified in him, God will also glorify him in himself, and glorify him at once.'" Compare 3:13-14; 8:28; and 12:34. Perhaps 1:51 also has reference to the passion: the glorious theophany ("'heaven opened, and the angels of God ascending and descending upon the Son of man'") takes place in the future ("'you will see'"), when the Son of man is lifted up and glorified.[18] However that may be, it is especially important to recall that, in the Synoptics, the Son of man enters into his glory at his Parousia, not at the passion (see, for example, Mark 13:26 and Matt. 25:31). Hence, John's use of "the Son of man" illustrates a transfer to the passion narrative of language that, in early Christianity (and perhaps in first-century Judaism, if there existed a pre-Christian conception of an eschatological Son of man), had its proper place in connection with discourse about the arrival of the consummation. A similar phenomenon, it should be remembered, is to be observed in Matthew. Matthew 26:62 and 28:18 seem to hold forth, in conjunction with the passion and resurrection of Jesus, what may be called a provisional or proleptic coming and enthronement of the Son of man.

---

17. Cf. Schnackenburg, *Gospel According to St. John*, 1:535-36; idem, "Der Menschensohn im Johannesevangelium," *NTS* 11 (1964-65): 130-31; and Matthew Black, "The 'Son of Man' Passion Sayings in the Gospel Tradition," *ZNW* 60 (1960): 5-7.

18. So A. J. B. Higgins, *Jesus and the Son of Man* (Philadelphia: Fortress Press, 1964), 157-61. Note also the interesting study of Stephen S. Smalley, "Johannes 1,51 und die Einleitung zum vierten Evangelium," in *Jesus und der Menschensohn: Für Anton Vögtle*, ed. R. Schnackenburg, J. Ernst, and J. Wanke (Freiburg: Herder, 1978), 300-313.

The transmutation of eschatology in John's Gospel is perhaps best illustrated in John 16:16–22, which reads as follows:

"A little while, and you will see me no more; again a little while, and you will see me." Some of his disciples said to one another, "What is this that he says to us, 'A little while, and you will not see me, and again a little while, and you will see me'; and, 'because I go to the Father'?" They said, "What does he mean by 'a little while'? We do not know what he means." Jesus knew that they wanted to ask him; so he said to them, "Is this what you are asking yourselves, what I meant by saying, 'A little while, and you will not see me, and again a little while, and you will see me'? Truly, truly, I say to you, you will weep and lament, but the world will rejoice; you will be sorrowful, but your sorrow will turn into joy. When a woman is in travail she has sorrow, because her hour has come; but when she is delivered of the child she no longer remembers the anguish, for joy that a child is born into the world. So you have sorrow now, but I will see you again and your hearts will rejoice, and no one will take your joy from you."

The sequence of this passage corresponds to the sequence of the eschatological transition: tribulation—redemption. The death of Jesus will bring weeping, mourning, grief, and tribulation. But as with birth, so with the passion: it is a prelude to joy. Grief will pass, and it will be turned into rejoicing, for the disciples will see Jesus and he will see them.

The terminology of John 16:16–22 recalls eschatological doctrine. *Thlipsis* denotes the eschatological tribulation elsewhere in the New Testament (e.g., Mark 13:19, 24; Rom. 2:9; Rev. 7:14) and is also so used in Dan. 12:1 LXX. The image of a woman in pain bringing forth her child was a well-known symbol for the eschatological transition in Judaism and the early church, and it is used in the Tanach in connection with the coming of the Day of the Lord.[19] The statement that the disciples will again see Jesus recalls to mind several Synoptic passages concerning the Parousia of the Son of man (for example, Mark 13:26 and 14:62); and "to see" the Messiah or the days of the Messiah was presumably a stock phrase (note Luke 17:22; Rev. 1:7; Justin, *Dialogue with Trypho* 14:8; 64:7; and *b. Sanh.* 98b). In view of all this, John 16:16–22 evidently offers yet one more instance of a peculiar use of eschatological language. The passion is as the great tribulation, the resurrection as the arrival of the age to come.

That the language of John 16:16–22 is drawn from eschatological teaching was already recognized by Augustine. In his commentary on John he understands the promise that the disciples will see Jesus to refer to the second advent.[20] (The "little while" of 16:16 is the time between the passion and the

---

19. See Bertram, "Ōdin, ōdinō," 668–74.
20. Augustine, *In Jo.* 101.6, noted by Raymond E. Brown, *The Gospel According to John (xii—xxi)*, AB 29A (Garden City, N.Y.: Doubleday & Co., 1970), 729.

Parousia.) This reading gains support from the description of the conditions attendant upon the disciples seeing Jesus. Raymond Brown writes:

> It is true that in John's view the promises of joy and peace (xvi 20–22, 24, 33) were to some extent fulfilled in the post-resurrectional appearances of the risen Jesus (xx 20, 21, 26), but do those appearances really grant "a joy that no one can take from you"? Much of what John reports in xvi 16ff. anticipates a more permanent union with Jesus than that afforded by transitory post-resurrectional appearances. Verse 23a promises the disciples plenary understanding so that they will have no more questions to pose. Such a depth of understanding was scarcely achieved in the brief post-resurrectional era within which Jesus appeared to them.[21]

It is unlikely, however, that the evangelist himself intended 16:19–22 to treat of eschatological matters. To quote Brown once more:

> In Johannine thought "seeing" Jesus and the joy and knowledge that are consequent upon this experience are considered as privileges of Christian existence after the resurrection. Jesus' promises have been fulfilled (at least to a significant extent) in what has been granted to all Christians, for the Last Discourse is addressed to all who believe in Jesus and not only to those who were actually present.[22]

Yet it is difficult to avoid the impression that John 16:19–22 is based upon a complex of sayings that originally had reference to the end and that the prospect of tribulation turned into joy was at one time a prophecy of the coming eschatological woes and the subsequent salvation.[23] But in John, this has become obscured because the passion has drawn to itself language descriptive of the messianic travail, while the resurrection has drawn to itself language descriptive of the Parousia.[24]

Our review of various Johannine texts that represent the passion of Jesus as though it were the eschatological turning point leads to three concluding observations. First, the realization of eschatological expectations is, in John, rooted in the passion narrative. The crucifixion is the hour of the Son of man, the hour of his glorification. It is when the Son of man is crucified that he draws all men to himself (12:32), reaching the goal of salvation history. Now, this understanding is usually thought to be especially John's own. Bultmann, as we have seen, could even claim that it contradicts earlier Christian thinking. But we have elsewhere argued that Mark and Matthew associate the death of Jesus with signs otherwise eschatological and thus imply an interpre-

---

21. Ibid.
22. Ibid.
23. See further, C. H. Dodd, *Historical Tradition in the Fourth Gospel* (Cambridge: Cambridge Univ. Press, 1963), 373.
24. Cf. ibid., 395–96.

tation of the crucifixion not so far removed from that of John. So John's discontinuity with earlier Christian tradition has been exaggerated. It may be less true to say that the reinterpretation of eschatology in John is indicative of an independent, deliberate theological act than that the fourth evangelist has simply elaborated or carried to its conclusion a tradition already established in the Synoptics. It may even be suggested that, as the crucifixion is the apex of the Fourth Gospel, the interpretation of that event as eschatological might well be the theological wellspring of the so-called "realized eschatology" of John.

Second, the Johannine reinterpretation of eschatology stands nearer to Matthew than to Mark. As is evident from the texts cited above, John not only looks back on the turning of the times but also understands his religious experience to mark the attainment of eschatological hopes. Eternal life has been bestowed, divine sonship granted, the resurrection experienced. John thinks himself to partake of the promises of the age to come; the eschatological transition—for him, the passion of Jesus—lies in the past. Matthew holds a comparable perspective. As argued previously, in the first Gospel, this age and the messianic age or the age to come overlap. Saints have been raised. The Son of man has received authority and entered into his glory. The prophecy in Matt. 26:62 has already met at least partial fulfillment. For Matthew, then, as for John, the work of Jesus entails that the eschatological redemption has in some sense come.[25] It is seemingly otherwise in Mark. His Gospel (at least in its present form) does not take its readers much beyond the "messianic woes." One is rather left, as it were, in the midst of the eschatological transition. The new age has yet to be entered, and the community still suffers the travails of the Messiah. Hence, Matthew and Fourth Gospel appear, if one may so put it, to be further along the eschatological time line than Mark.

Third, despite the contrast just noted, John's Gospel contains traces of the tradition according to which Christian experience partakes of the messianic birth pangs. This becomes evident when the parallels between Mark 13:5-13 and John 15:18—16:11 are set side by side. Jesus' prophecy of the church's future in John closely resembles Jesus' prophecy of the great tribulation in Mark:[26]

---

25. "Matthew does not have as fully 'realized' an eschatology as John, but he is moving in that direction." John P. Meier, *The Vision of Matthew* (New York: Paulist Press, 1979), 38.

26. Cf. Brown, *Gospel According to John*, 2:693-95.

| Mark 13:5-13 | John 15:18-16:11 |
|---|---|
| "You will be *hated* by all for my name's sake" (13:13) | "I chose you out of the world, therefore the world *hates* you" (15:19) |
| "They will deliver you up to councils; and you will be beaten in synagogues; and you will stand before governors and kings *for my sake*" (13:9) | "They will persecute you ... *on my account*" (15:20-21) |
| "Do not be anxious beforehand what you are to say; but say whatever is given you in that hour, for it is not you who speak, but *the Holy Spirit*" (13:11) | [Jesus will send *the Spirit* of truth and he will witness concerning Jesus (15:26-27; 16:7)] |
| [The persecution of Christians is a testimony (*martyrion*) and the gospel must first be preached to all the peoples (13:9-10)] | "You also are [my] witnesses" (*martyreite*) (15:27) |
| "Take heed that no one leads you astray" (13:5); cf. 13:23: "I have told you all things beforehand" | "I have said all this to you to keep you from falling away" (16:1) |
| "You will be beaten in *synagogues*" (13:9) | "They will put you out of the *synagogues*" (16:2) |
| "Brother will hand brother to *death*, and father son, and children will rise against parents and *kill* them" (13:12, au. trans.) | "Whoever *kills* you will think he is offering service to God" (16:2) |

It should be recalled that, for Mark, ecclesiology and eschatology are united: the time of the church and the time of the great tribulation coincide. This entails that Mark 13:5-14 is more than a prophecy of eschatological matters. It is also a prophecy of the church's future. The parallelism between John 15:18—16:11 and Mark 13:5-13 is thus all the stronger. Both passages offer the reader Jesus' forecasts concerning the age of the church. How then does one explain the broad similarity between our two texts?

John's Gospel, as argued previously, is further along the eschatological time line than Mark. The transition to the new time is more clearly relegated to the past in the former than in the latter. To be sure, John knows that in the world there is tribulation, but he also believes that Jesus has overcome the world (16:33), and this makes it difficult for him to identify the present age with the birth pangs of the new age. It may, therefore, be suggested that John has reinterpreted a traditional understanding of Christian existence. Acquainted with prophecies such as those embedded in Mark 13:4–12, he no longer understands them to be properly eschatological. One could, of course, argue that our suggestion should be turned on its head: John represents the more primitive tradition, Mark a later development. This would, presumably, be the argument of those who, like Glasson and Robinson, posit a contamination of the primitive Jesus tradition by foreign eschatological elements. Three considerations, however, weigh against this suggestion. First, the results of chapters 11–13 herein contradict the evolutionary theory propounded by Glasson and Robinson. The postulation of an originally pure tradition, uncontaminated by undesirable eschatological elements, cannot be maintained.[27] Second, Mark 13:5–13 and John 15:18—16:11 have in common prophecies of offense, hatred, death, and persecution. These prophecies are native to Jewish eschatological texts and occur in pre- and non-Christian descriptions of the coming tribulation. Given this fact, the supposition that the prophecies in Mark and John were originally eschatological is difficult to dispute. Third, it remains probable that John should be dated two or three decades after Mark, and it is thus natural—although admittedly not necessary—to regard the Johannine perspective as the later. We conclude, therefore, that John 15:18—16:11 reflects a tradition according to which the time of the church and the time of the great tribulation, which began with the passion of Jesus, are coincident.

---

27. See also Wilhelm Thüsing, "Erhöhungsvorstellung und Parusieerwartung in der ältesten nachösterlichen Christologie (Schluss)," *BZ* 12 (1968): 224–26.

# Six

# THE PAULINE EPISTLES

The relationship between Paul and the canonical gospels has been the subject of a long and inconclusive debate. It is our own view that the apostle was well acquainted with sayings of and stories about Jesus of Nazareth. But whether this be a fair conclusion or not, we are here concerned only to learn whether Paul was familiar with the line of interpretation that we have already met with in three Gospels. Did the apostle to the Gentiles believe that Jesus' end marked the inauguration of the eschatological turning point? Did he think of his Lord's death as belonging to the "messianic woes"? Did he view Jesus' resurrection as the onset of the general resurrection?

## The Church and the Great Tribulation[1]

Many have observed that Paul believed his own time to be that of the messianic woes.[2] In 1 Cor. 7:26 the apostle writes of *tēn enestōsan anagkēn,* "the present distress." Now, *anagkē* was used as an eschatological term (note Luke 21:23 and Zeph. 1:15 LXX), and the connotation of "the present distress" becomes evident in 1 Cor. 7:28–29: "But if you marry, you do not sin, and if a virgin marries she does not sin. But such will have tribulation [*thlipsin*] in the flesh, and I would spare you that. I mean, brethren, the appointed time has grown very short" (au. trans.). Heinrich Schlier remarks: "With his awareness of the shortening of the time, Paul obviously sees the afflictions of the last time breaking into the present, and his advice is designed to lessen the related *thlipsis* for his community."[3] In other words, Paul offers his counsel—

---

1. The following discussion assumes, against much recent work, the Pauline authorship of Colossians and 2 Thessalonians. Our results, however, could be established—although perhaps with less conviction—without reference to these two disputed writings.
2. Recently, J. Christiaan Beker, *Paul the Apostle,* 131, 145–46; A. J. Mattill, "'The Way of Tribulation,'" *JBL* 98 (1979): 535–38; and Ulrich Wilckens, *Der Brief an die Römer (Röm 1–5),* EKKNT VI/1 (Zürich: Benziger Verlag; Neukirchen-Vluyn: Neukirchener Verlag, 1978), 291.
3. Schlier, "*Thlibō, thlipsis,*" 145. Cf. Franzjosef Froitzheim, *Christologie und Eschatologie bei Paulus* (Würzburg: Echter-Seelsorge, 1978), 18–28.

remain in the unmarried state—on the presupposition that the present experience of the Corinthians is an eschatological experience: it partakes of the messianic woes. *Second Baruch* 10:13–14 is here relevant:

> And you, ye bridegrooms, enter not in,
> And let not the brides adorn themselves with garlands;
> And, ye women, pray not that ye may bear.
> For the barren shall above all rejoice,
> And those who have no sons shall be glad,
> And those who have sons shall have anguish.
>
> (*APOT*)

The final time of trouble will prove to be especially arduous for the married (cf. Mark 13:17 and Luke 23:29).

Paul's conviction concerning the eschatological character of the present time emerges in other texts. In 2 Thess. 2:7a, he writes that the mystery of lawlessness is "already at work." That is, the rebellion whose advent marks the final apostasy has already entered the world, even though its full manifestation belongs to the future (2:7b–9). Similarly, in Rom. 8:18 Paul speaks of "the sufferings of this present time." The contrast with "the glory that is to be revealed to us" together with the general eschatological orientation of 8:19–25 almost certainly imply that Paul here has in mind the sufferings of the final affliction—and these are "of this present time."[4] The use of the compound *sunōdinei* ("to be in travail with") confirms this assertion, for the imagery of birth was traditionally associated with the great tribulation.[5] Consider also 1 Thess. 3:4: "For when we were with you, we told you beforehand that we were to suffer affliction. . . ." This announcement to new converts in Thessalonica concerning the inevitability of tribulation was, one strongly suspects, founded upon eschatological doctrine.[6]

Colossians 1:24 probably points in the same direction. "Now I rejoice in my sufferings for your sake, and in my flesh I complete what is lacking in Christ's afflictions [*antanaplērō ta hysterēmata tōn thlipseōn tou christou*] for the sake of his body, that is, the church." This text, the interpretations of which are many and varied, is extremely difficult, to be sure, and any reading should be received with caution. But for our purposes it is significant that a number of recent commentators concur that Paul's words do not imply that some lack in

---

4. So also, Uwe Gerber, "Röm VIII, 18ff. als exegetisches Problem der Dogmatik," *NovT* 8 (1966): 60–64; and Wilckens, *Der Brief an die Römer*, 2:148–49, 151.

5. See 6 herein, n. 6.

6. Pertinent here is Ernst Bammel, "Preparation for the Perils of the Last Days: I Thessalonians 3:3," in *Suffering and Martyrdom in the New Testament*, ed. W. Horbury and B. McNeil (Cambridge: Cambridge Univ. Press, 1981), 91–100.

the vicarious work of Christ is to be supplied; nor does thought of a mystical union much eludicate the verse. Rather, the conception of the messianic woes which must precede the new age provides the best background for understanding Col. 1:24.[7]

*Thlipsis* is nowhere else in the New Testament demonstrably used of the sufferings of Jesus, but the word does frequently have reference to events expected in connection with the eschatological turning point, and the *thlipseōn tou christou* is reminiscent of *ḥeblô šel māšîḥa*. Further, as Eduard Lohse writes:

> The concept of a definite measure for the last days determines the phrase "what is lacking in Christ's afflictions." Just as God has set a definite measure in time (cf. *4 Ezra* 4:36f.; Gal. 4:4) and has determined the limitation of the tribulations at the end (cf. Mk. 13:5–27; par.), so he has also decreed a definite measure for the sufferings which the righteous and the martyrs must endure (I. En. 47:1–4; 2 Bar. 30:2). When this has been completed, the end is at hand; then the old aeon passes away and the wonderful new world dawns. For the present, however, this is not the case; something is still lacking in "Christ's afflictions." This lack is what the apostle through his sufferings is completing.[8]

Rev. 6:10–11 is here relevant. The souls under the altar of God cry out, "'O Sovereign Lord, holy and true, how long before thou wilt judge and avenge our blood on those who dwell upon the earth?'" They are then each given a white robe and told to rest a little longer, "until the number of their fellow servants and their brethren should be complete, who were to be killed as they themselves had been." The redemption will not come until a quota of suffering is met.

It is consistent with our conclusions thus far that Paul could write, "The wrath of God is presently being revealed from heaven" (Rom. 1:18, au. trans.). In Jewish and Christian eschatology, the great tribulation, which culminates in the great assize, marks the beginning of God's eschatological judgment, when the *orgē theou* is unleashed. This is especially clear in Luke 21:23 ("Great distress shall be upon the earth and wrath upon this people") and Rev. 6:16–17 ("'Fall on us and hide us from the face of him who is seated on the throne, and from the wrath of the Lamb; for the great day of their wrath has come....'"). The eschatological wrath of God begins to manifest itself in the

---

7. So e.g., Gerhard Delling, *"Plērēs ktl.,"* TDNT 6 (1968): 307; Henry Gustafson, "The Afflictions of Christ: What Is Lacking?" *BR* 7 (1963): 28–42; C. F. D. Moule, *The Epistles to the Colossians and to Philemon,* Cambridge Greek Testament (Cambridge: Cambridge Univ. Press, 1957), 75–79; and Franz Zeilinger, *Der Erstegeborene der Schöpfung* (Vienna: Herder, 1974), 82–94.

8. Eduard Lohse, *Colossians and Philemon,* Hermeneia, trans. W. R. Poehlmann and R. J. Karris (Philadelphia: Fortress Press, 1971), 71.

great tribulation. So the formulation in Rom. 1:18 is possible because the time of trouble has begun: Paul's time belongs to the pangs of the Messiah.[9]

## The Death of Jesus and the Great Tribulation

As argued earlier, the interpretation of the period between the first and second advents as the period of the messianic woes is met with in the Gospels. There it is brought into connection with the sufferings of Jesus: the passion introduces the eschatological time of trouble in which the church now suffers. One is led to ask if the same line of thought is presupposed or reproduced by Paul. That is, in the Pauline corpus, are the sufferings of Jesus as well as those of Christians part of the great tribulation? An affirmative answer has been given by others,[10] and at least three good reasons support their response.

First, the claim naturally follows from a central tenet of Pauline theology, namely, that the messianic age has dawned. Upon Paul the end of the ages has come (1 Cor. 10:11). In Christ there is a "new creation"; the old has passed away, the new has appeared (2 Cor. 5:17). Believers are even now rescued from "the present evil age" (Gal. 1:4). They have been transferred to the kingdom of God's beloved Son (Col. 1:13). The fullness of time has come (Gal. 4:4). The Messiah already reigns (1 Cor. 15:25). The conviction these statements share is important because if, for Paul, certain promises made for the messianic age or the age to come are realized in the present, and if the coming of Jesus Christ marks the inbreaking of God's kingdom, then the conviction that Christ died in the eschatological tribulation is implied almost inexorably—to wit: if the new age has dawned with the death of Jesus, and if the Christ has suffered, and if tribulation must introduce the new creation, then it follows that Jesus suffered the messianic woes.[11] Paul, to be sure, may not have drawn this inference. Yet as Gershom Scholem has written, "Jewish Messianism is in its origin and by its nature—this cannot be sufficiently emphasized—a theory of catastrophe"; it involves "the catastrophic and destructive nature of the redemption on the one hand and the utopianism of the content of realized

---

9. This conclusion may elucidate 1 Thess. 2:16. Assuming that 1 Thess. 2:15–16 is not an interpolation but perhaps a pre-Pauline tradition that the apostle has taken over (so Gerd Lüdemann, *Paulus und das Judentum*, TEH 215 [Munich: Chr. Kaiser, 1983]), it is significant that of *hē orgē* it is said, it "has come upon them [the Jews] at last!" "The wrath" is here God's eschatological wrath (so also Lüdemann), and the use of an aorist probably means that it has already begun to be revealed. The formulation is possible because the great tribulation, in which the eschatological wrath of God commences, has made its appearance.

10. E.g., C. K. Barrett, *The Second Epistle to the Corinthians*, HNTC (New York: Harper & Row, 1973), 61–62; and Gustafson, "Afflictions," 36.

11. Cf. (with differences) Albert Schweitzer, *The Mysticism of Paul the Apostle*, trans. W. Montgomery (New York: Seabury Press, 1968), 141–48.

Messianism on the other."[12] Could Paul, whose letters exhibit so many parallels to Jewish apocalypses, have ignored, in his interpretation of the Messiah's advent, an entire side of eschatological doctrine? 1 Corinthians 7:26-28 and 2 Thess. 2:3-10, among other texts, prove that he did not; so the inference made by us would have been near to Paul.

Second, not only has the believer, according to Paul, been crucified with Christ and undergone a death (Rom. 6:4-11; Gal. 2:19-20; 2 Cor. 4:10) but he yet suffers with Christ (Rom. 8:17: *sympaschomen*). Paul can even write of his ardent desire to know Christ and "share his sufferings" (Phil. 3:10); and in 2 Cor. 1:5 he declares, "The sufferings of Christ abound for us" (au. trans.). That the "sufferings of Christ" in 2 Cor. 1:5 and Phil. 3:10 are not only those of Paul but include the sufferings that Christ himself suffered follows from the context of Phil. 3:10: "That I may know him and the power of his resurrection, and may share his sufferings, becoming like him in his death." Reference is here made to the resurrection of Jesus and to his death. So Paul has in view the saving events, which entails that the sufferings of Christ are also known and shared by Paul. Thus, apostolic suffering and the sufferings of Christ are so closely bound together that they are both included in the one expression, "the sufferings of Christ" (*ta pathēmata tou christou*). But if, as we have urged, those who suffer "with Christ" suffer the messianic woes, then the suggestion that the same holds true for Christ himself follows naturally.

Third, although Col. 1:24 has probable reference to the messianic woes, for Paul and his readers the Messiah had already appeared, and he had suffered. So the original recipients of Colossians, reading of "Christ's afflictions," could hardly have avoided thinking of Messiah Jesus and of his passion and death. For them mention of the *thlipseis* of the Christ would not only have embraced present Christian experience interpreted as the messianic woes but also the afflictions of the earthly Christ. (Note that the "his" in Col. 1:24—"for the sake of his body"—has Christ as its only possible antecedent. As the "body" is the body of Christ Jesus, "Christ" is not simply the Jewish Messiah—as in *ḥeblô šel māšîḥa*—but Jesus Christ.) So "what is lacking in Christ's afflictions"—a phrase Paul uses without any explanation[13]—readily implies, within the context of a Christian writing, that the sufferings of Jesus stand at the inception of the final affliction. Further, *antanaplēroō* ("I complete") involves the idea of Christ leaving something for Paul to accomplish. So that which the apostle now suffers, the *thlipseis tou christou*, was also suffered by Jesus Christ.

---

12. Gershom Scholem, *The Messianic Idea in Judaism and Other Essays on Jewish Spirituality*, trans. M. A. Meyer and H. Halkin (New York: Schocken Books, 1971), 7.
13. The readers were probably already acquainted with the concept. Cf. Lohse, *Colossians and Philemon*, 71 n. 21.

## The Resurrection of Jesus and the
## Resurrection of the Dead

If the death of Jesus is, in the Pauline epistles, assumed to have been a death in the great eschatological tribulation, it is also true that Paul interpreted the resurrection of Jesus as part of the general resurrection of the dead. To begin with, in 1 Cor. 15:20 he calls Christ "the first fruits of those who have fallen asleep" (cf. 15:23). The first fruits denoted partly the first or beginning, and partly the best or main part of the crop; and it could represent not only the whole but symbolize the onset of a new period of time. As regards the meaning of the expression in 1 Corinthians 15, we may quote James D. G. Dunn. The metaphor of the first fruits here

> denotes the beginning of the harvest, more or less the first swing of the sickle. No interval is envisaged between the first fruits and the rest of the harvest. With the first fruits dedicated the harvest proceeds. The application of this metaphor to the resurrection of Jesus and the gift of the Spirit expresses the belief that with these events the eschatological harvest has begun; the resurrection of the dead has started, the end-time Spirit has been poured out.[14]

The same might be inferred from Paul's use of "firstborn" in Rom. 8:29 and Col. 1:18: Jesus is the "firstborn" among many brethren and the "firstborn" of the dead.[15]

Matters are even clearer when careful notice is taken of Rom. 1:3-4, which is widely held to embody a pre-Pauline confession. According to this tradition, Jesus was designated Son of God "in power according to the Spirit of holiness *ex anastaseōs nekrōn*." The RSV translates the last three words, "by his resurrection from the dead." The Greek, however, is not (as one might expect) *ex anastaseōs autou ek nekrōn*. There is no pronoun in Rom. 1:4. The phrase is simply *ex anastaseōs nekrōn*. "So," as Anders Nygren notes, "we are confronted with the peculiar fact that when Paul refers to the resurrection of Christ, he says, 'the resurrection of the dead.'"[16]

Should *ex anastaseōs nekrōn* be read as an abbreviation for *ex anastaseōs autou ek nekrōn*? Probably not; *anastaseōs nekrōn* was a technical term for the general resurrection of the dead.[17] Moreover, good sense can be made of a literal rendering of the expression: it preserves the primitive view that Jesus' resurrection betokened the onset of the eschatological resurrection—a convic-

---

14. James D. G. Dunn, *Jesus and the Spirit* (Philadelphia: Westminster Press, 1975), 159.
15. Acts 26:23 (Jesus *prōtos ex anastaseōs nekrōn*) and Rev. 1:5 (Christ is *prōtotokos tōn nekrōn*) suggest that Col. 1:18 picks up a pre-Pauline notion.
16. Anders Nygren, *Commentary on Romans* (Philadelphia: Fortress Press, 1949), 49.
17. Matt. 22:31; Luke 20:35; Acts 4:2; 17:32; 23:6; 24:21; 26:23; 1 Cor. 15:12, 13, 21; Heb. 6:2; 1 Pet. 1:13.

tion also reflected, as we have seen, by Paul's use of "first fruits" in 1 Cor. 15:20 and 23. Ernst Käsemann writes that Rom. 1:4 "does not isolate Christ's resurrection but rather understands it in its cosmic function as the beginning of the general resurrection."[18] Nygren and Ulrich Wilckens put forward similar judgments.[19] Matthew 27:51b–53 may profitably be recalled at this point.[20] According to this text, Jesus was not the only one to have been raised from the dead. His resurrection came to pass only as part of a more general resurrection. On the first day of the week, the holy ones emerged from their tombs, entered Jerusalem, and appeared to many. So in both Matt. 27:51b–53 and Rom. 1:4, the vindication of the Messiah is represented by an *anastaseōs nekrōn*. The formal confession passed on by Paul enshrines a conviction that in Matthew's Gospel has taken the form of a story.

## Conclusion

If Mark and Matthew and John preserve traditions that seemingly interpret the end of Jesus as the eschatological turning point, the same is true of Paul. Passages in the three Gospels and the Pauline epistles agree in seeing the eschatological time of trouble as a period extending (inclusively) from the death of Jesus to the consummation. They also agree in thinking of the resurrection of Jesus as the beginning of the general resurrection of the dead. Evidently, the texts we have been examining put us closely in touch with an interpretation of some influence.

Before leaving Paul, a final point should be made. It is this: the traditions that relate Jesus' death to the messianic woes and his resurrection to the general resurrection display every sign of being pre-Pauline. The *ex anastaseōs nekrōn* of Rom. 1:3–4 belongs to an ancient credal formulation. (No reconstruction of the primitive formula omits the phrase.) Paul's use of "firstborn" in Rom. 8:29 and Col. 1:18 finds its analogy in Acts 26:23 and Rev. 1:5, which probably indicates that the belief does not derive from Paul. The metaphor of Christ as "first fruits" has also been supposed to be pre-Pauline.[21] In Col. 1:24, which presupposes that Jesus' death belongs to the period of eschatological distress, the phrase *ta hysterēmata tōn thlipseōn tou christou* receives no explication. Paul—who did not found the community at Colossae—apparently assumes that his readers are familiar with the concept. Beyond this, the inter-

18. Käsemann, *Der Brief an die Römer*, 10.
19. Nygren, *Romans*, 48–51; Wilckens, *Der Brief an die Römer*, 1:65.
20. Cf. with what follows Hans-Werner Bartsch, "Zur vorpaulinischen Bekenntnisformel im Eingang des Römerbriefes," *TZ* 23 (1967): 329–39.
21. See James D. G. Dunn, *Unity and Diversity in the New Testament: An Inquiry Into the Character of Earliest Christianity* (Philadelphia: Westminster Press, 1977), 323.

pretation of the suffering and death of Jesus in terms of the messianic tribulation remains undeveloped in Paul. Nowhere is it taken up and expounded upon at length; it remains quite peripheral. This, too, is consistent with the presumption that we are dealing with pre-Pauline tradition. Otherwise we would expect the apostle to clarify ideas foreign to his readers.

# Seven

# THE REVELATION TO JOHN

The Apocalypse was almost certainly composed during a time of severe affliction. The book is addressed to those "who share ... in Jesus the tribulation and the kingdom and the patient endurance" (1:9). "Tribulation" and "suffering" characterize the present experience of the readers (2:9–10, 13; cf. 2:3; 12:17; 13:7). References to witnesses who have died for the faith are numerous (6:9–11; 12:11; 17:6; 18:24; 20:4; cf. 13:7). The inference, which has patristic support,[1] that the Apocalypse was penned in a period of persecution—either in the reign of Domitian or, less probably, in that of Nero—is well founded.[2]

The supposition that the seer, like some Jews and Christians before him, understood his own tribulation to be the great, messianic tribulation is also well founded.[3] *Thlipsis* characterizes the present, and in Revelation this word is a technical term for the final affliction (7:14; cf. 1:9; 2:9, 10, 22). Further, the multitude of Rev. 7:9–17, which has come out of the great tribulation (7:14), includes, without question, those Christians who have recently shed their

---

1. See the collection of texts in Fenton J. A. Hort, *The Apocalypse of St. John I—III: The Greek Text with Introduction, Commentary, and Additional Notes* (London: Macmillan & Co., 1908), xiv–xix.

2. It is hard to follow J. P. M. Sweet (*Revelation*, Westminster Pelican Commentaries [Philadelphia: Westminster Press, 1979]), 26, who denies that the Apocalypse was written in a time of heavy persecution. "The letters to the churches suggest that persecution was occasional and selective, and that the chief dangers were complacency and compromise." This is surely an overstatement. It is not so easy to tone down the apparent implications of Rev. 1:9; 2:2–3 (cf. 1:9), 9–10, 13, 19 (cf. 1:9); 3:10; 6:9–11; 7:14; 11:7; 12:1–6, 13–17; 13:7, 15; 14:13; 17:6; 18:24; and 20:4.

3. R. H. Charles, *A Critical and Exegetical Commentary on the Revelation of St. John*, 2 vols., International Critical Commentary (Edinburgh: T. & T. Clark, 1920), 1:21; Ernest F. Scott, *The Book of Revelation*, 5th ed. (London: SCM Press, 1939), 74–79; and Nigel Turner, "Revelation," in *Peake's Commentary on the Bible*, new rev. ed., M. Black and H. H. Rowley, ed. (New York and London: Thomas Nelson & Sons, 1962), 1046. According to Eduard Lohse (*The Formation of the New Testament*, trans. M. E. Boring [Nashville, Abingdon Press, 1981], 226), "The present, in which the author and his readers find themselves, is ... not neglected, but understood as a part of the series of eschatological events which have already begun. This reference to the present is clearly seen in the references to contemporary history (e.g., in chapter 13)."

blood as witnesses of Jesus. John may, admittedly, draw a distinction between the present tribulation and its intensification immediately before the end (3:10). But there is no cleavage between the two periods. The one stands as the climax of the other. G. R. Beasley-Murray offers the following comments on Rev. 1:9:

For John, as for the New Testament writers generally, the last times have arrived. They were introduced by the redemptive action of Jesus, and will shortly come to their climax in the unveiled kingdom of Jesus. As tribulation is the lot of Christians in this age (Jn. 16:33) and will give place to its intensification under the Antichrist (Rev. 11—13), so sovereignty with Christ marks their present existence (Rev. 1:6) and is to find its perfect expression in the kingdom of Christ (Rev. 2:26ff., 5:10, 20:4ff.). Tribulation and kingdom belong to the messianic pattern (Luke 24:26).[4]

This quotation raises the question of whether, as in Mark and Paul, the conviction that the sufferings of the faithful belong to the messianic travail is, in Revelation, found together with the belief that Jesus' passion inaugurated the great tribulation. An affirmative answer might be given on the basis of Rev. 1:9. Here *thlipsis* is "in Jesus." Paul's statements on the sufferings of Christ (2 Cor. 1:5; Col. 1:24; cf. Phil. 3:10), with their background in eschatological doctrine, come to mind. It is also significant that the noun *martys* serves to make Jesus the first in a line of witnesses who are called to give up their lives. Jesus was the first and faithful *martys* to shed his blood (Rev. 1:5; 3:14). Those who with John share tribulation in Jesus are also to be "martyrs" and even to give themselves over to death, as did the one named faithful and true (2:10; 5:9; 13:7; 17:6). Thus, within the perspective of an imminent end (1:3; 22:10, 12, 20), a continuous line runs from Jesus the *martys* to the recipients of the Apocalypse, who are called upon to conquer as did the Lamb, that they might join "those coming out of the great tribulation" (au. trans., 7:14).

Attention should also be directed to Rev. 12:1-6, which tells of a woman clothed by the sun:

And a great portent appeared in heaven, a woman clothed with the sun, with the moon under her feet, and on her head a crown of twelve stars; she was with child and she cried out in her pangs of birth, in anguish for delivery. And another portent appeared in heaven; behold a great red dragon, with seven heads and ten horns, and seven diadems upon his heads. His tail swept down a third of the stars of heaven, and cast them to the earth. And the dragon stood before the woman who was about to bear a child, that he might devour her child when she brought it forth; she brought forth a male child, one who is to rule all the nations with a rod

4. G. R. Beasley-Murray, *The Book of Revelation*, NCB (Grand Rapids: Wm. B. Eerdmans, 1974), 63–64.

of iron, but her child was caught up to God and to his throne, and the woman fled into the wilderness, where she has a place prepared by God, in which to be nourished for one thousand two hundred and sixty days.

It is unnecessary to pursue here the background of this passage in the history of religions or to consider whether, as seems likely, a Jewish source has been taken up into Rev. 12:1-6. It is instead our task to offer comments upon the text as it now stands and, in particular, to state what seem to be the christological presuppositions behind v. 2.

The woman introduced in Rev. 12:1 is not Mary, wife of Joseph and mother of Jesus, but a symbol of the people of God. In the Tanach, Israel or Zion is often represented by a female.[5] The twelve stars probably stand for the twelve tribes of Israel, as in Gen. 37:9. The male child is to be identified with Jesus Christ, for the description of him as the one who will rule over the nations with a rod of iron is taken from Ps. 2:9, and the second Psalm is referred, in the New Testament, to the Messiah who has come (Matt. 3:17; Luke 3:22; Acts 13:33; Heb. 1:5; 5:5). Revelation 19:15 confirms this. It is the Word of God, Jesus Christ, who is to rule the nations with a rod of iron. The picture in Rev. 12:1-5 is thus of Jesus the Messiah coming forth from the people of God, Israel.[6]

What is the function of verse 2 in Rev. 12:1-6? The woman, who symbolizes the people of God, is in labor and cries out to give birth, being in anguish to deliver. The figure of a woman in her labor pangs is a frequent symbol in extant apocalyptic literature when the subject is the eschatological transition, and it is used in the Tanach with reference to the Day of the Lord. That this usage has supplied the imagery of Rev. 12:2 has been recognized by many commentators. Anton Vögtle writes:

> That the seer understands the intense, acute pangs of birth as "messianic woes" and by this has especially in view the present persecution of Christians as the last great persecution is confirmed by the fact that the dragon just introduced recognizably produces not only the stress characteristic of the persecutor of the last time of affliction but also calls up the beast from the sea, which is the ruling and persecuting power of Rome.[7]

Isaiah 26:16—27:1 is especially interesting in this connection. In this text one

5. E.g., Isa. 1:8; 3:16-17; 4:4; 16:1; 37:22; 47:1; 52:2; 62:11; 66:8; Jer. 4:31; 6:2; 14:17; 18:13, 21; 31:4; 46:11; Hos. 2:2; Joel 1:8; Amos 5:2; Mic. 1:13. Cf. 4 Ezra 9:38—10:54.
6. See Josef Ernst, Die eschatologischen Gegenspieler in den Schriften des Neuen Testaments, BU 3 (Regensburg: Friedrich Pustet, 1967), 113-16; and Johannes Michel, "Die Deutung der apokalyptischen Frau in der Gegenwart," BZ 3 (1959): 301-10.
7. Anton Vögtle, "Mythos und Botschaft in Apocalypse 12," in Tradition und Glaube: Das frühe Christentum in seiner Umwelt: Festgabe für Karl Georg Kuhn zum 65. Geburtstag, ed. G. Jeremias, et al. (Göttingen: Vandenhoeck & Ruprecht, 1971), 404-5.

reads of the nation of Israel in labor (26:16-18), of a coming resurrection (26:19), of the unveiling of God's wrath (26:20-21), and of the Lord punishing Leviathan the fleeing serpent and slaying the dragon of the sea (27:1). This scriptural passage may stand behind Rev. 12:1-6, and it would have been read in the first century as a prophecy of eschatological events. In any event, if—as it seems—the birth pangs of Rev. 12:2 are in fact those of the messianic travail, then, according to the text, he who is to rule over the nations, Jesus the Messiah, was born or came forth in the time of the great tribulation.

André Feuillet has proposed that the birth recounted in Rev. 12:2 and 12:5 is identical with the death and resurrection of Jesus.[8] There is no mention of anything between the birth of the male child and his being caught up to God's throne. He is exalted to heaven as soon as he is born. It may, then, be no coincidence that in Rev. 1:5 the resurrection is thought of as a birth: Jesus is the "firstborn of the dead" (cf. Col. 1:18). Moreover, Ps. 2:9 is quoted in Rev. 12:5, and in this psalm the enthronement of the king is his birth or adoption by God (cf. Acts 13:33). As Rom. 1:3-4 shows, for early Christians Jesus had been installed as Son of God (in power) at or on account of the resurrection. The birth and ascent of the Messiah in Rev. 12:5 might, therefore, be taken as representing the passion and resurrection of Jesus. (The passion of Jesus is also represented as a painful birth in John 16:19-22.) But however that may be, it is sufficient for our purposes to observe that, in Rev. 12:1-6, the advent of Jesus the Messiah is located within the context of the messianic affliction. The Christ passes through the great tribulation and is then taken up into heaven. Is this not precisely the same conception we have discovered elsewhere in the New Testament? In Mark, Matthew, Paul, and certain traditions known to John, not only is the eschatological tribulation thought of as already inaugurated but its onset is traced back to the time of Jesus. Precisely the same thing may be said of the Revelation to John.

8. André Feuillet, "The Messiah and His Mother According to Apocalypse XII," in *Johannine Studies*, trans. T. E. Crane (Staten Island, N.Y.: Alba House, 1964), 258-92. Cf. George B. Caird, *The Revelation of St. John the Divine*, HNTC (New York: Harper & Row, 1966), 149-50. According to J. P. M. Sweet (*Revelation*, 197), *hērpasthē* "covers allusively Jesus' death and resurrection." *Harpazō* is not, admittedly, used elsewhere in the New Testament with reference to the resurrection of Jesus. But (1) the choice of the verb is dictated by the story line, not the traditional vocabulary of the church, and (2) given that the child is to be identified with Jesus Christ, to what other event of his history could the word refer?

*Eight*

# THE GOSPEL OF LUKE

The sources heretofore examined—Mark, Matthew, John, the epistles of Paul, and the Apocalypse—contain traditions in which the end of Jesus is interpreted as if it were the beginning of the fulfillment of eschatological expectations: the passion partakes of the messianic woes, and the vindication of Jesus belongs to the onset of the general resurrection. When we turn to Luke-Acts, no additional traces of this interpretation are to be found. Nowhere in Luke or Acts does the third evangelist portray the end of Jesus as if it marked the eschatological turning point. Indeed, the Markan materials that are susceptible of the eschatological interpretation and which Luke has made use of have been given a new meaning. Two illustrations of this may be offered. (1) The motif of darkness is no longer eschatological for Luke. On the one hand, he omits the reference to darkness in his version of the eschatological discourse (contrast Mark 13:24 and Luke 21:25). On the other hand, he introduces the motif in another connection. To "the chief priests and captains of the temple and elders" who come to arrest him, Jesus avows that "'this is your hour, and the power of darkness'" (22:52–53; cf. also Luke 1:79 and Acts 26:18). This statement probably provides the key to the Lukan understanding of 23:44: the sun's light fails precisely because the death of Jesus falls in the hour of evil and under the power of darkness. (2) While the darkness and the rending of the veil are separated in Mark (15:33 and 38), they are brought together in Luke, thus suggesting a thematic connection: "It was now about the sixth hour, and there was darkness over the whole land until the ninth hour, while the sun's light failed; and the curtain of the temple was torn in two" (23:44–45). But if 23:44 is no longer an eschatological sign (see above), neither probably is the rending of the veil. Further, the destruction of the temple in Luke-Acts—for the third evangelist, presumably an historical event of 70 A.D.—is seemingly not so much tied to the eschatological drama as to the guilt of the Jewish leaders. It is not God in his eschatological action who brings about the destruction of the temple but the leaders of the people by their rejection of Jesus; and when the temple is rent, this evidently means that men have brought upon themselves the destruction of the temple which is symbolized in Luke 23:45. Hence, there is for the evangelist a clear conceptual connection between the darkening of the sun and the rending of the veil. The Jewish leaders have crucified Jesus, and it is their hour and the power of darkness (23:44). But even in their hour of apparent triumph, the judgment which they bring upon themselves is sure, and the rending of the veil signifies the commencement of or foreshadows their certain demise (23:45). All of this is rather removed from the Markan interpretation of the darkness and the rending of the veil as eschatological occurrences.

If the end of Jesus is not, in Luke-Acts, presented in eschatological terms, what is the explanation for this? Four possibilities suggest themselves. (1) Perhaps Luke's consciousness of the delay of the Parousia explains matters. The understanding of Jesus' death and resurrection as initiating eschatology was, as we shall see, at least originally understood in a rather straightforward manner: the redemptive process had been set in motion, the messianic age or the age to come had begun to enter history. Such a conviction most naturally entailed a near culmination; for if the drama had opened, the last act could not be far off. Therefore, the longer the Parousia delayed, the more awkward it probably became to represent the passion and resurrection of Jesus as eschatological events. And if Luke, as many suppose, exchanged a *Naherwartung* for a *Fernerwartung*, this could explain the question under review. He simply saw too much distance between the time of Jesus and the final denouement for him to regard the former as the commencement of the latter. There is, however, a grave objection to this solution. In our estimation, it is not so obvious that Luke exchanged a *Naherwartung* for a *Fernerwartung*. The recent studies of A. J. Mattill in particular are deserving of mention in this respect.[1] He has forcefully argued that while the third evangelist did not expect Jesus to come at any moment, he did not give up hope that the redemption might come sooner than later. Indeed, according to Mattill, it may even be that Luke thought of the sufferings associated with mission as eschatological (cf. Acts 14:22). In any case, the author of Luke-Acts did not write for generations to come. As other Christians before him, he looked for his Lord to come in the not-too-distant future. If so—and we are convinced[2]—one cannot without hesitation fall back upon Luke's alleged abandonment of an imminent

---

1. A. J. Mattill, Jr., *Luke and the Last Things: A Perspective for the Understanding of Lukan Thought* (Dillsboro, N.C.: Western North Carolina Univ. Press, 1979); also "Naherwartung, Fernerwartung, and the Purpose of Luke-Acts: Weymouth Reconsidered," *CBQ* 34 (1972): 276–93.

2. Texts indicative of an early Parousia include Luke 9:27; 12:35–48; 13:1–9; 18:7–8; 21:32, 34–36; and Acts 3:19–21. Mattill also makes much of the use of *mellō* in Acts 17:31; 24:15 and 25.

expectation in accounting for his failure to see the end of Jesus as an eschatological event.

(2) According to Charles H. Talbert,[3] Luke-Acts was in part directed against Gnostic or proto-Gnostic tendencies.[4] This is a thesis that has some merit, and acceptance of it might bear on our problem.[5] Gnostic thinkers, in all probability, would have been interested in those traditions that set the passion and resurrection within an eschatological setting. The reason is obvious. Although Gnostic systems spoke of a future goal—the reunification of all light—they also had a very strong "realized eschatology." Hymenaeus and Philetus, who are said to have maintained that "the resurrection is past already" (2 Tim. 2:17–18), probably belonged to Gnostic or proto-Gnostic circles.[6] In *The Treatise on the Resurrection* from Nag Hammadi (1.43.25–50.18), the anonymous author addresses a certain Rheginos and tells him, "Flee from the divisions and the fetters and already you have the resurrection" (29, 14–15; cf. 45, 25–28).[7] Irenaeus writes concerning the Gnostic heretic Menander: "His disciples obtain the resurrection by being baptized into him, and can die no more, but remain in the possession of immortal youth" (*Adv. haer.* 1.23.5; cf. Justin, *1 Apology* 26.4). In the *Gospel of Thomas* 51 the disciples of Jesus ask their master, "When will the repose of the Dead come about, and when will the new world come?" He answers, "That which you look for has come, but you did not know it." In view of texts such as these,[8] it is plausible that Christian Gnostics drew inspiration from the traditions that associated the fate of Jesus with eschatological language and construed them as support for their "realized eschatology": they could appeal to certain traditions about Jesus as justifying the application of eschatological language to the experience of the

3. Charles H. Talbert, *Luke and the Gnostics: An Examination of the Lukan Purpose* (Nashville: Abingdon Press, 1966); idem, "An Anti-Gnostic Tendency in Lukan Christology," *NTS* 14 (1967): 259–71.

4. Talbert refers to Gnosticism (which for his purposes he identifies with a Christian heresy) with a capital *G*; others would have us write of it with a little *g*. We cannot here enter into the debate over the nature or definition of Gnosticism or of the relation between movements of the first and second centuries. If we use Gnosticism rather than gnosticism, this is only because we are assuming Talbert's position for the sake of discussion. It reveals no judgment on the vexed issues surrounding the emergence of Gnosticism.

5. In addition to what follows, see Charles H. Talbert, "The Redaction Critical Quest for Luke the Theologian," in *Jesus and Man's Hope*, 2 vols., ed. D. G. Buttrick (Pittsburgh: Pittsburgh Theological Seminary, 1970), 1:171–222; also Hans-Werner Bartsch, "Early Christian Eschatology," *NTS* 11 (1965): 387–97.

6. So, among others, Martin Dibelius and Hans Conzelmann, *The Pastoral Epistles*, Hermeneia, trans. P. Buttolph and A. Yarbro (Philadelphia: Fortress Press, 1972), 65–67, 112; and J. L. Houlden, *The Pastoral Epistles: I and II Timothy and Titus*, Pelican New Testament Commentaries (Middlesex: Penguin Books, 1976), 43, 122.

7. For discussion, see Malcolm L. Peel, *The Epistles to Rheginos: A Valentinian Letter on the Resurrection*, New Testament Library (Philadelphia: Westminster Press, 1969), 139–43.

8. For further references of a similar nature, see Hans-Martin Schenke, "Auferstehungsglaube und Gnosis," *ZNW* 59 (1968): 123–26.

individual. If so, and if Luke was—as Talbert and others have supposed—an enemy of Gnostic tendencies, then the evangelist may well have sought to reinterpret or altogether exclude from his narrative materials that could be used to support the Gnostic position. This would account for the fact that the traditions being examined in this dissertation do not show up in Luke-Acts.

Some support for this supposition might be found in Luke 19:11. On the way to Jerusalem, Jesus, as Luke has it, gave his disciples a parable in order to persuade them that the coming events in the capital would not coincide with the appearance of the kingdom of God. "Hearing these things he proceeded to tell a parable because he was near Jerusalem, and they supposed that the kingdom of God was just about to appear" (au. trans.). There follows the parable of the pounds (vv. 12–27), which tells of a nobleman who goes away to a distant land, leaving behind his servants. The implication is patent: the Messiah is not coming but going; an interval of time must pass before the kingdom of God is revealed.

Luke 19:11 is almost certainly redactional,[9] and if it is something other than historical memory, the verse may be a polemical barb aimed at Gnostics who, in accordance with their "realized eschatology," declared that the resurrection or ascension of Jesus had brought about the kingdom of God. That is, Luke perhaps uses the parable in 19:12–27 to refute the view he puts on the lips of the disciples—namely, that the kingdom came into view with the *analēmpsis* of Jesus in Jerusalem. It is certainly difficult to see in 19:11 a censure against eschatological enthusiasm in the Lukan community. Apart from the fact that Luke himself shares the hope that his Lord might soon come, the verse, given its context, most naturally treats not of post-Easter enthusiasm but of the events surrounding Jesus' exodus.

Acts 1:6 can be construed similarly. The disciples ask Jesus, "'Lord, will you at this time restore the kingdom to Israel?'" Jesus responds, "'It is not for you to know times or seasons which the Father has fixed by his own authority. But you shall receive power when the Holy Spirit has come upon you; and you shall be my witnesses in Jerusalem and in all Judea and Samaria and to the end of the earth'" (Acts 1:7–8). Perhaps the disciples' question mirrors the opinion of some who held that the ascension or Pentecost had coincided with the restoration of the kingdom of God, in which case Luke responds by having Jesus say that the time of the coming of the kingdom is not given for his followers to know (1:7) and that the ascension is not identical with the Parousia but only like it (see 1:9–11: Jesus will come again in the same way that he went into heaven).[10]

---

9. See Joachim Jeremias, *Die Sprache des Lukasevangeliums*, MeyerK (Göttingen: Vandenhoeck & Ruprecht, 1980), 277–78.

10. For other Lukan texts that can be understood as a refutation of the claim that the end of

(3) It is possible to urge, without having recourse to talk of Gnosticism, that Luke undertook to combat the excesses of a "realized eschatology." We have, after all, argued throughout these pages that members of the early church possessed, already before Paul's time, a "realized eschatology," and this had little if anything to do with Gnosticism or proto-Gnosticism. The case for this alternative could also appeal to Luke 19:11 and Acts 1:7 (see above).[11]

In support of this position, one could observe that other New Testament authors seem to have directed energies towards dampening an "over-realized eschatology" not clearly connected with Gnosticism. For example, many scholars have supposed that the Corinthians were possessed by the conviction that they knew in the present all the blessings of the future.[12] By this supposition these scholars explain why the Corinthians regarded themselves as perfect, as already filled and armed with wisdom and *gnosis* (1 Cor. 4:8, 10; 8:1); why they ignored proper sexual distinctions (11:1-16; 14:33-36) and felt themselves to be above the usual laws applicable to bodily existence (6:12-13; 8:4; 10:23); and why they did not look forward to the coming resurrection of the dead—they believed that Christians had already been raised up with Christ (15:1-57). We cannot here argue that this account of Paul's converts is correct, that an "over-realized eschatology" is the key to unlocking the main tendency of thought at Corinth. But the case for this has appealed to many and, if correct, strengthens the possibility that Luke, like Paul, combated an extreme claim of eschatological fulfillment. It should also be noted that opposition to an "over-realized eschatology" has been detected, although perhaps with less conviction, behind other canonical books, including Mark,[13] Philippians,[14] 2 Thessalonians,[15] and 1 Timothy.[16]

Jesus coincided with the Parousia, see Talbert "Redactional Quest," 178–91. For criticism, see Mattill, *Luke and the Last Things*, 125–30.

11. Luke himself, to be sure, had a "realized eschatology" of sorts. But the third evangelist drew a distinction between the "last days" (Acts 2:17) and "the Day of the Lord" (Acts 2:20). The days have come; the Day has not. Cf. Luke 17:22, 24, 26–31. For discussion, see Fred O. Francis, "Eschatology and History in Luke-Acts," *JAAR* 37 (1969): 49–63 and Franz Mussner, "'In den letzten Tage' (Apg 2,17a)," *BZ* 5 (1961): 263–65. Luke would not have dismissed every idea of eschatological fulfillment but only those traditions that were taken by some to imply either that the Day of the Lord had fully come or that the fate of the individual could be properly construed in eschatological terms.

12. Recently, Karl A. Plank, "Resurrection Theology: the Corinthian Controversy Re-examined," in *Perspectives in Religious Studies* 8 (1981): 41–54.

13. Theodore J. Weeden, "The Cross as Power in Weakness," in *The Passion in Mark: Studies on Mark 14—16*, ed. W. H. Kelber (Philadelphia: Fortress Press, 1976), 127–29.

14. Walter Schmithals, *Paul and the Gnostics*, trans. J. E. Steely (Nashville: Abingdon Press, 1972), 82–115.

15. See 151 herein.

16. Wiliam L. Lane, "I Tim. IV. 1–3—An Early Instance of Over-Realized Eschatology?", *NTS* 11 (1965): 164–67.

(4) It is just possible that the state of affairs under review is no reflection of the conscious work of the third evangelist. Perhaps Luke was simply sufficiently distant from the earliest communities to be unaware of the original significance of certain traditions that he had received, such as the signs and wonders at the cross. In this case, discussion of possible polemical purposes would not be to the point.

Which of the four alternatives should be endorsed? Reasons have already been given for laying aside the first. As for the fourth, it is difficult to substantiate and probably underestimates Luke's awareness of primitive Christian theology. One is therefore left with the second and third options, which in the end are not very far apart. On both views, Luke refrained from interpreting the death and resurrection of Jesus as the eschatological turning point because he opposed the extremes of a "realized eschatology" for which that interpretation offered support. Whether the proponents of this "realized eschatology" deserve to be labeled "Gnostic" is a question which we, given our present concerns, may refrain from answering.

# RECAPITULATION
# OF CHAPTERS 3—8

(1) Mark, Matthew, John, Paul, and the Apocalypse preserve an interpretation of the passion and resurrection of Jesus according to which the sufferings of the Messiah marked the inauguration of the messianic travail and his resurrection the onset of the general resurrection of the dead.

(2) This interpretation is part of a wider phenomenon, the so-called "realized eschatology" which, according to Dodd and others, characterized early Christian preaching. It is, in fact, the logical correlative to the early church's conviction that she enjoyed, in large measure, the benefits of the messianic age or the age to come. If the messianic age or the age to come has, in some sense, already come or begun to come, then it follows that the eschatological transition has taken place or is in the process of taking place.

(3) Is it possible to locate the origin of the interpretation we have uncovered? That it is found in so many different streams of the early church—Mark, Matthew, Paul, John, Revelation—indicates a fountainhead very near if not in earliest community. This conclusion is reinforced by Rom. 1:3-4, which presumably stems from the earliest Palestinian church, and by the fact that the interpretation is nowhere developed in the Pauline epistles but, rather, is assumed. Further precision on the question of genesis must be deferred until later.

(4) At this juncture it is necessary to enter into debate with Jürgen Becker's *Auferstehung der Toten im Urchristentum.*[1] According to Becker, in the oldest Christian materials the resurrection of Jesus "is not placed in the context of the general resurrection of the dead, particularly because, for the earliest community, with its intense *Naherwartung*, the death of the individual had no existential meaning."[2] The expectation of a general resurrection of the dead

---

1. Jürgen Becker, *Auferstehung der Toten im Urchristentum,* SBS 82 (Stuttgart: Katholisches Bibelwerk, 1976). Incidentally, portions of Becker's book read, amazingly enough, like a commentary on Kirsopp Lake's "The Date of Q," *Expositor* 7 (1909): 498–507. (Becker does not cite Lake.)

2. Becker, *Auferstehung,* 14.

played no role in the proclamation of John the Baptist or Jesus of Nazareth: "Damnation or salvation comes upon the living (*Naherwartung*)."[3] The same is to be said of the earliest Christian communities. Their prayer, "Maranatha," takes no account of a coming resurrection. In addition, the primitive formula, "God, who raised Jesus/him from the dead" (Rom. 4:24; 8:11; 2 Cor. 4:14; Gal. 1:1; Eph. 1:20; Col. 2:12; 1 Pet. 1:21), does not presuppose a general resurrection but, rather, speaks of Jesus as being raised *from* the dead. In Rom. 1:4, *ex anastaseōs nekrōn* is an abbreviation for *ex anastaseōs autou ek nekrōn*. The formula is entirely christological.[4] As for Paul, his earliest missionary preaching, as this is reflected in 1 Thess. 1:9–10, also passed over in silence any expectation of a coming resurrection.[5]

The doctrine of a general resurrection of the dead first came to prominence in Christian teaching when Paul faced a crisis in Thessalonica.[6] Saints had died. The Parousia had not yet occurred. The question arose: Would those who had died share in the messianic kingdom? Paul answered affirmatively by arguing that, at the Parousia, those who are alive will not anticipate those who have fallen asleep, for the trumpet of God will sound, and the dead in Christ will rise first. Then those remaining will be snatched up to be with the Lord (1 Thess. 4:13–18). Paul based his claim that believers will rise upon Jesus' prior resurrection: "For since we believe that Jesus died and rose again, even so, through Jesus, God will bring with him those who have fallen asleep" (v. 14). Here the resurrection of Jesus is, for the first time, brought into connection with the resurrection of believers.

In 1 Corinthians 15, in dialogue with an enthusiasm that left no room for future fulfillment, Paul further developed this connection.[7] In combating a theology that excluded a future resurrection, the apostle argued for the resurrection of the dead by drawing a parallel between the fate of Jesus Christ and the fate of the believer. How can one say that there is no resurrection of the dead (15:12)? If the dead are not raised, then Christ has not been raised (15:13). But he has been raised and is the first fruits (15:20, 23). As through one man (Adam) came death, so through another (Jesus Christ) has come the resurrection (15:21). As with the heavenly man, so with those who belong to him (15:48–49). The correlation drawn between the resurrection of Jesus and the general resurrection is here strengthened.

Becker's reconstruction immediately calls forth several criticisms. First,

3. Ibid., 15.
4. Ibid., 18–31.
5. Ibid., 32–45.
6. Ibid., 45–54. Contrast J. Plevnik, "The Taking Up of the Faithful and the Resurrection of the Dead in 1 Thessalonians 4:13–18," *CBQ* 46 (1984): 274–83.
7. Becker, *Auferstehung*, 66–105.

Matt 27:51-53 is nowhere brought into the discussion. This passage, which associates the passion of Jesus with a resurrection of holy ones, must be late if Becker's thesis is sound. But many have judged it to be early. In any event, the neglect of Matt. 27:51b-53 raises a question.

Second, Becker's analysis of Rom. 1:3-4 fails to persuade. When all has been said, the text states that Jesus was designated Son of God *ex anastaseōs nekrōn*, not *ex anastaseōs autou ek nekrōn*. Given that *anastaseis nekrōn* was a well-known, technical term, it remains the exegete's first task to attempt to make sense of the clause in the light of this fact. As the attempt produces, as we have argued, a plausible explication, alternative readings must remain less probable.

Third, Becker's case leans too heavily upon arguments from silence. Does the cry "Maranatha" really tell one anything about convictions concerning the resurrection in the early church? Does the expectation of a near Parousia necessarily or even probably exclude expectation of a resurrection? That the prayer makes no mention of the resurrection means little, if anything. It also makes no mention of much else. Further, is it clearly the case that the primitive formula "God, who raised Jesus/him from the dead" excludes the thought that Jesus' resurrection was part of a general resurrection?

Fourth, Becker's assertion that the resurrection played no role in the teaching of Jesus should be disputed. In a later chapter it will be urged that Jesus prophesied his own fate and interpreted that fate in eschatological terms. Specifically, he anticipated passing through the messianic travail and sharing in the resurrection of the dead. This conviction stands behind the passion predictions and is the wellspring of the pattern of suffering—vindication that runs throughout the Synoptics. Jesus expected to suffer and die. He also looked beyond death to vindication and spoke of resurrection.

Finally, Becker carries on his argumentation in isolation from a very pertinent consideration. The belief that Jesus' resurrection marked the onset of the general resurrection goes hand in hand with other traditions—such as those in the Markan passion narrative—that interpret the end of Jesus in eschatological categories. Becker does not persuade because he does not and cannot demonstrate that the widely attested interpretation of Jesus' death and resurrection as the eschatological turning point is a late development.

Becker's line of reasoning, we must conclude, exhibits major flaws, and they are sufficient to nullify his major thesis. It is, therefore, safe to conclude that the traditions reviewed in this part of our work have their roots in pre-Pauline Christianity.

*Nine*

# THE PROBLEMS
# OF "REALIZED ESCHATOLOGY"

Many have argued that the New Testament associates the Christ-event, especially the passion and resurrection of Jesus, with language that Judaism typically reserved for discourse about the last things. This conclusion is now a commonplace of critical scholarship and is supported by our work in previous chapters. But a problem immediately poses itself, a problem with which too few have seriously wrestled. The passion and resurrection did not, to state the obvious, coincide with the onset of the last things. Why then does the New Testament leave the impression that they did? Many students of the early church write as though the use of eschatological language to characterize the life, death, and vindication of Jesus was the most natural thing in the world. This is largely due, no doubt, to the widespread assumption that the Bible sometimes uses the language of eschatology to stress the import or significance of a past event or series of events—that is, as metaphor. What is the justification for this assumption? It owes, one suspects, as much to modern theological parlance as to the study of the Scriptures. Numerous Christian thinkers have, in recent times, employed language about the last things to characterize things other than the last. Specifically, it has been the particular predilection of twentieth-century theology to reinterpret statements about the last things in terms of the cosmic or the eternal (Karl Barth) or of existential decision or personal encounter (Rudolf Bultmann). Observe how in the following words of Bultmann "eschatological" becomes a cipher for that which is existentially significant.

> The cross in its redemptive aspect is not an isolated incident which befell a mythical personage, but an event whose meaning has "cosmic" importance. Its decisive, revolutionary significance is brought out by the eschatological framework in which it is set. In other words, the cross is not just an event of the past which can be contemplated, but is the eschatological event in and beyond time, in

so far as it (understood in its significance, that is, for faith) is an ever-present reality.[1]

Bultmann's use of "eschatological" has its parallels in the work of critical historians. Eduard Schweizer writes as follows concerning Mark 15:33:

> The darkness mentioned in Amos 8:9 ... shows the sweeping effect of Jesus' death. Not only the earth was affected, but the entire universe as well. What happened, therefore, is similar to what will accompany the Day of Judgment, according to 13:24. Therefore the death of Jesus is compared to that event....[2]

According to these sentences, Mark could introduce the darkening of the sun, a stock concomitant of the final judgment, to underline the "sweeping effect" of a past occurrence, the death of Jesus. The remark of Hans Conzelmann on the darkness at noon betrays the same supposition: "The aim is to stress the saving significance of Jesus' death by ref. to its eschatological and cosmic dimension."[3] The literature of New Testament studies is filled with statements similar to these of Schweizer and Conzelmann, statements which move without comment from the eschatological to the cosmic or to the significant.

Many modern theologians, having disposed of traditional beliefs concerning the last things, have sought to give new meaning to the New Testament's teachings on such matters by treating them so that they reflect existential or other contemporary concerns. The propriety of this attempt to render the Scriptures relevant is for our present purposes of no concern. The immediate problem is instead one of original intention. Perhaps Jews and Christians of the first century were as capable as Barth and Bultmann of employing the language of eschatology in a metaphorical manner, and perhaps this is the key to explaining the phenomenon Dodd encompassed with the term "realized eschatology." But this should not simply be assumed without discussion.

### The Argument of George B. Caird

George B. Caird, in his book on *The Language and Imagery of the Bible,* has recently pressed the following two points:

1. The biblical writers believed literally that the world had had a beginning and would have an end.
2. They regularly used end-of-the-world language metaphorically to refer to what they well knew was not the end of the world.[4]

---

1. Rudolf Bultmann, "New Testament and Mythology," in *Kerygma and Myth: A Theological Debate,* ed. Hans-Werner Bartsch, trans. R. H. Fuller (New York: Harper & Row, 1961), 36.
2. Eduard Schweizer, *The Good News According to Mark,* trans. Donald H. Madvig (Atlanta: John Knox Press, 1970), 352–53.
3. Hans Conzelmann, "Skotos ktl.," *TDNT* 7 (1971): 439.
4. George B. Caird, *The Language and Imagery of the Bible* (Philadelphia: Westminster

Because Caird argues these proposals, especially the second, with some care, and because, if he is correct, metaphor might be the key to "realized eschatology," his case invites our examination.

According to Caird, the authors of the Tanach believed that the world would, in the future, come to its literal end (Gen. 8:22; Ps. 102:25–26; Isa. 51:6). The phrase "the Day of the Lord" was sometimes used to designate this end. But the prophets also utilized the expression and the accompanying imagery of cosmic disaster and a return to primeval chaos to refer to contemporary crises such as the overthrow of Babylon, the annihilation of Edom, or the ravaging of Judah by a plague of locusts. That is, they used "the Day of the Lord" as a metaphor. The prophets had a "bifocal vision": with their near sight they foresaw on the horizon impending historical events; with their far sight they beheld the Day of the Lord. The superimposition of the two visions often produced a synthetic picture, of which Joel provides an illustration. In 1:1–12 the prophet tells of the destruction of the land caused by a plague of locusts. In 1:13–14 he summons his people, because the plague is God's judgment, to contrition and fasting. In 1:15 Joel speaks for the first time of the Day: "Alas for the day! For the day of the Lord is near, and as destruction from the Almighty it comes." In 1:16—2:27 he elaborates the themes introduced in 1:1–15 (including the Day; see 2:1, 2, 11) and delivers promises of salvation. Joel 3:1 (2:28) signals a major transition, and what follows readily draws to itself the label "eschatological." On Caird's reading this is natural. The "local manifestation of God's judgment has the power to call the nation to repentance because it is seen as an anticipation and embodiment of the universal judgment to come. So the foreground scene fades into a telephoto panorama of all nations gathered in the Valley of the Lord's Judgment."[5] Joel speaks of the present crisis as though it marked the arrival of the Day of the Lord. That Day, nevertheless, remains outstanding.

Caird's conclusions with regard to the apocalyptic literature are similar. In his judgment, the disparity between the world of the prophets and that of the apocalyptic seers has often been unduly exaggerated. Differences, do, of course, exist. There is, however, continuity with regard to the use of the language of eschatology, for the apocalyptic visionaries no more intended their eschatology to be taken literally than the prophets did. This is true, for example, of Daniel. The visions of the second half of the book reach their

Press, 1980), 256. Caird defines metaphor as "the transference of a term from one referent with which it naturally belongs to a second referent, in order that the second may be illuminated by comparison with the first or by being 'seen as' the first" (66).

5. Ibid., 260.

climax in the setting up of the abomination of desolation, the altar that Antiochus erected in honor of Olympian Zeus in the Jewish temple. The material leading to this climax constitutes a "realized eschatology"; for the future that Daniel allegedly prophesies is, for his readers, past or present: Antiochus has already entered Jerusalem, he has already razed the altar. Further—and this is for Caird the crucial point—to the extent that Daniel looks to the real future, it is only to the removal of the abomination and to the end of persecution.

For a moment, indeed, he uses the telephoto lens (12:1-3), but at once he brings us back to the foreground. Daniel asks how long it will be until the end and is given the symbolic figure of "a time, times and half a time." But this is only the interval that must elapse before "the shattering of the holy people ceases" (12:7); the end of the age is further off (12:13).[6]

In other words, the end of the present travail is near, but its extinction is not coincident with the end of the age.

In the New Testament, matters are similar. In Mark 13 the disciples ask their master when the stones of the temple will be thrown down. "'Tell us, when will this be, and what will be the sign when these things are all to be accomplished?'" (13:4). Scholars usually interpret the discourse that follows to pertain primarily to the end of the present age. But the question to which the chapter is directed is not, explicitly, When will the new age appear? Caird accordingly argues that the so-called Markan apocalypse addresses only the query that occasioned it and has to do not with the world's end but with the events of 70 A.D. "The disaster to Jerusalem will come within the lifetime of the present generation, and, when it arrives, they are to see in it the coming of the Son of man to whom God has entrusted the judgment of the nations" (Dan. 7:22; cf. John 5:27; 1 Cor. 6:2).[7] Mark 13:30 and 32 support this opinion. There is an apparent contradiction between 13:30, according to which the Son of man will come within a generation, and 13:32, according to which God alone knows the day and the hour. Caird asserts: "The paratactical Hebrew mind did not need to be told that the two sayings were at different levels: embodied in the historical event which Jesus predicted, the day would come within a generation; in its full, literal reality its time was known only to God."[8]

With regard to Paul, few scholars dispute that, to use Bultmann's term, eschatology is to some degree "historized,"[9] for the apostle frequently uses

6. Ibid., 263.
7. Ibid., 266.
8. Ibid., 267.
9. Rudolf Bultmann, *Theology of the New Testament*, vol. 1, trans. K. Grobel (New York: Charles Scribner's Sons, 1951), 307.

language appropriate to the last things when speaking of the Christ-event and of Christian experience. Most scholars elucidate this phenomenon by setting it within the context of a *Naherwartung:* the Christ-event is the beginning of the end of the age, and Christian experience gains its character from its unique position between the first advent and the final redemption, which lies just ahead. Caird disputes this explanation. Paul did not, he asserts, expect the redemption to come shortly. Not even Rom. 13:11–14 and 1 Corinthians 7 point in this direction. Thus, Paul's recourse to the language of eschatology was not determined by a conviction that the present would soon be swallowed up by God's eschatological kingdom but by a long biblical tradition that employed end-of-the-world language metaphorically. "Dodd was right in describing the beliefs of Jesus and the early church as realised eschatology, but wrong in thinking that this term adequately distinguished the events of the gospel story from other events, both before and after."[10]

Before offering criticism of Caird, it is necessary to distinguish two related but separate issues. The problem of metaphorical usage is not resolved by a judgment on the prosaic quality of the language of eschatology. To illustrate: Mark 13:24–25 reads, "'But in those days, after that tribulation, the sun will be darkened, and the moon will not give its light, and the stars will be falling from heaven, and the powers in the heavens will be shaken.'" Did the author of this sentence believe that the heavenly bodies would someday exhibit bizarre behavior, or did he instead intend, by means of a picture, to symbolize something? André Feuillet, like Caird, argues that Mark 13:24–25 prophesies the destruction of Jesusalem in 70 A.D. In his opinion, the language of Mark 13:24–25, although drawn from the eschatological teachings of Judaism, depicts through metaphor an occurrence in the middle of history.[11] On this reading, all literalism is certainly excluded: the sun and the moon and the stars did not, in 70 A.D., go dark and come crashing to the ground. But—and this must be emphasized—those who discern only engagement with the coming of the messianic era in 13:24–25 are not, as perusal of the commentaries makes evident, thereby committed to a literal explicaton. It is possible to interpret Mark 13:24–25 as pertaining to the messianic advent and still hold that the author was quite aware of the symbolic nature of his prophecy: when Mark wrote of the end, he knew himself to be doing something other than offering accurate information about future cosmological states. Our question, then, is not whether eschatological language should be interpreted literally but whether, as Caird and Feuillet suppose, its metaphorical application to things

10. Caird, *Language and Imagery,* 271.
11. André Feuillet, "La signification fondamentale de Marc XIII," *RevThom* 80 (1980): 199–202.

other than the last can be demonstrated and, if it can, whether this illuminates the phenomenon of "realized eschatology."

The New Testament does attach the language of eschatology to what is for us today the noneschatological, the passion and resurrection of Jesus. This our work in preceding chapters puts beyond doubt. But the question then becomes, Why did early Christians construe the Christ-event in the terms they did? Caird's answer is straightforward: they thereby made known the deep meaning of the event. The construction is metaphorical. The major reason for dissenting from this proposal is that it is difficult to avoid finding a *Naherwartung* in much of the literature of the early church, and this moves one to wonder to what extent the usage under review was bound up with belief in the near culmination of history. Few scholars would agree that the decisive revelation of God's eschatological kingdom is no near prospect in the Synoptics or Paul, and this entails a reading different from that of Caird. When a document depicts the present or immediate past in apparently eschatological terms, talk of metaphor is appropriate only if the redemption remains distant; for as we shall see straightaway, if it is thought to be proximate, the present becomes the time immediately before the redemption and hence naturally draws to itself the language of eschatology.[12] This has nothing to do with metaphor.

It is beyond the scope of this investigation to demonstrate that Paul and other members of the primitive church shared a belief in the age's near end. But assuming for the moment and for the sake of discussion that this was in fact the case, one can interpret the depiction of the Christ-event as the eschatological turning point without recourse to talk of metaphor. A proximate end entails that the present be counted as the prelude to the new era, and given such a view of the present, the appearance of signs and wonders could easily indicate the literal beginning of the end. (That the eschatological renewal could be thought of as a process over an extended period of time is evident, above all, from the Apocalypse of Weeks [1 *Enoch* 93:1-10 and 91:11-17];[13] we have also encountered the same conception in *Jubilees* 23; see 17-19 herein). Thus, unusual disturbances of nature (such as one finds in Mark 15:33 and Matt. 27:51) could, in view of the prophecies made in the apocalypses and the New Testament, mark the presence of the great tribulation; and the report of a resurrection or a story like that in Matt. 27:51b-53 could betoken the onset of the general resurrection. On the premise that the end is at hand, one can read signs and wonders as genuine eschatological events. The observation is

12. Cf. Scholem, *Sabbatai Ṣevi*, 262-66, 688.
13. See Jacob Licht, "Time and Eschatology in Apocalyptic Literature and in Qumran," *JJS* 16 (1965): 177-82.

the more telling as Caird's examples of the past or present being characterized in eschatological terms are drawn from documents that, on the reading of most scholars, contain a *Naherwartung*. One might, therefore, dismiss Caird with the following assertion. Over the centuries, Jewish eschatology developed and changed, and by the time one reaches the intertestamental literature, there are few instances of past or present occurrences being characterized in eschatological terms unless, at the same time, the messianic age or the age to come is thought of as near.

There are, however, texts that command caution. In *Bib. Ant.* 11:3 (a passage not cited by Caird), one reads that, when God gave the Law to Moses,

> the mountains burned with fire and the earth shook and the hills were removed and the mountains overthrown: the depths boiled, and all the habitable places were shaken: and the heavens were folded up and the clouds drew up water. And flames of fire shone forth and thunderings and lightnings were multiplied and winds and tempests made a roaring: the stars were gathered together and the angels ran before, until God established the law of an everlasting covenant with the children of Israel, and gave unto them an eternal commandment which should not pass away.[14]

*Fourth Ezra* 3:18–19 and *b. Zebaḥim* 116a offer similar pictures of the same event.

The three passages just cited tell in favor of Caird's thesis, for they recount an event of the distant past—one unconnected with the end—in language reminiscent of descriptions of the eschatological turning point.[15] Difficulties nonetheless remain with taking such texts as the clue to comprehending the New Testament's "realized eschatology." The darkness in Mark's passion narrative probably rests, as we have seen, upon Amos 8:9. Since early Christians viewed the passion of Jesus as the literal fulfillment of numerous scriptures, why should Mark 15:33 be understood any differently? That is, does not the verse record the actual fulfillment of a prophecy having to do with the Day of the Lord? If so, one cannot at the same time construe it as metaphor. By the same reasoning, a like conclusion obtains for the extensive correlation we observed between Zechariah 9—14 and Mark 11—16. Zechariah's prophecy was systematically employed because it had been fulfilled by Jesus, not because the Christ-event was being compared to that which will happen on the Day of the Lord. Again, the story of a resurrection of holy ones in Matt.

14. Montague Rhodes James, *The Biblical Antiquities of Philo: Now First Translated from the Old Latin Version* (New York: Macmillan Co., 1912; New York: Ktav, 1971 repr.), 107.

15. Also relevant are those rabbinic texts that speak of the Exodus as the achievement of a redeemed state similar to that of the future world. See on this Ira R. Chernus, *Redemption and Chaos: A Study in the Symbolism of the Rabbinic Aggada* (Ann Arbor, Mich.: University Microfilms, 1978), 111–69.

27:51b–53 is scarcely metaphorical. The attempt to find parallels for such an interpretation certainly leaves the hands empty. No ancient Jewish source known to this writer parades the significance of an event of the past by adorning it with a resurrection. Hence it is most natural to read Matt. 27:51b–53 as announcing the onset of the general resurrection.

If the so-called "realized eschatology" of the New Testament resists ready explanation in terms of metaphor, the reason is not far to seek. The early church believed Jesus to be the Messiah. This is crucial. The coming of the Messiah was bound up with the last things, and to claim that the Messiah had come was to claim that the prophetic promises of the Tanach had begun to meet their fulfillment. It entailed that the messianic age or the age to come was near and thus that the terrors or wonders of eschatological expectation must be present or very near to hand. The implication is unavoidable. If the coming of the Messiah was a genuine eschatological event, then the early church's characterization of that event as the eschatological turning point should be taken at face value. Surely, then, Caird's stricture against Dodd—the "realized eschatology" of the early church does not distinguish the events of the gospel story from other events, both before and after—is not justified. Talk of "realized eschatology" cannot be adequately translated into talk of metaphor.

## "Realized Eschatology" and Jewish Parallels

As our work in chapter 2 shows, early Christians were not the only group in antiquity to claim that the final events had begun to unfold. The conviction that the great tribulation had arrived is, as we have seen, found in several Jewish documents of the period 165 B.C.—135 A.D. In this regard the New Testament offers nothing new. Moreover, as several authorities have noted, the so-called "realized eschatology" of the New Testament also has its parallels. At Qumran the description in 1QSa of the messianic banquet matches that of the actual meal of the Essene community (1QS VI, 4–6). Thus, "in its central religious act, the sect understands itself as an anticipation of the Age to Come."[16] We have also observed how *Jubilees* 23, on one reading, places the turning point in the present: the terrors of the great tribulaton have come and gone, and the new age is dawning. R. H. Charles could write, "The writer of Jubilees, we can hardly doubt, thought that the era of the Messianic kingdom had already set in."[17]

---

16. Krister Stendahl, "The Scrolls and the New Testament: An Introduction and Perspective," in *The Scrolls and the New Testament*, ed. K. Stendahl (New York: Harper & Brothers, 1957), 10.
17. *APOT*, 2:9.

Neither the belief that the great tribulation had broken in upon the present nor the belief that the blessings of the eschatological future could be anticipated is unique to Christianity.[18] But having said this, one must add a caveat. In teaching that the Messiah has come, that resurrections have taken place (Matt. 27:51b–53), that the sun has hidden its face (Mark 15:33), and that the judgment has been accomplished (John 3:15; 5:24; 12:31), the New Testament does set itself apart. There is really no adequate parallel to the claim that the decisive turning point lies in the past. At Qumran, the advent of the messianic figures and of the judgment remains outstanding. Even *Jubilees* 23, on our reading, falls short of the New Testament's bold assertions. The author of this pseudepigraphon is comparatively restrained in his depiction of the present. Although he sees it as a time of renewal, and although he expects it to blossom swiftly into the full-fledged messianic age, his claims are not nearly so extravagant as those of the New Testament. Krister Stendahl has correctly written that, as concerns the redemptive drama, "the Christian church was one act ahead of the Essenes."[19] For "the Essenes" one could substitute any intertestamental group or document, and the statement would remain true. If it be only of degree, the New Testament does confront the scholar with an apparent singularity. Therefore, the marshaling of Jewish parallels, although highly instructive, will not of itself fully illuminate the rise of "realized eschatology."

David Aune's book on *The Cultic Setting of Realized Eschatology in Early Christianity*[20] might leave one with a different impression. According to Aune, the phenomenon referred to by the term "realized eschatology" not only has parallels in Judaism but "is a relatively common phenomenon in comparative religions."[21] Insofar as eschatology is protology, a return to the primal state from which humanity fell, the proleptic experience of the new age in the early church is nothing exceptional. The terms "realized eschatology" and "realized protology" (functionally equivalent concepts) stand for a prevalent way of conceptualizing religious experience in which devotees are taken up "in illo tempore" (Mircea Eliade). The locus of this experience is the cult. Aune's concern is to demonstrate that "realized eschatology" within early Christianity—he looks at John, Ignatius, the Odes of Solomon, and Marcion—had its birth within cultic worship. He is persuaded that, "apart from the recognition of this fact, realized eschatology as a datum in early Christian

---

18. Cf. Nils A. Dahl, "Eschatology and History in Light of the Qumran Texts," in *The Crucified Messiah and Other Essays* (Minneapolis: Augsburg Pub. House, 1974), 140–41.

19. Stendahl, "Scrolls and the New Testament," 15.

20. David Eduard Aune, *The Cultic Setting of Realized Eschatology in Early Christianity*, NovTSup 28 (Leiden: E. J. Brill, 1967).

21. Ibid., 8.

religious thought cannot be adequately understood."[22] In other words, the key to right comprehension of the early church's "realized eschatology" is to be found in cultic experience.

If we follow a different line of investigation herein, this is not because we wholly dispute Aune's major thesis. The "realized eschatology" of the new Testament does fall into a category familiar to the history of religions, and there can be little doubt concerning the importance of the cult for creating and maintaining experience that can be conceived as proleptic participation in the golden age. Aune, however, leaves several important questions unresolved. For example, while he concerns himself firstly with the cult, the focus of much of the "realized eschatology" of the New Testament is not Christian experience but the Christ-event. That is, the New Testament not only interprets present experience in eschatological categories but also so interprets a past series of events: the life, death, and resurrection of Jesus. One must therefore ask: Was it cultic experience which led to an eschatological interpretation of the Christ-event, or did an eschatological interpretation of the Christ-event encourage one to interpret cultic experience as the attainment of prophetic promises? Certainly, one is not necessarily dealing here with two exclusive approaches. Perhaps the case is like to the dilemma of the chicken or the egg. Aune himself writes: "The theoretical and practical expression of religious experience are inextricably intertwined, and . . . primacy cannot be imputed to one or the other."[23] But this is a generality, and our work leads us to conclude that, as concerns early Christianity, primacy lies with the theoretical or doctrinal element. As we shall demonstrate in chapter 12, an interpretation of the Christ-event determined the conceptualization of cultic experience in terms of "realized eschatology," not the other way around. To the extent that we can establish this, to that extent is Aune's work deficient as a comprehensive explanation of "realized eschatology."

One further point should be made. Aune leaves unexplored the formative period in the development of "realized eschatology." His investigation, after a chapter on the Dead Sea Scrolls, immediately passes on to the Fourth Gospel. But John, as we have seen, stands at the end of a development that can be traced back through traditions in the Synoptics and Paul to pre-Pauline Christianity. Insofar as Aune does not inquire into this line of development, his work needs to be supplemented.

## The Resurrection

For some scholars, the sufficient cause of "realized eschatology" was belief

22. Ibid., 220.
23. Ibid., 9.

in Jesus' resurrection. Joachim Jeremias made these remarks: "Nowhere in Jewish literature do we have a resurrection to *doxa* as an event of history. Rather, resurrection to *doxa* always and without exception means the dawn of God's new creation. Therefore the disciples must have experienced the appearances of the Risen Lord as an eschatological event, as a dawning of the turning point of the world."[24] This logic, at first glance, seems compelling. But the premise—"Judaism did not know of any anticipated resurrection as an event in history"—is perhaps not true. What does one make of *T. Job* 39:9(12)—40:6(4)? In this passage from a pseudepigraphon of the first century A.D. or B.C., Job explains to those who have come to bury his children that they will not find their bodies, for the children have already been taken up into heaven—which fact is confirmed to all by the sight of them crowned beside the heavenly glory. Theirs is no mere resuscitation, a return to earthly life. Here the bodies of individuals are taken up into the heavens and given to partake of the heavenly glory; all this in the middle of history.

Even if *T. Job* 39:9(12)—40:6(4) be not thought sufficient of itself to overturn Jeremias's generalization, he has begged the question. If resurrection to *doxa* as an event of history had no precedent in Judaism, why was it not more natural to see in the exaltation of Jesus something akin to the assumptions of Enoch, Moses, and Elijah?[25] If resurrection was a purely eschatological category, and if the resurrection of an individual alone was so implausible, why not interpret the vindication of Jesus as a bodily assumption to heaven like that of previous heroes? Why bring in the category of resurrection at all? Jeremias does not help us here. The reason? Adequate answers to our queries will only come when one ceases to speak of Judaism in general and begins to inquire into what the disciples of Jesus in particular believed before Good Friday. We have at our disposal documents that ostensibly relate what Jesus (and therefore his disciples) hoped would happen. Should not these be the primary guides for conjectures concerning how the first Christians would have interpreted their Easter experiences?

### Hans-Werner Bartsch

Hans-Werner Bartsch has in a number of publications argued that, according to the most primitive interpretation of the Easter experiences, the

24. Joachim Jeremias, *New Testament Theology: The Proclamation of Jesus*, trans. J. Bowden (New York: Charles Scribner's Sons, 1971), 308-9.

25. Cf. David Flusser, "Salvation Present and Future," in *Types of Redemption: Contributions to the Theme of the Study-Conference held at Jerusalem 14th to 19th July 1968*, Studies in the History of Religions 18, ed. R. J. Zwi Werblowsky and C. Jouca Bleeker (Leiden: E. J. Brill, 1970), 53.

Parousia, the coming of the Son of man, had already occurred.[26] The prophecy of Jesus before the Sanhedrin (Mark 14:62: "'You will see the Son of man seated at the right hand of the Power, and coming with the clouds of heaven'") was originally believed to have been fulfilled in the resurrection—otherwise, the saying would have been dropped. And those who came to the tomb of Jesus saw, as the original conclusion of the passion narrative once recounted, the splendor of the Son of man.[27] In accordance with this, Matt 28:2–4 preserves an early tradition which contains imagery common to apocalyptic writings,[28] and Bartsch proposes that "the angel of the Lord" (28:2) is secondary: Matt. 28:2–4 was originally about an appearance of the Son of man as Lord.[29] Traces of the same interpretation of Easter are also present in Matt. 28:18 ("'All authority in heaven and on earth has been given to me'") which, through allusion to Dan. 7:14 LXX, makes plain that the prophecy concerning the Danielic Son of man came to fulfillment in the resurrection of Jesus.

As time passed, belief in the final arrival of the kingdom of God could not endure, and the Parousia became again an object of hope. Traces of this transformation of doctrine are preserved in the New Testament in two polemical barbs. When Luke has Jesus, on his way to Jerusalem, correct the disciples, who supposed that the kingdom of God was about to appear (Luke 19:11), the evangelist is combating the primitive notion, which lived on in some circles, that "the Passion of Jesus in Jerusalem was already bringing in the Parousia."[30] And when, in Mark 16:7, the angel commands the women to tell the disciples and Peter that Jesus goes before them into Galilee, then this serves to refute those who maintained that Peter saw in the appearance of the risen Lord the fulfillment of the promise of Mark 14:62. Against those who interpreted the appearances as the Parousia, the present polemical text of Mark affirms that the coming of the Son of man remains to be accomplished in Galilee.

Bartsch supports his reconstruction by observing that the passion narratives of Mark and Matthew are full of traditions that seem to place the passion of Jesus within an eschatological context. Many of these we ourselves have

26. See the works cited in nn. 27, 29, 30, and 31, this chap.; also in n. 20 on 68; "Historische Erwägungen zur Leidensgeschichte," *EvT* 22 (1962): 449–59; "Inhalt und Funktion des Urchristlichen Osterglaubens," *NTS* 26 (1980): 180–96; and "Die Passions- und Ostergeschichten bei Matthäus," in *Entmythologisierende Auslegung: Aufsätze aus den Jahren 1940 bis 1960*, TF 26 (Hamburg: Herbert Reich, 1962), 80–92.

27. See esp. Bartsch, "Der ursprünglich Schluss der Leidensgeschichte: Überlieferungs-geschichtliche Studien zum Markus-Schluss," in *L'Évangile selon Marc*, BETL 34, ed. M. Sabbe (Louvain: Louvain Univ. Press; Gembloux, Belg.: J. Duculot, 1974), 401–33.

28. Cf. our conclusion herein, 47–48.

29. Cf. Hans-Werner Bartsch, *Auferstehungszeugnis: Sein historisches und sein theologisches Problem*, TF 41 (Hamburg: Hervert Reich, 1965), 12.

30. Idem, "Early Christian Eschatology," 393.

examined, especially in chapters 3 and 4, and we can concur with the thrust of Bartsch's argument. But why did primitive Christianity interpret the resurrection as the Parousia and see the passion of Jesus as the eschatological turning point? To answer this question, Bartsch turns back to the proclamation of Jesus. According to Bartsch, Jesus is presented to us in the oldest layers of the passion history as the eschatological prophet, who in line with contemporary expectation believed that the culmination of his ministry in Jerusalem would coincide with the onset of the kingdom of God.[31] When the disciples interpreted their master's death and resurrection as the fulfillment of eschatological promises, they were claiming that the expectations of Jesus had met their fulfillment in his own fate. The resurrection meant that Jesus' prophecies concerning the kingdom of God and the Son of man had come to pass. Thus, the "realized eschatology"—a term Bartsch does not use—of the post-Easter period did not have as its point of departure the "realized eschatology" of the pre-Easter period; the note of fulfillment was not simply a continuation of Jesus' stress on the presence of salvation. On the contrary, "realized eschatology" arose out of the conviction that, with the resurrection, the purely future eschatological expectations of Jesus had passed from promise to fulfillment. "Early Christianity ... proclaimed the fulfillment of that which Jesus announced in his preaching."[32]

In our estimation, Bartsch's conjecture concerning the genesis of "realized eschatology" is close to correct, and the present investigation will undertake to demonstrate this in detail. Many of the words of Jesus on eschatological matters were believed to have been fulfilled in the passion and resurrection. Bartsch, however, has not been an influential figure. Discussions of his work are few and far between. In the English-speaking world especially, his contributions are rarely cited. The cause of this is not far to seek. Bartsch has aligned himself with too many questionable assumptions and conclusions. These unfortunately overshadow the genuine contribution he has to make. For instance, it is difficult to credit the claim that, with the resurrection, the Parousia was believed to have taken place, and Bartsch's reasoning for this is nowhere close to persuasive. Would Mark 14:62 really have been preserved only if it had already met fulfillment? Could not the tradition have handed on a prophecy that would, as Christians assumed, soon come to pass? Further, Bartsch's estimation of Matt. 28:2-4 and 28:18b is suspect. There is no compelling cause for thinking that the former originally described not an angel but the risen Lord, and the latter is hardly admissible as primitive

31. Cf. idem, *Jesus: Prophet und Messias aus Galiläa* (Frankfurt am Main: Stimme, 1970), 57.
32. Ibid., 117.

testimony. It is, in addition, no encouragement for Bartsch that the appearances of the risen Lord in the Gospels have, as they now stand, few points of contact with eschatological expectation.[33] It may also be observed that the old tradition in 1 Cor. 15:3-8 does not use the language of eschatology to recount the appearances of Jesus.

Bartsch nowhere considers the possibility of what one might call a "partially realized eschatology," and this is perhaps what leads to the false conclusion that the Parousia was believed to have occurred already. It is probable that the primitive Christian preaching proclaimed that many prophecies had attained fulfillment, and just as probable that it held forth many as outstanding. "Realized eschatology" and intense eschatological expectation were not mutually exclusive. It was possible to paint the passion of Jesus with eschatological colors and yet expect the Son of man to come on the clouds in the future; and this reading of the evidence commends itself because it is able to take into account at the same time the data upon which Dodd and Bartsch have called, as well as the data upon which Hahn and Tödt and others have pinned their cases. Early Christianity did not proclaim that the Parousia had taken place. Instead it preached that the last things were unfolding, that certain promises had been fulfilled, that others would soon come to pass.

Bartsch must also draw criticism for his failure to explain with any thoroughness the development of early Christian eschatology on the presupposition that belief in an accomplished Parousia lies at the beginning of the church. Like Glasson and Robinson, he is forced to account for the emergence of the doctrine of the second advent. How did the church soon come to cast its hope upon the Parousia if it originally saw in the resurrection the realization of the Parousia? In this connection Bartsch speaks, without much elaboration, of "the suffering of the community"[34] and of confrontation with "concrete reality."[35] This is a surprisingly brief and inadequate solution to a problem that Glasson and Robinson have deemed sufficiently involved to require book-length treatment; and being assertion, not argument, it will certainly not persuade many. Furthermore, Bartsch's reconstruction involves—if one may judge by the sociology of religion—an improbability. Rarely does a closely knit, vital religious movement tolerate major alteration of its belief-structure. Doctrinal convictions will endure despite every apparent disproof, including suffering and "concrete reality." If early Christianity had declared the occur-

---

33. Further, as Wilhelm Michaelis has observed (in "Horaö ktl.," *TDNT* 5 [1967]: 356 n. 204), "The fact that the beginning of the appearances is not described as coming from heaven rules out any idea that the ref. is to the Parousia...."
34. Bartsch, *Auferstehungszeugnis,* 25.
35. Bartsch, "Der ursprünglich Schluss der Leidensgeschichte," 420.

rence of the Parousia, it is likely that, despite every obstacle, the belief would have persisted indefinitely. And if early Christian thinking had in fact evolved away from a "realized eschatology," expectation would presumably have come to cluster around prophecies that, unlike the Parousia, had not previously been clearly proclaimed as realized.

In view of our rather severe criticism, we should reiterate our agreement with Bartsch's attempt to root the community's so-called "realized eschatology" in an interpretation of the eschatological expectations of the pre-Easter period. This is indeed a thesis that throws a flood of light upon the New Testament. But the statement, "Early Christianity . . . proclaimed the fulfillment of that which Jesus announced in his preaching," however true, passes over the most important question: Why? Why did the primitive community proclaim the fulfillment of that which Jesus had announced in his preaching? Why did the followers of Jesus interpret his eschatological prophecies so that they found their fulfillment in his own fate? Bartsch has, it seems to us, only indicated the task that lies ahead.

## August Strobel

Before turning to our own proposals, it will prove well to examine one last contribution, August Strobel's *Kerygma und Apokalyptik*.[36] This book, although first a study of the historical Jesus, is in some ways reminiscent of Bartsch's work and is pertinent to our present task. The work is characterized by a critical attitude toward much contemporary scholarship, and in some respects it marks a return to the position of Schweizer. It does not suffice, according to Strobel, to speak of the eschatological message of Jesus. The proclamation of Jesus can only be adequately described by the word "apocalyptic." Attempts to deny this do not persuade. The thought of Jesus "moved in the context of the official, common-apocalyptic expectation, [which was] perhaps stronger in the district of Galilee, with its probably in part specific piety. The expectation of the apocalyptic reversal of things was undoubtedly common."[37] Failure to recognize this conclusion inevitably leads to reconstructions of Jesus created in accordance with modern consciousness.

The words of Luke 19:11, to which Strobel refers several times, contain an historical memory, and Jesus shared the hope of his disciples. He, thinking like an apocalyptic pacifist, went up to Jerusalem expecting the kingdom of

---

36. August Strobel, *Kerygma und Apokalyptic: Ein religionsgeschichtlicher und theologischer Beitrag zur Christusfrage* (Göttingen: Vandenhoeck & Ruprecht, 1967). Note also Strobel's essay on "Discipleship in the Light of the Easter-Event," in *The Beginnings of the Church in the New Testament*, ed. F. Hahn, A. Strobel, and E. Schweizer, trans. Iain and Ute Nicol (Minneapolis: Augsburg Pub. House, 1970), 40–84.

37. Strobel, *Kerygma und Apokalyptik*, 101.

God to appear immediately. His expectation was more or less tied to a fixed date (cf. Mark 13:28–30; 14:24); and believing himself to be the Son of man, he anticipated (along the lines of *1 Enoch* 71) not death and resurrection but exaltation.[38]

Strobel supports his reconstruction of Jesus' proclamation by taking notice of passages in the New Testament which interpret the Christ-event in eschatological categories. Unlike Bartsch, he does not assert that the Parousia was believed to have occurred.[39] But Christians did interpret the cross as the exaltation of Jesus and the resurrection as the first act of Jesus' expected return. They also painted the passion with colors usually reserved to depict the Day of the Lord. Mark 15:33, the darkness at noon, is especially important here (cf. Amos 8:9). Strobel also argues that the apostle Paul saw the crucifixion as the "turn of the aeons"[40] and that the use of "the Lord's day" for Easter Sunday derives from the LXX translation of *yôm yhwh*.[41] Thus, what "Jesus expected as a public act of God, was proclaimed and experienced by the early community as a hidden but real act of God."[42]

Several of Strobel's conclusions recall those of Bartsch, and concerning the point of primary concern for us the two concur: certain eschatological hopes were proclaimed as realized because it was believed that the fate of Jesus fulfilled certain eschatological expectations of the pre-Easter period. But unfortunately, Strobel's work also resembles that of Bartsch in that it invites a good deal of criticism. (1) Even if he is not primarily concerned with explaining the rise of "realized eschatology" in the post-Easter church, one may rightly express disappointment that Strobel, given the nature of his conclusions, nowhere enters into dialogue with Dodd or others in the English-speaking world who have addressed this problem. In this he is like Bartsch. (2) Few scholars would countenance talk of an "official, common-apocalyptic expectation"; there was too much diversity for such a phrase to be justified. Few would accept Strobel's portrait of a Jesus completely at home in the world of the apocalypses; what, to mention nothing else, of Jesus' statements on the presence of the kingdom of God? (3) An expectation of the coming of the kingdom of God in the near future and an anticipation of death or martyrdom would not have been mutually exclusive for Jesus. It in any case remains highly probable, despite Strobel's doubts, that Jesus anticipated death and resurrection (see chap. 12 herein). The importance of this point becomes

38. Ibid., 41, 43, and 58–84, respectively.
39. Ibid., 112.
40. Ibid., 92–93.
41. Ibid., 43. Later Christian tradition held that the Parousia would occur on the Lord's Day, that is, on Sunday. See, e.g., the *Book of John Concerning the Falling Asleep of Mary*, 37.
42. Strobel, *Kerygma und Apokalyptik*, 191.

evident in our next criticism. (4) According to Strobel, although Jesus nourished the hope that history would come to its conclusion during his lifetime, and although Jesus did not expect to meet death, it was precisely in the passion that the early community saw the decisive eschatological moment. It is not clear how these two facts are to be harmonized. The crucifixion did not fulfill the hopes of Jesus as Strobel presents them. Why then was it regarded as their confirmation? In other words, while Strobel desires to explain the eschatological interpretation of the passion by reference to the expectations of Jesus, those expectations were, given Strobel's conclusions, to all appearances only canceled or at least left unfulfilled by the passion—and seemingly all the more so given the scandalous nature of crucifixion in the ancient world (cf. 1 Cor. 1:18, 23). As is the case with Bartsch, it remains unclear why the disciples of Jesus proclaimed the fulfillment of what their master held forth only as eschatological promise.

## The Present Thesis

No satisfactory explanation of the "realized eschatology" of the early church has yet been offered. The phenomenon is not an instance of metaphor, and one cannot convincingly explicate its genesis by reference to Jewish documents or to faith in the resurrection. The solution of Bartsch and Strobel—that the primitive community saw in the passion and the events of Easter the fulfillment of eschatological promises of Jesus—although suggestive, is, for reasons noted above, bound up with difficulties. We believe, however, that it is possible to circumvent these difficulties and sustain the thesis Bartsch and Strobel share, and such is the object of this book.[43]

The intertestamental literature, as already observed, does not offer any precise parallel to the so-called "realized eschatology" of the New Testament. But insofar as the great tribulation is, in some Jewish texts, already part of present experience, and insofar as promises concerning the Day of the Lord are to some degree brought into the present, something decisive is shared with the New Testament—namely, the conviction that prophecies have been and

43. Walter Schmithals also agrees with Strobel and Bartsch: "In the preaching of the church, that salvific deed of God which Jesus announced as outstanding is proclaimed as realized. The expectation of Jesus becomes seen and known as fulfilled in his own fate—above all in his death on the cross. The continuity and discontinuity of Jesus and the church is the continuity and discontinuity of expectation and fulfillment"; see "Jesus von Nazareth in der Verkündigung der Kirche," in *Jesus Christus in der Verkündigung der Kirche: Aktuelle Beiträge zum notwendigen Streit um Jesus* (Neukirchen-Vluyn: Neukirchener Verlag, 1972), 22–23. See also "Jesus und die Wirklichkeit des Reiches Gottes," 101–4 in the same volume, and Schmithals's essay on "Jesus und die Apokalyptik," in *Jesus Christus in Historie und Theologie: Neutestamentliche Festschrift für Hans Conzelmann zum 60. Geburtstag*, ed. G. Strecker (Tübingen: J. C. B. Mohr [Paul Siebeck], 1975), 70–75. We have not treated Schmithals at length because he himself cites Strobel and adds little to the discussion.

are being fulfilled. One knows that the great tribulation has entered the here and now because present conditions match prophecies delivered by Daniel or Moses or Ezra or some other figure from the past. It is the same with the "realized eschatology" of Qumran or *Jubilees* 23. Prophecies of the coming age are construed so that they appear to match present realities. In the intertestamental literature, the realization of eschatology is, in short, the realization of prophecy.

The same may be said of the New Testament. On the one hand, as chapters 3—9 of this work make manifest, in at least some early Christian circles, language otherwise typically reserved in Judaism for discourse about the last things came to be associated with the end of Jesus. Jesus' resurrection was interpreted not as an isolated event but as part of the general resurrection of the dead, and his death was understood as if it were a death in the great tribulation of the latter days. On the other hand, Jesus understood his own ministry within eschatological categories. As we shall argue in chapter 11, he reckoned with the possibility of suffering, even death, in the coming crisis, the great tribulation, and looked beyond that to the resurrection of the dead. One thus observes a correspondence between the eschatological expectations of Jesus and a post-Easter interpretation of the passion and resurrection. This is no coincidence. Jesus anticipated suffering, death, and resurrection, and in fact he did suffer and die. According to the testimony of the Easter witnesses, he was also vindicated by God. Hence, the course of events naturally suggested that the expectations of Jesus had, at least in part, come to fulfillment, and this inevitably led to an interpretation of the passion and resurrection in eschatological categories and to the birth of a "realized eschatology." Further, as social psychology demonstrates, people strongly tend to interpret their experiences in terms of their own previously established categories and prior expectations, even when these are seemingly confuted. It is, therefore, not surprising that, although the kingdom of God did not arrive as hoped, the early church held on to their interpretation of Jesus' passion and resurrection in pre-Easter—that is, in eschatological—categories.

To establish our thesis, two topics demand investigation: (1) post-Easter interpretations of the death and resurrection of Jesus, and (2) the eschatological expectations of Jesus. The first we have already explored at length. It is thus now necessary to turn to the second.

## Ten

# JESUS AND
# THE KINGDOM OF GOD

Until recently, critical scholarship has been almost unanimous that in the proclamation of Jesus the kingdom of God (*hē basileia tou theou*) signifies primarily not the territory God rules but his dynamic activity as ruler. It has also tended to agree that the kingdom should somehow be considered both present and future, and formulations such as "already and not yet" or "eschatology in the process of realization" have been offered as descriptive of this state of affairs. Professor Norman Perrin indeed came to assert that it may not be "legitimate to think of Jesus' use of kingdom of God in terms of 'present' and 'future' at all"[1]—an assertion we shall have to examine soon enough. But first we must briefly introduce the evidence that has led to the contemporary consensus.

A number of dominical parables testify to the kingdom's future. For example, the parables of the mustard seed,[2] of the seed growing secretly,[3] of the leaven,[4] and (perhaps) of the sower[5]—the so-called parables of growth—have as their presupposition, if not object, supreme faith in God's future. They teach: "What God has begun he will bring to a triumphant conclusion."[6]

In their original setting, the parables of growth probably supplied comfort or reassurance in the face of disillusionment with the present. How could one believe that the promises of God were already being fulfilled? How could Jesus be the expected one? An answer is given in these parables which direct the hearer to known truths. God often raises the great from the small. Harvest is the fruit of seedtime. The grand end can be the sequel to a seemingly

1. Norman Perrin, *Jesus and the Language of the Kingdom: Symbol and Metaphor in New Testament Interpretation* (Philadelphia: Fortress Press, 1976), 40.
2. Mark 4:30-32; Matt. 13:31-32 = Luke 13:18-19 (Q); *Gospel of Thomas* 20.
3. Mark 4:26-29.
4. Matt. 13:33 = Luke 13:20-21; *Gospel of Thomas* 96.
5. Mark 4:1-9 = Matt. 13:1-9 = Luke 8:4-8; *Gospel of Thomas* 9.
6. Norman Perrin, *Rediscovering the Teaching of Jesus* (New York: Harper & Row, 1967), 158.

inconsequential beginning. Reminded of such truths, one can pass beyond superficial perception of current circumstances, and the present can open itself to the consolation brought by trust in God's sure future; for the present is in truth the beginning of that future. In other words, because the kingdom of God has a future dimension, the faithful may find hope for better things to come.

The coming of the kingdom of God is also unambiguously set forth as a future event in the parable of the weeds among the wheat (Matt. 13:24–30) and in the parable of the dragnet (Matt. 13:47–50). According to the former, just as wheat and tares may presently grow together, their separation taking place in the future at harvest, similarly God at the judgment will separate good and evil and thereby set things aright. Further, men cannot make this segregation before the time; patience is therefore inculcated. The parable of the dragnet makes a like point. That which will happen when the kingdom comes resembles the sorting of a catch of fish. Prior to the sorting of the catch, good and bad are mixed. Just so is it in Israel before the judgment. But God, like the fisherman, will make a separation and thus create a holy community purged of all wickedness. Both Matt. 13:24–30 and 47–50 answer a question about evil and the world, and both answer by referring to the future.

Several dominical sayings confirm the conclusions drawn from the parables. Here we need consider only two in any detail. The first is Luke 11:2a = Matt. 6:10a, "Thy kingdom come." This petition is almost certainly authentic and was originally an integral part of the Lord's Prayer. Of its general implication there can be no doubt. Whether interpreted as a prayer for others to experience the coming of the kingdom, or as a petition that the present experience of the disciples come to consummation, or as both of these, "Thy kingdom come" is a decided reference to the future; it acknowledges the magnificence of the future and prays for it to enter the present. Matthew 8:11 = Luke 13:28–29 is also an authentic saying which looks towards things to come: "I tell you, many will come from east and west and sit at table with Abraham, Isaac, and Jacob in the kingdom of heaven." As most scholars conjecture, the initial context for this utterance was almost certainly Jesus' table fellowship with outcasts, with "tax collectors and sinners." Significant for our purposes is the distinction implicitly drawn between the present and the future. The present table fellowship around Jesus is only an anticipation of the coming messianic banquet. The future will see the consummation of what is now known only proleptically. So the present is marked by anticipation; one looks forward to sitting at table with the patriarchs in the kingdom of God.

Beyond the materials already introduced, Jesus' expectation of a future fulfillment presents itself, among other places, in his teaching on the signs that

will precede the coming of the kingdom,[7] in the recurrent motif of eschatological reversal,[8] in sayings about entering the kingdom,[9] and in the beati-
tudes—which, like the parables of growth, tell of a future that sustains life in
the present.[10] The expectation of a future fulfillment, it is no exaggeration to
say, runs throughout the sayings of Jesus; it is a fundamental datum of the
synoptic tradition.

If, on exegetical grounds, a strong element of futurity appears in Jesus'
preaching on the kingdom of God, this result is confirmed by the use of "reign
(of God)" in contemporary Jewish literature. Although the term is not frequent, it carries a future reference in more than one text. Note, for example,
*As. Mos.* 10:1: "And then his [God's] Kingdom shall appear throughout his
creation, and then Satan shall be no more, and sorrow shall depart with him"
(*APOT*). The *Sibylline Oracles* III, 46–48 ("But, when Rome shall rule over
Egypt ... then the mightiest kingdom of the immortal king over men shall
appear") and 767 ("And then indeed he will raise up his kingdom for all ages";
*APOT*) are also pertinent, as is the well-known line from the Kaddish prayer:
"May he establish his kingdom in your lifetime and in your days, and in the
lifetime of the whole house of Israel, speedily and at a near time."[11] The
prophetic targums likewise speak of the reign of God as something yet to
come.[12] For example, in *Tg. Zech.* 14:9 and *Tg. Obad.* 21 it is written that "the
kingdom of the Lord will be revealed upon all those dwelling on the earth."
And from Qumran, 1QSb IV, 25–26 states, "May you attend upon the service
in the Temple of the kingdom and decree destiny in company with the Angels
in the Presence" (cf. also 1QM VI, 6). Thus, a connection between the
kingdom of God and eschatological hopes was known in ancient Judaism, and
this encourages one to see the same connection in the sayings of Jesus.

If the futurity of the kingdom of God is firmly established, it is no less true
that Dodd's case for "realized eschatology" in the teaching of Jesus has much
in its favor.[13] In Luke 11:20 = Matt. 12:28, the authenticity of which is little
doubted, Jesus declares that "'if it is by the finger of God that I cast out

7. E.g., Mark 13:28–32 = Matt. 24:32–36 = Luke 21:29–33; and Luke 12:54–56.
8. Notice may be taken of Mark 8:35 = Matt. 16:25 = Luke 9:24 = John 12:25; Mark
10:23–25 = Matt. 19:23–24 = Luke 18:24–25; Mark 10:31 = Matt. 19:30; Matt. 23:12; Luke
14:11; 18:14.
9. Mark 10:15 = Matt. 18:3 = Luke 18:17 = John 3:3, 5; Mark 10:23–25 = Matt. 19:23–24
= Luke 18:24–25; Mark 9:47 = Matt. 18:9; Matt. 7:21; 21:31–32; 23:13.
10. Matt. 5:3–13; Luke 6:20–23.
11. See Ismar Elbogen, *Der jüdische Gottesdienst in seiner geschichtlichen Entwicklung,* 3d
ed. (Frankfurt am Main: J. Kauffmann, 1931), 92–93.
12. Bruce D. Chilton, "Regnum Dei Deus Est," *SJT* 31 (1977): 261–70; Klaus Koch,
"Offenbaren wird sich das Reich Gottes," *NTS* 25 (1979): 158–65.
13. See now Eta Linnemann, "Zeitansage und Zeitvorstellung in der Verkündigung Jesu,"
in *Jesus Christus in Historie und Theologie,* 247–54.

demons, then the kingdom of God *ephthasen eph hymas.*'" The extensive
debate this verse has called forth seems to have issued in a consensus. One
should translate it "the kingdom of God has come upon you." Luke 17:21b
("the kingdom of God *entos hymon estin*") probably has a similar meaning ("is
in the midst of you"), as may Matt. 10:7 = Luke 10:9, 11 and Matt. 4:17 =
Mark 1:15. In addition to these explicit statements, Mark 2:19 ("'Can the
wedding guests fast while the bridegroom is with them?'") seems to imply that
the disciples of Jesus do not fast because the kingdom of God is present in the
person of Jesus. And the similes in Mark 2:21–22 convey that the old is now
passing; the new—which is most probably to be identified with the kingdom of
God, whose power now works to displace the old order[14]—has already arrived.
For Jesus, even now is it true that Satan has been cast out of heaven (Luke
10:18) and bound (Mark 3:27). Even now is there in the midst of Israel
something greater than Solomon, something greater than Jonah (Matt. 12:41–
42 = Luke 11:31–32). Even now can the sons of Abraham open their eyes and
see that which the prophets and the righteous only longed to see (Matt. 13:16–
17 = Luke 10:23–24).

Once one has discovered this side of the tradition, how does one account for
it, given the sayings that presuppose the futurity of the kingdom of God? The
options are several and a decision difficult, but perhaps the most satisfactory
solution involves recourse to talk of an extended time. Not unlike the program
in Deutero-Isaiah—a section of Scripture which presumably had some influence on Jesus[15]—the advent of God's kingdom did not, for Jesus, belong to a
moment but constituted a series of events that would cover a period of time.
According to Lloyd Gaston,

> Deutero-Isaiah certainly does not imply the coming of the Kingdom "in a
> moment, in the winking of an eye" (1 Cor. 15:52). One can even speak of the
> coming of salvation in Deutero-Isaiah as a process: already the prophet hears the
> angels going forth (Isa. 40:3–5) to prepare the way for the procession back to
> Jerusalem, but this will take some time.[16]

A similar conception is present in *Jubilees*. As already observed, in this
pseudepigraphon the age of blessedness enters onto the stage of history a step
at a time. *Jubilees* 23:26–27 reads:

14. Cf. Joachim Gnilka, *Das Evangelium nach Markus*, 2 vols., EKKNT 2 (Zürich: Benziger
Verlag; Neukirchen-Vluyn: Neukirchener Verlag, 1978, 1980) I:116.
15. See now Werner Grimm, *Die Verkündigung Jesu und Deuterojesaja*, ANTJ 1, 2d rev. ed.
(Berne: Peter Lang, 1981), and A. E. Harvey, *Jesus and the Constraints of History*
(Philadelphia: Westminster Press, 1982), 120–53.
16. Lloyd Gaston, *No Stone on Another: Studies in the Significance of the Fall of Jerusalem in
the Synoptic Gospels*, NovTSup 23 (Leiden: E. J. Brill, 1970), 414.

And in those days the children shall begin to study the laws, and to seek the commandments, and to return to the path of righteousness. And the days shall begin to grow many and increase amongst those children of men till their days draw nigh to one thousand years, and to a greater number of years than (before) was the number of days. (*APOT*)

The Apocalypse of Weeks, *1 Enoch* 93 and 91:12–17 (Maccabean period?), also views the eschatological transition as a protracted process. Its schematization of history consists of ten weeks:

| | |
|---|---|
| First week: | from Adam to Enoch |
| Second week: | from Enoch to Noah |
| Third week: | from Noah to Abraham |
| Fourth week: | from Abraham to the giving of the Torah |
| Fifth week: | from the giving of the Torah to the first temple |
| Sixth week: | concludes with the destruction of the temple |
| Seventh week: | a period of great wickedness; at its conclusion the elect become apparent and receive knowledge |
| Eighth week: | Israel is judged |
| Ninth week: | the nations are judged |
| Tenth week: | the angels are judged |

Jacob Licht has offered the following diagram of this numerical scheme, which makes plain that the last things stretch out over the span of several periods of time:[17]

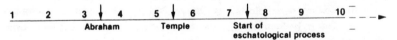

We need only add that the author of the Apocalypse of Weeks thinks of himself and of his community as in the end of the seventh week. The eschatological process is already underway.

The phenomenon common to Deutero-Isaiah, *Jubilees* 23, and the Apocalypse of Weeks supplies the best background for understanding the relationship between the future and the present in the synoptic tradition.[18] The seeming contradiction between the presence of the kingdom of God and its futurity is dissolved when one realizes that Jewish thinking could envision the final events—the judgment of evil and the arrival of the kingdom of God—as extending over time, and as a process or series of events that could involve the present. When Jesus announces that the kingdom of God has come and is

17. See Jacob Licht, "Time and Eschatology," 178–79.
18. Charles, *APOT* 2:315, observes that the great renewal in *T. Levi* 18 is also "gradual"; but here the present is not yet properly eschatological time. In *Apocalypse of Abraham* 29 we read of how "the Age of the righteous *beginneth* to grow."

coming, this means that the last act has begun but has not yet reached its climax; the last things have come and will come. Already, in the person and activity of Jesus, the kingdom of God is present. Even though the consummation remains outstanding, in him eschatological promises are being fulfilled. The kingdom of God is conceived as "a total event . . . composed of several significant parts which together make up that whole"[19]—and several of the episodes that constitute that total event have already transpired. So, as Jürgen Becker puts it, "the present [is] no longer the short time before the expected end but already itself the eschatological time."[20] Despite current infatuation with the criterion of dissimilarity, the great advantage of this interpretation is that it provides the proclamation of Jesus with a foundation and precedent in ancient Judaism.

According to David Flusser, Jesus "is the only Jew of ancient times known to us, who preached not only that men were on the threshold of the end of time, but that the new age had already dawned."[21] This oft-quoted statement invites qualification. Jesus is perhaps the only Jew of ancient times known to us who preached, in so many words, the presence of the kingdom of God. But for the author of *Jubilees* 23, the age of renewal had already dawned; see 17–19 herein. Note should also be taken of *1 Enoch* 93 and 91:12–17. The writer of this apocalypse placed himself in a very special time. He believed that the time of apostasy was fast coming to its close, that the "righteous of the eternal planting" had already been elected, and that to them the holy one was presently giving "sevenfold instruction concerning all His creation" (93:10; *APOT*). That is, he believed that blessings of the new age were already being bestowed. We have here the "eschatological reversal" of an "ordinary situation."[22] Perhaps similar convictions lie behind *1 Enoch* 90 and portions of the Qumran *Hôdāyôt*.[23]

## The Kingdom of God: Its Character

The data heretofore reviewed imply, despite the presence of the kingdom, a disjunction between the present and the future. Jesus speaks of a time to come,

19. Robert F. Berkey, "ΕΓΓΙZEIN, ΦΘANEIN, and Realized Eschatology," *JBL* 82 (1963): 184.
20. Jürgen Becker, *Das Heil Gottes: Heils- und Sundenbegriffe in den Qumrantexten und im Neuen Testament*, SUNT 3 (Göttingen: Vandenhoeck & Ruprecht, 1964), 206.
21. David Flusser, *Jesus*, trans. R. Walls (New York: Herder & Herder, 1968), 90.
22. Michael Stone, "Lists of Revealed Things in Apocalyptic Literature," in *Magnalia Dei: The Mighty Acts of God: Essays on the Bible and Archaeology in Memory of G. Ernest Wright*, ed. F. M. Cross, Jr., W. E. Lemke, and P. D. Miller, Jr. (Garden City, N.Y.: Doubleday & Co., 1976), 424–42.
23. For *1 Enoch* 90 see the interpretation of Bo Reicke, "Official and Pietistic Elements of Jewish Apocalypticism," *JBL* 79 (1960): 139–42; on the *Hôdāyôt*, see Kuhn, *Enderwartung*.

brought about through the supernatural intervention of God, wherein the present order will be reversed. The last will be first, the first last. The poor will be blessed, the rich will wail. Those doing the will of the Father in heaven will enter the kingdom; those not doing his will will be thrown into Gehenna. These promises, unless perceived through existentialist glasses or interpreted as symbols for that which is beyond history and hence indescribable, are scarcely intelligible apart from belief in a literal end or renewal of the world. According to the synoptic testimony, the definitive establishment of God's visible kingdom *en dynamei* will be once and for all, and it will be the end of sin and evil. The decisive divine action will annul the wicked works of humanity and bring to an end the rule of Satan. The kingdom of God must therefore mark a radical turning point, introduced perhaps by a "cosmic catastrophe,"[24] as already in Isa. 24:17-23 (cf. Dan. 2:44). Even if, as seems likely, Jesus did not use the terminology of the two ages,[25] he believed that, on the far side of judgment and resurrection, the kingdom of God would bring the otherwise unattainable.[26]

This writer cannot concede the legitimacy of the existentialist analysis or discover much reason for referring the eschatological imagery of the canonical Gospels to some realm beyond history (although he would be most happy to do so). But it must be admitted that a sophisticated use of literary criticism and a strict application of the popular criteria for determining the authenticity of synoptic logia at present forbid many from concluding that Jesus' proclamation of the kingdom was bound up with a belief in the disruption of the natural course of history. Here the work of Norman Perrin stands pre-eminent, and to it we must now turn.

In his book on *Jesus and the Language of the Kingdom*,[27] Perrin has argued that, with Jesus, the kingdom of God was neither an idea nor a conception but a symbol that functioned to evoke a "myth." More precisely, it was a "tensive symbol" that evoked "the myth of the activity of God." Picking up on the work of Philip Wheelwright and Paul Ricoeur,[28] Perrin defines a tensive symbol in opposition to a "steno-symbol." The former has "a set of meanings that can

24. Karl Ludwig Schmidt, "Basileus ktl.," *TDNT* 1 (1964): 585.
25. Cf. Anton Vögtle, *Das Neue Testament und die Zukunft des Kosmos* (Düsseldorf: Patmos-Verlag, 1970), 145-48. According to Volz, *Die Eschatologie*, 64-66, the terminology of the two ages did not develop before 70 A.D.
26. On whether Jesus expected a temporary messianic kingdom to be followed by the age to come (as in *4 Ezra*), see Dale C. Allison, Jr., "A Millennial Kingdom in the Teaching of Jesus?" *IBS* 7 (1985): 46-52.
27. Norman Perrin, *Jesus and the Language of the Kingdom* (Philadelphia: Fortress Press, 1976).
28. Philip Wheelwright, *Metaphor and Reality* (Bloomington, Ind.: Indiana Univ. Press, 1962); idem, *The Burning Fountain* (Bloomington, Ind.: Indiana Univ. Press, 1968); Paul Ricoeur, *The Symbolism of Evil*, trans. E. Buchanan (Boston: Beacon Press, 1967).

neither be exhausted nor adequately expressed by any one referent." The latter has "a one-to-one relationship to that which it represents, such as the mathematical symbol pi."[29] In Jewish apocalyptic and in the early church, the kingdom of God functioned primarily as a steno-symbol. Concerning the Jewish apocalypses, the

> seer [typically] told the story of the history of his people in symbols where each symbol bore a one-to-one relationship with that which it depicted. This thing was Antiochus IV Epiphanes, that thing was Judas Maccabee, the other thing was the coming of the Romans, and so on. But if this was the case, and it certainly was, then when the seer left the known facts of the past and present to express his expectations of the future, his symbols remained "steno-symbols," and his expectation concerned singular concrete historical events.[30]

On the Christian side, Luke 17:20-37 is typical. This text interprets the kingdom of God in terms of the Son of man, now identified with Jesus; here a steno-symbol (Son of man) defines with precision the content of eschatological expectation.

The proclamation of Jesus confronts one with something altogether different. On his lips the kingdom of God was a tensive symbol and evoked "the myth of the activity of God," the form of this remaining open or unexhausted by any one apprehension of the reality represented. Jesus offered no picture of the future. Indeed, the forms of language of which he was fond (proclamatory sayings, parables, proverbial sayings, prayer) resist translation into formal discourse; they are not readily put into propositional statements.[31] Moreover, as the preaching of Jesus itself made real the experience of God as king, questions concerning the time of the kingdom's coming are misdirected (cf. Luke 17:20-21).

Perrin's case, inadequately introduced by the previous paragraphs, is full of interesting observations and provocative claims. But the observations, however stimulating, do not establish the claims, which are based upon three sayings about the kingdom (Luke 11:20; 17:20-21; Matt. 11:12), the Lord's Prayer, several proverbial sayings, and the parables. Perrin writes that competent scholarly opinion recognizes the authenticity of at least these portions of the tradition, and this is true. At the same time, most scholars would also wish to add considerably to this list. Many, if not most, for example, would probably maintain that talk about the Son of man has roots in the teaching of Jesus. But

---

29. Perrin, *Jesus and the Language,* 30.
30. Norman Perrin, "Eschatology and Hermeneutics: Reflections on Method in the Interpretation of the New Testament," *JBL* 93 (1974): 11.
31. But note the different opinion of Madeleine Boucher, *The Mysterious Parable: A Literary Study,* CBQMS 6 (Washington, D.C.: Catholic Biblical Association of America, 1977), 30.

an admission of the dominical authorship of certain sayings about the Son of man would probably require a modification of Perrin's central determination, the tensive character of the kingdom of God in the sayings of Jesus. Now, it is not our purpose here to argue for the authenticity of the Son of man sayings or of any other synoptic logia that are inconsistent with Perrin's portrait of Jesus. For now, we simply observe that Perrin's work, if correct, demands not only that *at least* the three kingdom sayings, the Lord's Prayer, several proverbs, and the parables be dominical; it also demands that *not much more* should be attributed to Jesus. As soon as one leaves the three kingdom sayings, the Lord's Prayer, the several proverbs, and the parables, Perrin's analysis finds little foothold and much to contradict it. That is, the argument only holds up if one shares Perrin's fairly skeptical stance with regard to the historical integrity of the Gospels.[32]

Beyond this general difficulty, one must stress that, in the apocalypses, the distinction between a tensive symbol and a steno-symbol is not, as Perrin himself admits, perfectly vivid.[33] This is important. When Perrin turns to the Gospels, he writes as though use of the kingdom of God as a tensive symbol stands in unreconcilable opposition to its use as a steno-symbol. Such is not obviously the case if the distinction between the two types of symbols is not hard and fast. In line with this, John J. Collins's instructive article on "The Symbolism of Transcendence in Jewish Apocalyptic," which is a response to Perrin's characterization of the nature of symbolic language in apocalyptic literature, persuasively demonstrates that, in the Jewish apocalypses, the literal and symbolic can be one: a steno-symbol can function as a tensive symbol.[34] To illustrate: the four great beasts of Daniel 7 are the kingdoms of Babylon, Media, Persia, and Greece. But Dan. 7:17 ("'These four great beasts are four kings'") does not adequately express the seer's intent, for the simple interpretation does not contain the evocative power of the vision. Although the beasts are steno-symbols—this beast is that kingdom—the vision conveys much more. It "communicates the universal and transcendent dimensions of the kingdoms, and gives them a signification and dimension which is not evident in the interpretation. If we must describe the symbol of the beasts in Wheelwright's terms, then we should not call it a steno-symbol but a tensive symbol of ancestral vitality."[35] Collins's observations raise a question. If tensive symbols and steno-symbols can show up side by side in the apocalyptic literature,

---

32. A similar criticism could be made against James Breech, *The Silence of Jesus* (Philadelphia: Fortress Press, 1983).
33. Perrin, *Jesus and the Language*, 31.
34. John J. Collins, "The Symbolism of Transcendence in Jewish Apocalyptic," in *Papers of the Chicago Society of Biblical Research* 19 (1974): 12–22.
35. Ibid., 16.

why not also in the teachings of Jesus? According to Perrin,"Earliest Christianity used the symbol Son of man to evoke the myth of apocalyptic redemption where Jesus had used the symbol Kingdom of God to evoke the myth of the activity of God."[36] But is not "the myth of apocalyptic redemption" simply an instance of the broader category, "myth of the activity of God"? The two "myths" do not, despite the impression left by Perrin, exhibit any necessary antagonism. Was it not possible for one who prayed the Lord's Prayer (in which the kingdom of God is a tensive symbol) to believe concurrently that the Son of man (a steno-symbol) would someday come to the ancient of days with the clouds of heaven? It is probably simplistic to contrast Jesus' use of the kingdom of God as a tensive symbol with the later use of the kingdom of God as a steno-symbol. That Jesus used the phrase "kingdom of God" as a tensive symbol does not exclude his having used it or some other eschatological term as a steno-symbol.

Jesus "used the symbol of Kingdom of God to evoke the myth of the activity of God." Is this an adequate statement? In sayings that Perrin treats as dominical, Jesus proclaims that one person will lose his life, another save it; that the exalted will be humbled, the humble exalted; that the first will be last, the last first; that some will enter the kingdom of God, others find themselves cast out and thrown into hell. Such pronouncements as these permit one to define further "the myth of the activity of God." The teaching of Jesus has to do with the eschatological manifestation of God's kingship. The future of which he speaks is not simply open and uncircumscribed: it is eschatological and will reveal God's kingship to all peoples. When Perrin writes that "earliest Christianity used the symbol Son of man to evoke the myth of apocalyptic redemption where Jesus had used the symbol Kingdom of God to evoke the myth of the activity of God," the contrast is unduly exaggerated. "The myth of the activity of God" is, in the sayings of Jesus on the kingdom of God, more properly, and to use Perrin's terms, "the myth of eschatological redemption." Further, this eschatological redemption involves concrete expectations and a temporal element. Concerning this last, Perrin's attempt to eliminate the problem of time is difficult to fathom.[37] The sayings on eschatological reversal tell of that which will become evident only in time. They are promises that the kingdom of God will turn the present upside down. This is not to deny the present experience of God as king. Rather, if God presently discloses his kingly activity, it is that very disclosure which implies, nay requires, a future fulfillment, a coming, irresistible climax at which God will make manifest to

---

36. Perrin, *Jesus and the Language*, 59.
37. Even Perrin, when discussing Luke 11:20, has recourse to the word "anticipate" (ibid., 43).

all his innermost nature and thence assume his role as undisputed sovereign.[38] This is particularly evident in many of the parables. Talk of "already and not yet" or of "eschatology in the process of realization" is hard to circumvent. If Jesus' preaching on the kingdom involved a temporal element, it also involved concrete expectations. Perrin does not come to this conclusion in part because he tends to underinterpret texts. According to Matt. 12:41-42 = Luke 11:31-32, the queen of the south and the men of Nineveh will arise at the judgment and condemn the generation of Jesus. In *Rediscovering the Teaching of Jesus*, Perrin affirms:

> The reference to the queen of the South and the men of Nineveh arising at the judgment is no more than a conventional way of speaking of a future moment at which Jesus' ministry will be vindicated. It is this, but it is no more than this, and in particular it says nothing about the form of this future moment, nor about the time element involved, beyond the fact that it is future.[39]

On this reading, the verses mean no more than that "Jesus' ministry will be vindicated." The saying implies expectation neither of the coming assize of Jewish expectation nor of a resurrection. Why not? Because the words seeming to suggest such are "no more than a conventional way of speaking." This is hardly compelling reasoning. An individual does not usually choose a conventional form of expression unless it fittingly conveys his intention. No reason is given for the supposition that the unqualified use of a customary way of speaking does not naturally involve the acceptance of what that way of speaking normally implies. Indeed, with regard to Luke 11:31-32 = Matt. 12:41-42, the exegete readily assumes that it does not offer picturesque details of the future moment of vindication because these could be taken for granted, the point of the passage lying elsewhere. Despite Perrin, the double saying about the queen of the south and the men of Nineveh refers to common Jewish expectations, the final judgment and the resurrection,[40] and this entails that Jesus' hopes for the future took specific form.

---

38. Cf. David Hill, "Towards an Understanding of the 'Kingdom of God,'" *IBS* 3 (1981): 73.

39. Perrin, *Rediscovering the Teaching*, 195.

40. According to George B. Caird, "Eschatology and Politics: Some Misconceptions," in *Biblical Studies: Essays in Honor of William Barclay*, ed. J. R. McKay and J. F. Miller (Philadelphia: Westminster Press, 1976), 75-77, there is in Matt. 12:41-42 = Luke 11:31-32 no reference to the resurrection: *egeirō* and *anistēmi* can both mean simply "to appear," and here they are used of witnesses appearing in court to give testimony (cf. Mark 14:57). But both Matthew and Luke use a future tense, and *en tē krisei* and *geneas tautēs* usually have eschatological content in the Jesus tradition. Note also that the scene painted by the saying from Q presupposes a universal judgment, for it involves the Queen of Sheba, the Ninevites, and the Israel of Jesus' time.

Our criticisms of Perrin permit us to revert to a more traditional formulation. For Jesus, the future of the kingdom of God was bound up with a belief—widely held in first-century Judaism—in the end or transformation of the world. Notwithstanding his use of the kingdom of God as a so-called tensive symbol, Jesus' sayings on the kingdom portend a decisive, future epiphany of God as king.

## "When Will These Things Be?"

Jesus also proclaimed that the kingdom of God was temporally near. There are first the explicit statements of temporal proximity. "'Truly, I say to you, there are some standing here who will not taste death before they see that the kingdom of God has come with power'" (Mark 9:1). "'Truly, I say to you, this generation will not pass away before all these things take place'" (Mark 13:30). "'Truly, I say to you, you will not have gone through all the towns of Israel, before the Son of man comes'" (Matt. 10:23). The case for the authenticity and independence of these three sayings is not easily dismissed. Yet it is admittedly possible that they are variants of an original, single pronouncement which some would assign to an early Christian prophet. Fortunately, then, our verdict on the issue at hand does not hinge upon this set of sayings.[41] The Synoptics contain, in addition to the explicit statements on the temporal proximity of the kingdom, (1) parables admonishing people to watch for the coming of the Lord or of the Son of man[42]; (2) pronouncements of eschatological woes on contemporaries[43]; (3) parables that are best interpreted as warnings in the face of imminent catastrophe[44]; (4) sayings about *hē genea autē*, "this generation"[45]; and (5) a host of miscellaneous traditions that alike announce or presuppose that the final fulfillment of God's saving work is nigh.[46] Any attempt to deny the authenticity of all of this material probably

41. This against the impression left by Barry S. Crawford, "Near Expectation in the Sayings of Jesus," *JBL* 101 (1982): 225–44.
42. Mark 13:34–36; Matt. 24:45–51 = Luke 12:42–46; Matt. 24:43–44 = Luke 12:39–40; cf. *Gospel of Thomas* 21; Matt. 25:1–13; Luke 12:35–38; cf. *Gospel of Thomas* 103.
43. E.g., Mark 13:17 = Matt. 24:19 = Luke 21:23; Matt. 11:20–24 = Luke 10:12–15; Luke 6:24–26; 13:1–5; 23:27–31.
44. E.g., Matt. 7:24–27 = Luke 6:47–49; Matt. 11:16–17 = Luke 7:31–32; Luke 12:16–21; 13:25–27; 16:19–31; Matt. 25:1–13.
45. E.g., Mark 8:12 = Matt. 12:39; 16:4 = Luke 11:29; Mark 9:19 = Matt. 17:17 = Luke 9:41; Mark 8:38; Matt. 23:34–36 = Luke 11:49–51; 17:25. Note Martin Hengel, "Kerygma oder Geschichte? Zur Problematik einer falschen Alternative in der Synoptikerforschung aufgezeigt an Hand einiger neuer Monographien," *TQ* 151 (1971): 334; and E. Lövestam, "The *hē genea autē* Eschatology in Mk 13,30 parr.," in *L'Apocalypse johannique et l'Apocalyptique dans le Nouveau Testament*, ed. J. Lambrecht, BETL 53 (Louvain: Louvain Univ. Press, 1980), 403–13.
46. E.g., Mark 13:33 = Matt. 24:42; 25:13 = Luke 21:36; Mark 13:28–29 = Matt. 24:32–33 = Luke 21:29–31; Mark 14:24 = Matt. 26:29 = Luke 22:16, 18; Mark 1:15 = Matt. 4:17; 10:7

cannot be carried through consistently without committing one to a critical silence—in spite of Eta Linnemann's recent attempt to do just this.[47] Linnemann concedes that Jesus frequently spoke of eschatological subjects, yet denies that he spoke of the kingdom of God as close in time. But against this, it suffices to ask, Would one speak of eschatological matters as often and as urgently as did Jesus if one did not strongly believe that they impinged upon the immediate future?

One suspects that the endeavors to eliminate a *Naherwartung* from dominical tradition and indeed to exclude altogether any temporal reference—"not temporal, but experiential"[48]—are are little more than signs of the ever-present desire to modernize Jesus. Such endeavors must overlook the plain sense of many passages and postulate a discontinuity between Jesus and the Baptist and between Jesus and the church, for both John and the first Christians held a *Naherwartung*. If the texts are given their simple and natural sense, it is evident that Jesus hoped that the kingdom of God would come soon. One might attempt rebuttal by appealing to Mark 13:32 ("'But of that day or that hour no one knows, not even the angels in heaven, nor the Son, but only the Father'"). But as Ernest C. Colwell has written, "Actually this passage and its parallels say no more than, 'No one knows *exactly* when it will come.' A modern preacher would say, 'No man knows the minute and the second,' but Jesus' watch had neither a minute nor a second hand. The hour was the small, exact unit of time for Jesus and his friends."[49] Our conclusion cannot, moreover, be resisted by protesting that the Synoptics do not contain an *Interimsethik*.[50] As Richard H. Hiers has incisively argued, this remonstration regularly rests upon a caricature of Schweitzer or upon a confusion of the distinct domains of history and theology.[51] Even less can one account for the *Naherwartung* of the Jesus tradition by doing honor to early Christian prophets, concerning whom we know far less than many imagine. The many attempts to assign various synoptic sayings to inspired congregational prophets speaking in the name of the Lord have, in our judgment, been quite ill grounded.[52]

---

= Luke 10:9, 11; Mark 13:37; Luke 18:1-8; 21:34-36.

47. See n. 13 above and Linnemann's "Hat Jesus Naherwartung gehabt?," in *Jésus aux origines de la Christologie*, ed. J. Dupont (Gembloux, Belg.: J. Duculot, 1975), 103-10.

48. Perrin, *Rediscovering the Teaching*, 205.

49. Ernest C. Colwell, *An Approach to the Teaching of Jesus* (Nashville: Abingdon Press, 1947), 93.

50. According to C. H. Dodd, *The Parables of the Kingdom*, new rev. ed. (New York: Charles Scribner's Sons, 1961), 79, the ethical teaching of Jesus "appears to contemplate the indefinite continuance of human life under historical conditions."

51. Richard H. Hiers, *Jesus and the Future: Unresolved Questions for Eschatology* (Atlanta: John Knox Press, 1981), 50-61.

52. Especially telling are the following three studies: James D. G. Dunn, "Prophetic 'I'-Sayings and the Jesus Tradition: The Importance of Testing Prophetic Oracles in Early

## Conclusion

For Jesus, the kingdom of God, the eschatological establishment of God's kingly rule, was due to come in its fullness soon. And when it came, after the judgment and the resurrection, the world would be new, the powers of evil eliminated, and the will of God accomplished perfectly. If Jesus spoke of the kingdom as already present, that was because, in his eyes, the powers of the coming age had, in his person and ministry, already begun to invade and thus transform the here and now: the night was giving way to the light of a new day.

Christianity," *NTS* 24 (1978): 175-98; David Hill, *New Testament Prophecy,* New Foundation Theological Library (Atlanta: John Knox Press, 1979), 160-85; and David E. Aune, *Prophecy in Early Christianity and the Ancient Mediterranean World* (Grand Rapids: Wm. B. Eerdmans, 1983), 233-45.

*Eleven*

# THE DEATH OF JESUS
# AND THE GREAT TRIBULATION

According to a common verdict, while Jesus accepted traditional beliefs about resurrection, judgment and eschatological tribulation, these must be regarded as marginal, as things he was not interested in depicting or expounding at length.[1] This evaluation of the evidence is undoubtedly correct, to some degree, and Bultmann has rightly written: "Jesus does take over the apocalyptic picture of the future ... [but] he does so with significant reduction of detail."[2] Such a conclusion, however, is to be disassociated from the opinion (criticized in the previous chapter) that the hope of Jesus is sufficiently summarized as faith in vindication and judgment. The words of Jesus offer much more than this.

## The Prospect of a Great Tribulation

The prospect of a final time of trouble, which would mark the transition between this age and the messianic age or the age to come, was widespread in first-century Judaism. Firmly rooted in the Old Testament, it frequently found its way into the intertestamental literature; and as the New Testament and rabbinic sources indicate, Christians and rabbis also reckoned with the advent of a terrible tribulation before God's decisive victory.[3] One is, therefore, initially inclined to the possibility that the belief (even though it does not appear to have been universal) would likewise have been held by Jesus. The Synoptics do nothing but confirm this initial inclination: notice of a coming catastrophe occurs often in them. Jesus proclaims that the kingdom of God does not come without violence (Matt. 11:12 = Luke 16:16), and he speaks of the time preceding its coming as marked by a decisive struggle between God and Satan (Mark 3:27). He calls for preparation as for a storm (Matt. 7:24–27 =

1. Cf. Hans Conzelmann, *Jesus,* trans. R. Lord (Philadelphia: Fortress Press, 1973), 74–77.
2. Bultmann, *Theology of the New Testament,* 1:6.
3. Note Mark 13; 1 Cor. 7:25–31; Revelation 6—9, 11—19; *m. Soṭa* 9:15; and *b. Sanh.* 96b–97a.

Luke 6:47–49). He announces that woes and weeping lie ahead (Luke 23:27–31), that the time to come holds days not of peace but of the sword (Matt. 10:34 = Luke 12:51), that the holy place in Jerusalem will be visited with destruction (Luke 19:41–44). He warns the faithful that they will be forced to take flight (Matt. 10:23) and prophesies that families will be divided, son against father and daughter against mother (Matt. 10:35–36 = Luke 12:52–53). The disciples of Jesus are enjoined to pray for preservation in trial (Matt. 6:13 = Luke 11:4).

The value of the material cited in the preceding paragraph has called forth various judgments from different scholars, but one cannot easily dismiss this entire side of the tradition. At least several of the texts are almost certainly dominical, which means that Jesus probably did foresee a coming tribulation. As many people of his day, he apparently expected the new age to come to birth amid distress and affliction.

## The Prospect of Suffering and Death

Before exploring further the role of the expectation of a great tribulation in Jesus' teaching, it is necessary—for reasons that will become apparent soon enough—to establish that Jesus anticipated suffering and an untimely death. Although sometimes contested, especially in conjunction with skepticism concerning the formal passion predictions, the balance of the evidence favors this conclusion, which has gained strong support from several recent studies.[4] The following considerations seem most cogent. To begin with, four observations made by C. H. Dodd and repeated by others after him merit our assent.

> We may observe (1) that the whole prophetic and apocalyptic tradition, which Jesus certainly recognized, anticipated tribulation for the people of God before the final triumph of the good cause; (2) that the history of many centuries had deeply implanted the idea that the prophet is called to suffering as a part of his mission; (3) that the death of John the Baptist had shown that this fate was still a part of the prophetic calling; and (4) that it needed, not supernatural prescience, but the ordinary insight of an intelligent person, to see whither things were tending, at least during the latter stages of the ministry.[5]

In addition to these general considerations, a number of sayings indicate that Jesus enjoined his followers to reckon seriously with the possibilities of suffering and death—for instance, Mark 8:34–35; 9:1; 13:9–13; 10:38–39; Matt. 10:28 = Luke 12:4–5; Matt. 10:34–36 = Luke 12:51–53; Matt. 10:37–39 = Luke 14:25–27. If the authenticity of any of these texts be acknowledged, then it becomes probable that Jesus himself expected to suffer and die before

---

4. See the review essay of John P. Gavin, "Jesus' Approach to Death: An Examination of Some Recent Studies," *TS* 41 (1980): 713–44.

5. Dodd, *Parables of the Kingdom*, 40.

his time, for surely he would have anticipated for himself a fate not dissimilar to that which would befall those around him. In line with this, the Synoptics contain a mass of material that clearly looks forward, explicitly or implicitly, to Jesus' death—for example, Mark 8:31; 9:12b; 9:31; 10:33-34; 10:38-39, 45; 12:1-11; 14:3-9, 21, 22-25, 32-42; cf. John 12:1-8; Mark 14:27; Luke 12:49-50; 13:31-33; 17:25; 24:6-7. While the genuineness of many of these verses may justly be queried, at least Mark 10:38-39; Luke 12:49-50; and Luke 13:31-33 lay rather good claim to preserving original material. It is, consequently, safe to conclude that Jesus anticipated suffering and an untimely death.

## The Death of Jesus and the
## Great Tribulation

Having argued that Jesus believed in a coming time of trouble and that he anticipated suffering and death, it remains to relate these two prospects—to wit: Jesus spoke of the nearness or even presence of the eschatological tribulation and in all probability expected to meet his own end in it. This proposal follows first from the common reckoning that the great tribulation would occasion severe persecution for the saints.[6] According to our records, Jesus expected to die, hoped that the kingdom of God was near, and assumed that the eschatological tribulation had already set in or was at hand. These convictions can hardly have been unrelated. Indeed, they are most naturally associated: Jesus will have entertained the possibility of dying in the period of distress. Consonant with this inference is the fact that the Synoptics do not permit one to sever the suffering of Jesus from the suffering of his disciples. To quote Dodd again:

> The impression which we gather from the Gospels as a whole is that Jesus led His followers to the city [Jerusalem] with the express understanding that a crisis awaited them there which would involve acute suffering both for them and for Him. The most striking of such passages is Mk. x. 35-40. Here the sons of Zebedee are assured that they shall drink of the cup of which their Master drinks, and be baptized with His baptism. The purport of the words is not doubtful. The disciples are to share the fate of their Master, and surely to share His fate in the crisis which lies immediately before them.[7]

Presumably, Jesus predicted that at least some of his followers would meet death amid the eschatological woes. Forecasts of tribulation for the disciples are frequently found in eschatological contexts, as is the case in Mark 8:34—

---

6. There is in the Gospels no trace of an expectation that the tribulation of the latter days will not touch the righteous. This is in contrast to the teaching of several Jewish texts; see 20-22 herein.

7. Dodd, *Parables of the Kingdom*, 41-42. Note also John 11:16.

9:1 and 13:9-13. But Jesus does not somehow stand outside the circle of his followers, whom he considers to be his true family (cf. Mark 3:35). Their lot must be his, and that means tribulation and possibly death for Jesus himself. Thus, the passages just cited, if authentic, should be interpreted in a collective sense; they encompass the fate of the master as well as the fate of the disciple. Our view of things owes much to Schweitzer, to Dodd, and to Jeremias. But Schweitzer, without sufficient warrant, argued that Jesus, in the latter stages of his ministry, expected to take up in his own person all the afflictions of the final tribulation.[8] Dodd erred by referring eschatological prophecies to a realm beyond history.[9] For his part, Jeremias has not established that Jesus saw his death as the necessary *prelude* to, not *a part of,* the messianic woes.[10] We shall seek to show that Jesus, already during the days of his ministry, interpreted the present, as had other Jews before him, as the eschatological time of trouble. In this we concur with Oscar Cullmann. He has correctly asserted (although without adequate argument) that Jesus (1) thought of the birth pangs of the end as already coming into operation during his earthly life and (2) believed that "his death itself ... would be [the] decisive manifestation of those pangs."[11] It is now our task to prove this.

## Not Peace but a Sword

Although the wording of Luke 12:51-53 and Matt. 10:34-36 differs considerably, a common origin in Q is not in doubt; the texts of both Matthew and Luke can be explained as redactional adaptations of something close to the following: "Do you think that I came to give [*balein*] peace on the earth? I did not come to give [*balein*] peace but a sword. For I came to divide a man against [his] father and a daughter against [her] mother and a daughter-in-law against [her] mother-in-law."

There are sound reasons for supposing that this saying, as a unit, goes back ultimately to Jesus. (1) Matthew's *balein eirēnēn* is not good Greek but does have an equivalent in the Hebrew idiom *hiṭṭîl šālôm.*[12] Further, Matt. 10:34b is easily translated back into Aramaic.[13] (2) Matthew 10:35-36 = Luke 12:52-53 is based upon Mic. 7:6: "For the son treats the father with contempt, the

8. Albert Schweitzer, *The Quest of the Historical Jesus: A Critical Study of Its Progress from Reimarus to Wrede,* trans. W. Montgomery (New York: Macmillan Co., 1968), 330-97.
9. Dodd, *Parables of the Kingdom,* 21-84.
10. Joachim Jeremias, *New Testament Theology,* 318-22.
11. Oscar Cullmann, *Salvation in History,* trans. S. G. Sowers (London: SCM Press, 1967), 229-30.
12. Cf. Adolf Schlatter, *Der Evangelist Matthäus: Seine Sprache, sein Ziel, seine Selbständigkeit* (Stuttgart: Calwer Verlag, 1948), 349.
13. Cf. Eduardo Arens, *The HΛΘON-Sayings in the Synoptic Tradition: A Historico-Critical Investigation,* OBO 10 (Göttingen: Vandenhoeck & Ruprecht, 1976), 84.

daughter rises up against her mother, the daughter-in-law against her mother-in-law; a man's enemies are the men of his own house." Now, Mic. 7:6 was not an important text for the early church. Apart from our passage and Mark 13:13 = Matt. 10:21, which may be a secondary development of the more original saying preserved in Q, it is nowhere cited in any extant Christian literature of the first century. (3) Many early Christians understood Jesus to be the bringer of peace; see Luke 2:14; 19:38; Acts 10:36; Rom. 5:1; Eph. 2:14–18; Heb. 7:2. Because the statement that Jesus "came not to bring peace but a sword" stands, at least on the surface, in tension with this theologoumenon of the early church, one hesitates to locate its origin in the post-Easter period. (4) The saying on familial division coheres with other hard sayings of Jesus. According to Matt. 10:37 = Luke 14:26, the one who does not hate father or mother or son or daughter is not worthy of Jesus. According to Mark 10:29, for some the call of Jesus means leaving brother and sister and mother and father and children. According to Matt. 8:21–22 = Luke 9:59–60, the decision to follow Jesus even comes before the obligation to bury one's father. The prophecy of discord in Matt. 10:35–36 = Luke 12:52–53 is one more expression of the conviction that lies behind these sayings: the eschatological crisis puts all family ties in jeopardy. Our text is furthermore in accord with the harsh prospects persistently predicted for the messengers of Jesus; see, for example, Matt. 10:38 = Luke 14:27 and Matt. 10:39 = Luke 17:33; and the declaration that Jesus came not to bring peace but a sword is consistent with the numerous synoptic sayings that see the present heading toward conflict and crisis; see, for instance, Matt. 23:37–39 = Luke 13:34–35; Luke 19:41–44; and 23:28–31. (5) It is quite unlikely that the prophecy based on Mic. 7:6 ever existed by itself. It almost demands an introduction. Since it gains this through the saying on the sword, and as the two parts of our saying can be interpreted together, it is best to assume that we are dealing with a unit. (6) In the words of Franz Mussner, "In view of the tendency, especially observable in Acts, to present Christianity as politically harmless, [the possibilty that] the *machaira*-saying is a product of the Christian community appears to be excluded. Such 'misleading sayings' go back to Jesus himself."[14]

What meaning should one assign to Matt. 10:34–36 = Luke 12:51–53 on the lips of Jesus? A consideration of Jewish parallels leaves little room for doubt. The passage is, as already observed, dependent upon Mic. 7:6, and this verse was drawn upon to describe the discord of the latter days. *M. Soṭa* 9:15 reads as follows: with the footprints of the Messiah, "Children shall shame the elders, and the elders shall rise up before the children, for the son dishon-

---

14. Franz Mussner, "Wege zum Selbstbewusstsein Jesu," *BZ* 12 (1968): 166.

oureth the father, the daughter riseth up against her mother, the daughter-in-law against her mother-in-law; a man's enemies are the men of his own house." Similar statements are to be found in *Jub.* 23:16, 19; *1 Enoch* 56:7; 70:7; 99:5; 100:1–2; Mark 13:12; *4 Ezra* 5:9; 6:24; *2 Apoc. Bar.* 70:3, 7; *b. Sanh.* 97a; and *b. Soṭa* 47b. The conviction that the great tribulation would turn those of the same household against one another was evidently widespread. Talk of the sword within prophecies of eschatological affliction or of the day of judgment was also widespread. See Isa. 66:16; Sir. 39:30; Wis. 5:20; *Jub.* 9:15; *1 Enoch* 62:12; 63:11; 90:19; 91:11–12; 4QPsDanAᵃ (= 4Q244);[15] *Pss. Sol.* 15:8(7); *Sib. Or.* III, 797–99; IV, 174; *2 Apoc. Bar.* 27:6; 40:1; Luke 21:24; and Rev. 6:4. And the sword could serve as a symbol for the holy war of the last times.[16]

It is, then, against the background of Jewish eschatological teaching that Matt. 10:34–36 = Luke 12:51–53 should be understood. The saying comprehends the ministry of Jesus in terms of the eschatological time of trouble. Jesus has not come to bring peace but a sword—that is, division. His appearance coincides with—or, rather, causes—a crisis that divides Israel, even the members of one household. So the eschatological trial, the time of the sword and of the fulfillment of Mic. 7:6, has broken in with the appearance of Jesus, and before the kingdom of God comes, before peace will be finally and fully established, all must pass through tribulation and judgment (cf. Acts 14:22; *Barnabas* 7:11). As chaos and darkness came before the first creation (Gen. 1:2), so division and strife must come before the second creation: the last things are as the first (cf. *Barn.* 6:13). Thus, and for the present, Jesus and those around him know not concord but the eschatological conflict. Revelation 6:4, which also contains the antithesis peace/sword, offers a good parallel. Here the time of tribulation and judgment has come, which means the giving of a sword and the taking of peace. "And out came another horse, bright red; its rider was permitted to take peace from the earth, so that men should slay one another; and he was given a great sword." The absence of peace and the presence of the sword are signs of the great tribulation.

## The Kingdom of God and Violence

"The Law and the prophets were until [*mechri* or *heōs*] John; from then the kingdom of God has suffered violence [*biazetai*] and violent men [*biastai*] take

---

15. See Joseph Fitzmyer, "The Contributions of Qumran Aramaic to the Study of the New Testament," in *A Wandering Aramean: Collected Aramaic Essays*, SBLMS 25 (Missoula, Mont.: Scholars Press, 1979), 90–93, 102–7.

16. On the eschatological holy war, see Hans Windisch, *Der messianische Krieg und Urchristentum* (Tübingen: J. C. B. Mohr [Paul Siebeck], 1909).

it by force [*harpazousin autēn*]." This or something very much like it probably stood in Q (cf. Matt. 11:12-13 = Luke 16:16).[17] Can we trace it back to Jesus? (1) Luke 16:17 ("'But it is easier for heaven and earth to pass away, than for one dot of the law to become void'") is clearly an attempt to soften the radical implications of Luke 16:16. This is evidence that the statement was, at least for Luke, potentially too extreme; and if Luke 16:17 was conjoined to 16:16 in Q (a disputed issue), the statement was already considered too extreme by Luke's tradition. (2) It is John the Baptist who is presented as marking the shift in salvation history. Would not a later formulation almost certainly have made Jesus the center of reference? (3) That Jesus, who held John in esteem, would speak of the Baptist as marking a turning point is not exactly surprising. Did not the Baptist, in a novel way, and in view of the coming judgment, seemingly dismiss the significance of Abrahamic descent (Matt. 3:10 = Luke 3:9)? (4) The very obscurity of *hē basileia tou theou biazetai kai biastai harpazousin autēn*, a phrase which Luke has rewritten, speaks for antiquity. It is certainly difficult to trace in the line any theological conviction characteristic of the primitive community. (5) Matthew 11:12-13 = Luke 16:16 reflects a positive view of John that is more in line with the thinking of Jesus than of the church, for it does not relegate the Baptist to a bygone era. Although Matthew's "from the days of John the Baptist until now" and Luke's "from then" are grammatically ambiguous and can be read either exclusively or inclusively, recent work strongly favors an inclusive reading for both Matthew and Luke as well as Q.[18] Thus, the saying sets John and Jesus on the same stage of salvation history; that is, the Baptist is here included in the new order. This is significant because sayings that imply a high estimate of the Baptist belong to the earliest stages of the tradition; for the church, in dialogue with a Baptist sect, tended to play down the importance of the Baptist and subordinate his work to that of Jesus. Matthew 11:12-13 = Luke 16:16 is therefore probably not a formulation of the community.

The interpretation of Matt. 11:12-13 = Luke 16:16 depends primarily upon the meaning ascribed to *biazetai*, which can be read either as a middle or a passive. The middle is excluded here because, although "the kingdom of God breaks in with power, with force" is a possible translation, *biazetai* is parallel to *biastai*, and the latter clearly refers to hostile action against the kingdom. That is, the kingdom is the object of some action done to it.

17. So also Siegfried Schulz, *Q: Die Spruchquelle der Evangelisten* (Zurich: Theologischer Verlag, 1972), 262.
18. See Walter Wink, *John the Baptist in the Gospel Tradition*, SNTSMS 7 (Cambridge: Cambridge Univ. Press, 1968), 46-57; David R. Catchpole, "On Doing Violence to the Kingdom," *IBS* 3 (1981): 78-79; and Paul Hoffmann, *Studien zur Theologie der Logienquelle* (Münster: Aschendorff, 1972), 60-65.

As Gottlob Schrenk has shown, *biazetai* is best taken as a passive *in malam partem:* the kingdom of God is violently hampered or opposed or attacked.[19] This corresponds with the current extrabiblical usage of *biazomai* and with the second half of the logion. The natural signification of *biastēs* is violent one or violator, and *harpazō* means to take something forcefully.[20] Matthew 11:12 = Luke 16:16b thus declares that violent men forcibly take the kingdom, which permits the second half of the saying to explicate the first: the kingdom of God is violently attacked because violent men forcibly seize it.

But what can that mean? The rabbinic sources know of a violence that brings in the kingdom of God[21]; but the sources are late, and the thought of violently forcing God to bring his kingdom is foreign to the teaching of Jesus. The closest parallels, as Otto Betz has shown, are to be found at Qumran.[22] For the Essenes, the eschatological tribulation, which had already begun, was primarily conceived of as the fighting of a holy war. On the one side stood God, his angels, and the pious on earth, on the other Belial, his spirits, and the godless inhabitants of the world. The clearest presentation of this conflict is to be found in the Scroll of the War of the Sons of Light against the Sons of Darkness (1QM). But other scrolls also contain reference to the great conflict of the latter days (for example, 1QH III, 34–36; VI, 29–35; 4QFlor; and 1QSb V, 20–29). Given the Essenes' understanding of the present and of the near future as the time of eschatological conflict and distress, the formulations in 1QH II, 10–11 and 21–22 take on particular significance for the interpretation of Matt. 11:12–13 = Luke 16:16. 1QH II, 10–11 reads in part, "I have become the cause of the iniquity of the wicked, a source of slander on the lips of the violent ['ryṣym]; the scoffers grind their teeth. I have become a derision for the transgressors." 1QH II, 21–22 reads in part, "Violent ones ['ryṣym] have sought after my life because I have held to Thy covenant." In these two places the hymnist, who is living in the eschatological time of distress and who characterizes himself as an interpreter of mysteries and a source of knowledge and understanding, is oppressed at the hands of the violent ones. The parallel with our synoptic saying is striking. Both John and Jesus preached the kingdom of God, and both faced opposition. Indeed, John suffered martyrdom, and Jesus anticipated no less for himself. The suggestion thus lies near to hand that Matt. 11:12–13 = Luke 16:16 originally had to do with the kingdom of God, represented by its two great heralds, John and Jesus, and with the hostile

19. Gottlob Schrenk, "Biazomai, biastēs," *TDNT* 1 (1964): 610–11.
20. Thus, ibid., 613–14.
21. See SB I:599.
22. Otto Betz, "Jesu heiliger Krieg," *NovT* 2 (1957): 125–29.

response directed towards them and their followers. At Qumran, the time immediately before the new age was one of conflict and struggle, the time when violent ones oppressed the pious and their leaders; so, too, in the eyes of Jesus, the coming of the new age was to be preceded by violence done against the kingdom of God and its people. The saying on violence thus sets John and Jesus within the eschatological time of distress. It speaks of those who, through their opposition to the heralds of the kingdom, close that kingdom to others (cf. Matt. 23:13). Compare Matt. 13:19, where the evil one comes and snatches (*harpazei*) the word of the kingdom that has been sown in the heart. Compare also *Genesis Rabbah* on 32:3: R. Phinehas ben Ḥama (ca. 300) is reported to have said that God will not arise until the poor are oppressed or robbed. Perrin was right: "In Matt. 11:12 the use of Kingdom of Heaven . . . evokes the myth of the eschatological war between God and the powers of evil and interprets the fate of John the Baptist, and the potential fate of Jesus and his disciples, as a manifestation of the conflict."[23]

The proposed interpretation gains support from other texts. In Matt. 10:34–36 = Luke 12:51–53, already examined, Jesus announces that he has come to bring not peace but a sword, and that he has come to set individuals of the same household against one another. Here the language of combat and division is drawn upon in an attempt to bring home the meaning of the contemporary situation. As in our interpretation of Matt. 11:12–13 = Luke 16:16, the time of Jesus, the man who heralds the redemption, is pictured as one of violence, even war. Mark 3:27, the parable of the strong man, also provides an instructive analogy, as does the Beelzebul controversy, to which it is joined in Mark (3:22–26). "No one can enter a strong man's house and plunder his goods, unless he first binds the strong man; then indeed he may plunder his house" (Mark 3:27). This verse presupposes the same battle as that represented in the saying on violence but views it from the other side. In Matt. 11:12–13 = Luke 16:16, the kingdom of God is on the defensive, and the violent ones are on the offensive; here Satan (the strong man) is on guard, and the kingdom of God (in the person of its representative) is the aggressor. Here the final conflict between God and Satan is comprehended as the despoiling of Satan; there the eschatological time of distress is spoken of in terms of a violent assault against the forces of good (cf. Matt. 16:18?). For Jesus, as for the apocalyptic literature in general, the great redemption must be preceded by a conflict between two mighty kingdoms, the kingdom of God and the kingdom of Satan. Further, this conflict has already been joined, from the days of John the Baptist until now. (We recall that a number of Jewish texts also interpret

23. Perrin, *Jesus and the Language*, 46.

the present as the time of the great tribulation.) And although the kingdom has suffered violence through the assault of its enemies, those who hinder the eschatological work of God and God's ministers, it is the kingdom of Satan that is coming to an end; it is the strong man that is being plundered (Mark 3:27).

## Fire on the Earth

In Luke 12:49–50 Jesus declares, "'I came to cast fire upon the earth; and would that [*ti thelō ei*] it were already kindled! I have a baptism [*baptisma*] to be baptized with [*baptisthēnai*]; and how I am constrained until it is accomplished!'" These two verses may derive from Q, even though there is no parallel in Matthew.[24] The two lines, which show no signs of Lukan redaction,[25] are evidently ancient. *Ti thelō ei* is difficult and best explained as an Aramaism.[26] Further, the saying falls easily, according to C. F. Burney, into Aramaic poetical form.[27] Luke 12:49–50 seems to be, in the words of Matthew Black, an instance of "literal translation Greek."[28]

Concerning authenticity, three points are telling. First, Luke 12:49-50 contains a hint that Jesus shrank from his prospective fate ("'I am torn between conflicting feelings [*synechomai*] until it be completed'"[29])—a detail not easily assignable to the early church. Second, the use of baptism with reference to coming martyrdom has its parallel in Mark 10:38-39. Jesus asks the sons of Zebedee if they are able to drink the cup that he drinks or to be baptized with the baptism with which he is baptized. They answer, We are able. Jesus then says to them, "'The cup that I drink you will drink; and with the baptism with which I am baptized, you will be baptized.'" It is hard to assail the claim that here we have a real prophecy of Jesus, which entails the likelihood that Jesus envisioned his fate as a baptism. Finally, the enigmatic logion looks too indefinite to be a post-Easter construction.

The interpretation of Luke 12:49–50 depends upon the meanings one gives to fire in verse 49 and to baptism in verse 50. Concerning fire, several lines of evidence converge and encourage one to think that Luke 12:49 refers to the

---

24. Cf. Josef Ernst, *Das Evangelium nach Lukas*, RNT (Regensburg: Friedrich Pustet, 1977), 412.
25. See Joachim Jeremias, *Die Sprache*, 223; contrast Arens, HΛΘON-*Sayings*, 65–66. Against Arens, Luke 12:50 is hardly redactional.
26. See C. C. Torrey, *Our Translated Gospels: Some of the Evidence* (New York: Harper & Brothers, 1936), 31, 34.
27. C. F. Burney, *The Poetry of Our Lord* (Oxford: Clarendon Press, 1925), 90, 92.
28. Matthew Black, *An Aramaic Approach to the Gospels and Acts*, 3d ed. (Oxford: Clarendon Press, 1967), 275.
29. Translation of Joachim Jeremias, *The Parables of Jesus* (New York: Charles Scribner's Sons, 1972), 163–64.

eschatological judgment. To begin with, everywhere else in the Synoptics, with the exception of Mark 9:21 (the possessed boy who throws himself into the fire) and Luke 22:25 (Peter warming himself in the courtyard), *pyr*, "fire," has to do with the last assize. Next, John the Baptist came onto the scene preaching of the coming one who would baptize with fire (Matt. 3:11 = Luke 3:16): he will clear his threshing floor with his winnowing fork and then gather the wheat and burn the chaff with unquenchable fire (Matt. 3:12 = Luke 3:9). Trees not bearing fruit will be cut down and thrown into the fire (Matt. 3:10 = Luke 3:9). Fire was, for John, the outstanding symbol of the coming judgment, and Jesus heard John preach. In the third place, fire is both prominent and significant in the Pseudepigrapha, and there it is, among other things, a concomitant of the final judgment and an instrument of punishment of the dead.[30] Lastly, fire is already associated in Scripture with the idea of eschatological destruction: Isa. 66:24; Mal. 3:19(4:1); Jth. 16:17. This association was natural in view of the use of fire elsewhere in connection with God's wrath and punishment, in connection with suffering and judgment, and in connection with the Day of the Lord.[31]

Given the associations between fire and the eschatological judgment in the Tanach and later Jewish literature, in the preaching of John the Baptist and the Synoptic Gospels, one should probably seek an understanding of Luke 12:49–50 with this association in mind. Before going any further, however, we must first examine the word on baptism in Luke 12:50. It would be natural, in the light of Mark 10:38–39 and the fate that did in fact befall Jesus, to equate baptism with martyrdom; and such an equation might receive partial justification from the link Paul is able to draw between baptism and death in Romans 6. But matters are not so easily resolved. The concept of martyrdom as a baptism in blood is unattested before the late second century A.D.[32] Moreover, the Hebrew and Aramaic *ṭbl*, unlike the Greek *baptizein*, nowhere bears the meaning of "to drown" or "to perish."[33] How then does one explain Jesus' statement about his own baptism?

We begin with a conclusion of Otto Kuss. "The image of baptism is ... in the sense presupposed in Mark 10:38–39; Luke 12:50 not demonstrable in the Old Testament; but it finds there related conceptions."[34] Kuss cites Ps.

30. E.g., *Jub.* 9:15; *1 Enoch* 10:6; 54:1–2, 6; 90:24–25; 91:9; 100:9; 102:1; *Pss. Sol.* 15:4–5; *Sib. Or.* III, 53–54; IV, 159–60; *4 Ezra* 7:36–38; 13:10–11; *2 Apoc. Bar.* 37:1; 44:15; 59:2; *4 Macc.* 9:9; 12:12; *3 Apoc. Bar.* 4:16; *T. Zeb.* 10:3; *T. Jud.* 25:3.

31. For texts and discussion, see Vinzenz Hamp, "'s," *TDOT* 1 (1977): 424–28; and Friedrich Lang, "Pyr ktl.," *TDNT* 6 (1968): 934–37.

32. Eduard Lohse, *Märtyrer und Gottesknecht*, FRLANT n.f. 46 (Göttingen: Vandenhoeck & Ruprecht, 1955), 211–13.

33. See Albrecht Oepke, "Baptō ktl.," *TDNT* 1 (1964): 530, 536.

34. Otto Kuss, "Zur Frage einer vorpaulinischen Todestaufe," in *Auslegung und Verkün-*

18:17(16); 32:6; 42:7(8); 69:1-2, 14-15(15-16); 124:4-5; 144:7(8); Job 22:11; Isa. 8:7; and 43:2. Water (or a flood) is in these texts a symbol of calamity, as in Ps. 42:7(8) ("All thy waves and thy billows have gone over me") and Isa. 43:2 ("'When you pass through the waters I will be with you; and through the rivers, they shall not overwhelm you'"). It is presumably against the background of such passages as these that Luke 12:50 (and Mark 10:38-39) should be read. The saying on baptism tells us that Jesus anticipated for himself a difficult end and expressed this anticipation in terms of a metaphor that recalled well-known scriptural imagery, imagery especially prominent in the Psalms. He expected to be overcome as in a flood, to be baptized with a baptism.[35]

If Luke 12:50 is correctly interpreted as a figurative prophecy of coming calamity, and if Luke 12:49 is a foreboding prediction of eschatological judgment, the question of how these two verses should be related immediately arises. It may be answered by observing that, as symbols of judgment, fire and water are closely linked in a number of Jewish sources. From the Tanach, notice may be taken of Isa. 43:2:

> "When you pass through the waters I will be with you;
>     and through the rivers, they shall not overwhelm you;
> when you walk through fire you shall not be burned,
>     and the flame shall not consume you."

Isaiah 30:27-28 also juxtaposes fire and flood:

> Behold, the name of the Lord comes from far,
>     burning with his anger, and in thick rising smoke;
> his lips are full of indignation,
>     and his tongue is like a devouring fire;
> his breath is like an overflowing stream
>     that reaches up to the neck;
> to sift the nations with the sieve of destruction,
>     and to place on the jaws of the peoples a bridle that leads astray.

Compare also Ps. 66(65):10-12 and Isa. 30:30, where God's judgment comes as a fire and as a cloudburst. From later times note *Sib. Or.* III, 689-91 (God will carry out his judgment with fire and cataclysms of rain) and Jos. *Ant.* 1.2.3 (Adam prophesied that God would destroy the world once by fire, another time by water; cf. *Adam and Eve* 49:3 and 2 Pet. 3:5-7). Of special importance is the fact that, in the apocalyptic literature and at Qumran, fire and water are joined to become one symbol. In Dan. 7:10; 1QH III, 29-36; *1 Enoch* 14:19;

---

digung: *Aufsätze zur Exegese des Neuen Testaments* (Regensburg: Friedrich Pustet, 1968), 169.

35. For the use of "to baptize" in extrabiblical materials with reference to a threatening situation see Gerhard Delling, "ΒΑΠΤΙΣΜΑ ΒΑΠΤΙΣΘΗΝΑΙ," *NovT* 2 (1957): 99-101.

17:5; 67:13; *Sib. Or.* III, 54, 84; Rev. 19:20; 20:10, 14–15; 21:8; *4 Ezra* 13:10–11; and *2 Enoch* 10:2, we read of a river or flood or lake of fire. Most of these texts have the last judgment in view: a stream of fire comes forth from God and consumes the wicked (cf. Ps. 50:3; 97:3) or the condemned are thrown into a lake of fire. The rabbis also spoke of the eschatological flood of fire (note *Mek.* on Exod. 18:1; *b. Zeb.* 116a). And presumably, when John the Baptist warned of the coming one who would baptize with fire, he had in view this fiery stream. Now, the warning of the Baptist is for us of particular importance, for here the fire of judgment is delivered through a baptism: *baptisei en pyri.* If Jesus also spoke of baptism and of fire in the same utterance, as Luke 12:49–50 attests, it is altogether likely that conceptions similar to those of the Baptist were in mind. Certain Synoptic texts confirm this. In more than one place Jesus likens the coming tribulation to a flood (Matt. 7:24–27 = Luke 6:47–49; Matt. 24:37–39 = Luke 17:26–27) and warns of the coming fire of judgment (Mark 9:43, 48, 49). Indeed, in Luke 17:26–30 (Q), whose substance we take to go back to Jesus,[36] the threat of fire is paired with the threat of a flood.

> "As it was in the days of Noah, so will it be in the days of the Son of man. They ate, they drank, they married, they were given in marriage, until the day when Noah entered the ark, and the flood came and destroyed them all. Likewise as it was in the days of Lot—they ate, they drank, they bought, they sold, they planted, they built, but on the day when Lot went out from Sodom fire and brimstone rained from heaven and destroyed them all—so will it be on the day when the Son of man is revealed."

Drawing our previous conclusions together and bringing them to bear upon Luke 12:49–50, we may say that the verses have to do with two distinct but related prospects: the eschatological judgment (v. 49) and the portending flood that will overtake Jesus (v. 50). The two prospects can be related because Jesus sees the eschatological tribulation, which is the beginning of God's judgment on the world, as the context of his own suffering. That is, the eschatological time of trouble brings persecution and suffering for the saints, and it will bring these for Jesus himself: the fire and the flood will come upon all. Compare Mark 9:49: *"Every one* will be salted with fire." Thus, it is said that Jesus shrinks from the prospect: How I am torn between conflicting feelings! One is reminded of the words of Ulla and Rab in *b. Sanh.* 98b concerning the terrors of the latter days: "Let him [Messiah] come, but let me not see him!" The messianic travail will be so severe that one scarcely wishes to be found in it. As Jeremias has written: "Jesus is the bringer-in of the New Age. But he knows—and this troubles him deeply—that the way to New Creation lies

36. Cf. A. J. B. Higgins, *The Son of Man in the Teaching of Jesus,* SNTSMS (Cambridge: Cambridge Univ. Press, 1980), 65–68.

through disaster and destruction, through purging and judgment, through the deluge of fire and water."[37] The only other Synoptic text in which Jesus speaks of a coming baptism is Mark 10:38–39. Here baptism is joined to the figure of a cup: "'The cup that I drink you will drink; and with the baptism with which I am baptized, you will be baptized.'" In the Tanach, the figurative use of "cup" ($pot\bar{e}rion/k\hat{o}s$) is frequently found in texts treating of God's wrath or judgment. Instances include Pss. 11:6; 75:7–8(9); 116:13; Isa. 51:17, 22; Jer. 22:15, 17, 27–28; 49:12; 51:7; Lam. 4:21; Ezek. 23:31–32; and Hab. 2:16. From later sources see *Pss. Sol.* 8:14–15; 1QpHab. XI, 14; Rev. 16:19; 17:4; 18:6; and *Midr. Hab.* 11:14–15. Thus, in both Luke 12:49–50 and Mark 10:38–39, Jesus connects his prospective baptism with a standing symbol of God's judgment, with fire in Luke, with cup in Mark. This is no coincidence. Both texts presuppose, to quote Eduard Schweizer, "a 'universal baptism' by which Jesus in some sense assumes the eschatological sorrow as part of his own destiny...."[38] That is, both texts tell us that Jesus foresaw for himself a frightful end which he (1) spoke of as a baptism and (2) believed would take place in the eschatological time of distress, when God would pour out the cup of his wrath and send forth a consuming fire.

### The Son of Man

Within the confines of the present work, it would hardly be possible to set forth adequately the course of the modern discussion on the Son of man in the teaching of Jesus. For this we must refer to surveys others have made.[39] Herein we can only state our own conclusions on the labyrinthine issues, offer reasons for them, and relate them to our claim that Jesus believed in the nearness or even presence of the eschatological tribulation and expected to suffer in it.

To begin with, one is, against the weight of German scholarship, disinclined to assume that "Son of man" was a well-established title in first-century Judaism used to refer to a central figure of the eschatological judgment. The Similitudes of Enoch (*1 Enoch* 37—71), which in the past have been the principal source for this supposition, cannot bear the burden of proof. Many are persuaded that the Similitudes are not pre-Christian.[40] Much more

---

37. Jeremias, *Parables of Jesus*, 164.
38. Schweizer, *Good News According to Mark*, 211.
39. Recent surveys include S. Legasse, "Jésus historique et le Fils de l'homme: aperçu sur les opinions contemporaines," in *Apocalypse et Théologie de l'Espérance*, LD 95 (Paris: du Cerf, 1977), 277–98; and William O. Walker, Jr., "The Son of Man: Some Recent Developments," *CBQ* 45 (1983): 584–607.
40. See the review of David Suter, "Weighed in the Balance: The Similitudes of Enoch in Recent Discussion," *RelSRev* 7 (1981): 217–21.

important, even if they are, certainly Perrin and others are correct in concluding that the Son of man in *1 Enoch* is no independent conception with a title which is itself a sufficient designation of that conception. Rather, the Similitudes depend upon an exegesis of Daniel 7, as the definite article attests: the Son of man is always *that* Son of man—that is, the one in Daniel 7. It is the same with *4 Ezra* 13: here there is no unambiguous title but instead Danielic imagery which helps to paint a vision of the Messiah.[41] Thus, until further evidence is forthcoming, it appears methodologically unsound to approach the synoptic data with the assumption that most first-century Jews, upon hearing the term "Son of man" would immediately have thought of a transcendent redeemer figure, the judge of the last day. The most one can say is that the phrase, within the appropriate context or with the appropriate markers, could cause one to recall the theophany of Daniel 7.

We are also disinclined to resolve the riddles of the Son of man by following Geza Vermes and his conclusions concerning *br nš'* or *br nš* in Galilean Aramaic. According to him, *br nš'/br nš* was sometimes employed as a circumlocution; that is, it could serve as a substitute for the personal pronoun "I" and was used especially in contexts alluding to danger or death, or where humility or modesty was appropriate.[42] Only those sayings of Jesus that can be explained in terms of this idiom are dominical; the others have been added by the church, largely under the influence of Daniel 7. But as Joseph Fitzmyer has observed, the data upon which Vermes has drawn are perhaps too late. Earlier texts, including those found at Qumran, know only the sense of "someone" or "a human being" for *br 'nš*.[43] Further, Vermes's reading of the later texts is not always the most persuasive—many of his texts can easily be read as general statements[44]—and the only certain instance of *br nš* being used as a straightforward surrogate for "I" is found in Cairo Targum B (on Gen. 4:14)—but the material in question is of uncertain date, and *br nš* is itself a late form, *br 'nš(')* presumably being the form used at the time of Jesus.[45] For the first century it may be that, to quote Jeremias,

> Bar *'enāšā* ... keeps it generic or indefinite significance, "the (or a) man, and therefore also I," "the (or a) man like myself," even where the speaker does

41. Perrin, *Rediscovering the Tradition*, 167–70.

42. Geza Vermes, *Jesus the Jew: A Historian's Reading of the Gospels* (Philadelphia: Fortress Press, 1981; London: Fontana, 1973), 160–91; idem, "The Present State of the Son of Man Debate," *JJS* 29 (1978): 123–34; idem, "'The Son of Man' Debate," *JSNT* 1 (1978): 19–32; idem, "The Use of *br nš/br nš'* in Jewish Aramaic," in Black, *Aramaic Approach*, 310–33.

43. See Joseph Fitzmyer, "The New Testament Title 'Son of Man' Philologically Considered," in *Wandering Aramean*, 145–53.

44. Cf. P. Maurice Casey, *Son of Man: The Interpretation and Influence of Daniel 7* (London: SPCK, 1979), 224–27.

45. Joseph Fitzmyer, "Another View of the 'Son of Man' Debate," *JSNT* 4 (1979): 58–59.

include himself. This can be demonstrated from Matt. 4.4 (*ho anthrōpos*) and John 8.40 (*anthrōpos*). That means that while *bar 'ᵉnāšā* (like our "one") can include the speaker, it is not a periphrasis for "I."[46]

Whether Jeremias be correct or not, it remains true that Vermes's explanation of Synoptic texts is frequently unconvincing. Jesus is reported to have said, "'The sabbath was made for man, not man for the sabbath; so the Son of man is lord even of the sabbath'" (Mark 2:27–28). On Vermes's view, a circumlocutional use of *bar ᵉnāšā*, with Jesus as the self-referent, makes good sense of this verse. But a generic use of the term offers a much more satisfactory reading: the sabbath was made for man, and man is therefore lord of the sabbath. A generic use of the term also seems to be just as plausible for the other Son of man sayings Vermes regards as dominical, including Matt. 8:20 = Luke 9:58; Matt. 11:19 = Luke 7:34; Matt. 12:32 = Luke 12:10; and Mark 2:10.

P. Maurice Casey has claimed that in Aramaic a speaker could use a general statement about man (*br 'nš*) in order to say something about himself.[47] *Br 'nš(')* was not, however, against Vermes, a simple circumlocution for "I" but *always included a more general reference*. In view of the previous paragraph, this estimation of the evidence seems to be better founded than that of Vermes, and thus Casey's contribution must be weighed seriously. He allows as primary only those Son of man sayings that can be given a generic reading. Jesus said that "a man has power to forgive sins on earth," that "man came not to be served but to serve," that "every word spoken against a man will be forgiven." Casey even finds a generic statement behind the passion predictions: a man will die but he will rise again at three days, in a little while. If a saying cannot be given a generic interpretation—that is, if it cannot be explained in terms of Aramaic idiom—it should be attributed to the activity of the post-Easter community. In particular, every allusion to Daniel 7 is secondary.

In agreement with Casey, it is plausible enough that Jesus sometimes used *br 'nš(')* idiomatically and that the Greek, *ho huios tou anthrōpou*, does translate too literally in several instances a general expression that could include the speaker. Mark 2:27–28 and Matt. 12:32 = Luke 12:10 are in this regard likely candidates. But the view according to which Jesus also sometimes spoke of the Son of man with an eye toward Daniel 7 does not easily go away. Among other things, there is the persistent presence of the definite article. The Synoptics consistently have *ho huios tou anthrōpou;* we never run across a *huios anthrōpou*. In the opinion of Barnabas Lindars, *ho huios tou anthrōpou* must, because of its persistence and awkwardness, be a translation

---

46. Joachim Jeremias, *New Testament Theology*, 261 n. 1.
47. Casey, *Son of Man: Interpretation*, 224–40.

which goes back to a definite place and time in the history of the tradition.[48] It was adopted quite intentionally, in order to represent a particular christological conception, the identification of Jesus with the Danielic Son of man. In other words, the Greek phrase in the Gospels does refer to Daniel 7, but the reference is present only in the Greek and had no basis in the Aramaic, in which *br 'nš(')* simply meant "the man." The link between Jesus and the one like a son of man was forged at the point of transition from Aramaic- to Greek-speaking communities. Casey argues similarly, but with a difference. "In Greek the definite article is used to indicate a particular, previously known entity. To any early Christian, Jesus was a particular, previously known entity." For this reason, one translating a saying with the *br 'nš(')* idiom and "selecting the most important level of meaning of such a saying, that at which Jesus is saying something about himself, would use the articles on the ground that the entity represented by *br 'nš(')* was a particular, previously known entity." And he would feel justified in the use of the article "because of the so-called 'generic' use of the article in Greek."[49] Having, however, once translated the Aramaic by the awkward *ho huios tou anthrōpou*, it became possible to see an allusion to Dan. 7:13, and the church did not miss the opportunity to make the most of the coincidence.

Although there is nothing that absolutely prohibits Lindars's suggestion that *ho huios tou anthrōpou* was first formulated with the intent to recall Dan. 7:13, it seems more likely that Casey is here to be followed. The consistent use of the article is not to be explained on theological grounds. On the other hand, one hesitates to follow Casey all the way, for he has not satisfactorily clarified the status of *br 'nš(')* in first-century Aramaic. He conjectures, on the basis of later usage, that the emphatic and absolute states were interchangeable.[50] But with C. F. D. Moule,[51] one wonders whether it was not possible at that time to distinguish between the emphatic and absolute states—whether one could not, through use of the definite article or a demonstrative pronoun, advert to a specific referent. Unfortunately, the sources cannot really answer the question. While the Bible and the Dead Sea Scrolls by and large use the emphatic state to express determination, caution is to be recommended with regard to generalizations about first-century usage.[52] Moule, nevertheless, has raised a question which becomes especially interesting when notice is taken of the Son

48. Barnabas Lindars, "Jesus as Advocate: A Contribution to the Christological Debate," *BJRL* 62 (1980): 480–82.
49. Casey, *Son of Man: Interpretation*, 230.
50. Ibid., 227–28.
51. C. F. D. Moule, *The Origin of Christology* (Cambridge: Cambridge Univ. Press, 1977), 15.
52. See Fitzmyer's review of Black's *Aramaic Approach, CBQ* 30 (1968): 427.

of man in *1 Enoch*. In *1 Enoch* 37—71, there is an initial reference to Daniel 7 which does not use a definite article (46:1: "another being whose countenance had the appearance of a man"; *APOT*). Thereafter we read only of "*that* Son of man" or "*the* Son of man." Subsequent references to the Son of man hark back to *1 Enoch* 46:1 and to the imagery of Daniel 7 there used. Moule postulates something similar for the Jesus tradition. The definite state was a way of alluding back to Daniel's human figure. Jesus used the definite article or a demonstrative pronoun to direct his hearers back to the well-known scene of Daniel 7 with its "one like a son of man." "In Dan. 7 the seer sees *a* human figure ... but Jesus, referring back to this symbol, with all its associations, speaks of his own vocation and that of his friends in terms of '*the* Son of Man': it is for him and for them to be or to become that figure." This result is, Moule claims, buttressed by a remarkable fact, namely, that before the New Testament there is only a single instance of the definite article used with the singular "*the* Son of man." And this, in 1QS XI, 20, "appears to be an afterthought, for the he (*h*) of the definite article is placed above the first letter of 'Man' (that is, over the a (') of *adam*)."[53] This is in striking contrast to the New Testament, where there is only one example of the phrase without the article. Now, whether Moule is correct or incorrect in reading as much as he does into the definite article is difficult to say. But his thesis does provide an alternative. Perhaps the definite article belies the solutions of Vermes and Casey, who explain *ho huios tou anthrōpou* as an overly literal translation of a common idiomatic expression; perhaps it is a sign that Daniel 7 stands at the beginning, not at the end, of the tradition.

In line with such a suggestion, we should reflect upon an observation of C. M. Tuckett: "Every culture has its accepted shorthand ways of speaking and writing; e.g., in England, 'the war' means the 1939–45 war, even though the word 'war' is quite general."[54] Even if *br 'nš(')* simply meant "man," and even if the absolute and emphatic states were interchangeable, could Jesus not have used the expression in such a way as to give it special content? One might compare the Johannine use of "I am." Certainly, the simple Greek phrase *egō eimi* is common enough and not necessarily overloaded with significance; yet because of its associations in the Fourth Gospel, *egō eimi* becomes pregnant with meaning, gaining the status of a title. Jesus, in like manner, might have used *br 'nš(')*, a common expression, in an uncommon manner, making it take on for himself and for his audience extraordinary associations, associations not present in everyday speech.

If our conclusions thus far have been tentative, we can be more certain

53. Moule, *Origin of Christology*, 16.
54. C. M. Tuckett, "The Present Son of Man," *JSNT* 14 (1982): 73 n. 14.

about another issue. Daniel 7 has left few traces in the New Testament outside of the Gospels; and apart from the Apocalypse, there are few if any references to the Danielic Son of man. To be sure, scholars have made up the lack by telling us that, despite all appearances, the primitive community of Palestine had as its lifeblood a Son of man Christology. But despite the long-running popularity of this affirmation, it is woefully ill-founded. It forces one to suppose that "from this Christology not a single formula of the community, neither a kerygma, nor a confession, nor a prayer, outside (or for that matter within) the Gospels would have survived!"[55] The implausibility of this is enormous. By way of contrast, references to Daniel 7 and to the Son of man do certainly occur in materials attributed to Jesus. Moreover, there are Synoptic passages in which the Son of man is not mentioned but allusion to Daniel 7 is made. For instance, the absolute use of *basileia* with *dounai* in Luke 12:32 ("'Fear not, little flock, for it is your Father's good pleasure to give you the kingdom'"), a saying we should probably assign to Jesus,[56] recalls Dan. 7:18 and 27, where the saints of the most high are given the kingdom. And the original form of Luke 22:28-30 = Matt. 19:28, which perhaps did not mention the Son of man (contrast the present text of Matthew) and which *may* go back to Jesus, also depends upon Daniel 7. Luke speaks of thrones (cf. Dan. 7:9), of the kingdom (cf. Dan. 7:18, 27), and of the judgment (cf. Dan. 7:10), and the Matthean parallel adds a reference to glory (cf. Dan. 7:14). Given the lack of reflection upon Daniel 7 outside the Gospels, the repeated use of the Son of man in the Synoptics, and the likelihood—established apart from the Son of man sayings—that Jesus was influenced by Daniel 7, those who believe Jesus himself spoke of the Son of man with reference to Daniel 7 have grounds for their conviction.

We are all the more confirmed in this verdict because there is at least one Son of man saying that (1) has high claim to go back to Jesus and (2) probably draws upon the imagery of Dan. 7:13-14. One is on relatively safe ground when considering Luke 12:8-9 = Matt. 10:32-33. This is a saying from Q with a parallel in Mark 8:38. The Markan version is usually regarded as secondary. The original probably came close to the following:[57]

> Truly I say to you, he who acknowledges me before men, the Son of man will acknowledge before the angels of God; but he who denies me before men, the Son of man will deny him before the angels of God.

55. Leonard Goppelt, *Theology of the New Testament: Jesus and the Gospels*, vol. 1, trans. J. Alsup (Grand Rapids: Wm. B. Eerdmans, 1981), 180.

56. Cf. Joachim Jeremias, "Poimēn ktl.," *TDNT* 6 (1968): 501.

57. Translation of Greek reconstruction by Rudolf Pesch, in "Über die Autorität Jesu: Eine Rückfrage anhand des Bekenner- und Verleugnerspruchs Lk 12, 8f par.," in *Die Kirche des Anfangs: Für Heinz Schürmann*, ed. R. Schnackenburg, J. Ernst, and J. Wanke (Freiburg: Herder, 1978), 39.

In the opinion of some, Matthew, who has "I" rather than "Son of man," is closer to Q. But the Markan parallel has *ho huios tou anthrōpou*, and Matthew has elsewhere apparently substituted "I" for "the Son of man," as a comparison of Mark 8:31 = Matt. 16:21 and Luke 6:32 = Matt. 5:11 shows. Another point of dispute concerns the voice of the second clause. Luke 12:9 is in the passive, Matt. 10:33 in the active. Perhaps Luke is here more faithful to the original, but given the active voice in the first clause and in Mark 8:38, Luke, it may be conjectured, altered the voice in order to make a smoother link with Luke 12:10, the word about forgiveness for words spoken against the Son of man: as *ho huios tou anthrōpou* occurs in Luke 12:8 and 12:10, retention of the title in 12:9 would have meant its awkward repetition three times in three verses.

Concerning the authenticity of our saying, there are two alternatives. According to most scholars, Luke 12:8-9 = Matt. 10:32-33 is a dominical utterance. But others have argued, with a nod towards Ernst Käsemann's study of prophetic "sentences of holy law," that the logion had its *Sitz im Leben* in Christian prophecy; it is an instance of the proclamation of the eschatological *ius talionis*. We cannot here enter into a discussion of Käsemann's thesis, which has had a favorable reception with many. The following observations must suffice. (1) All talk of early Christian prophets speaking in the name of the risen Lord and having their utterances later taken for words of the earthly Jesus rests upon very weak pillars.[58] (2) Form criticism cannot assign the so-called "sentences of holy law" to a community of Christian prophets on grounds of form alone because, among other things, the *ius talionis* form has parallels in the genre of sapiential exhortation.[59] (3) "While it may well be true that sacred law played a decisive part in the life and ordering of the primitive church, this does not by any means imply that Jesus Himself may not have equally well used this form, as in other respects also He made use of traditional modes of expression in the formulation of His words."[60] (4) The form of a two-part pronouncement, in which one clause states an activity of man and the other an eschatological activity of God, and in which the same verb is used in both clauses, can almost certainly be ascribed to Jesus (note Matt. 6:12 = Luke 11:4; Luke 6:37-38; and Luke 14:11 = 18:14 = Matt. 23:12). In view of these considerations, one does well to stay in the company of those who regard Luke 12:8-9 = Matt. 10:32-33, which has Semitic coloring,[61] as a genuine word of Jesus.

---

58. See herein 113, n. 52.
59. See Klaus Berger, "Die sogennanten 'Sätze heiligen Rechts,'" *NTS* 17 (1970): 10-40.
60. Thus, Ferdinand Hahn, *Titles of Jesus in Christology*, 29-30.
61. Wilhelm Michaelis, "Homologeō ktl.," *TDNT* 5 (1967): 208 n. 27.

The saying finds no better background than that provided by Daniel 7. Luke 12:8-9, like Daniel 7, has to do with the last judgment. Luke 12:8-9, like Daniel 7, has as its central figure the Son of man. Luke 12:8-9, like Daniel 7, makes this figure an agent of judgment.[62] Luke 12:8-9, like Daniel 7, sets the stage with heavenly hosts or angels. Further, Daniel 7 is the Tanach's most detailed, most colorful, and most powerful picture of the great assize, and presumably any allusion to the heavenly court and the last judgment might have sent Jewish hearers, steeped as they were in the Bible, back to the *locus classicus*. Moreover, the prepositional use of *emprosthen*, "a standard expression for standing before the judge,"[63] occurs in Luke 12:8 and has its parallel in Daniel 7:13 (*qdm*). As the one like a son of man comes before (*qdm*) the Ancient of days and his host, so Jesus will confess and deny men before (*emprosthen*) the angels of God (cf. Rev. 3:5). Finally, as Pesch has observed, Luke 12:8-9 envisions a situation of persecution. "The 'forensic' stamp of the saying is significant (*homologeō, arneomai, emprosthen*), and the invitation to the personal confession of Jesus and the warning of denying him plainly speak to a situation in which Jesus was rejected, a situation with which his disciples met." Thus, "only within the situation of 'martyrdom' in which personal testimony is advanced is the invitation to 'confession' and the warning of 'denial' understandable."[64] Now, Daniel 7 also deals with persecution; see 7:21 and 25. Hence, there is one more point of correlation between the saying about confessing and denying the Son of man and Daniel 7. We conclude, accordingly, that Luke 12:8-9 in all probability preserves an authentic word of Jesus in which the Son of man is to be identified with the figure of Dan. 7:13–14.

One additional point may be made in favor of this verdict. Those who question whether Jesus spoke of the Son of man with reference to Daniel 7 or to an established figure of Jewish expectation must suppose that the church formulated a good number of new Son of man sayings. This is true even of those who explain the *br 'nš(')* sayings in terms of Aramaic idiom; for the postulated idiomatic usage accounts only for a handful of the total number of logia. But what evidence is there that christological terms were readily put into the mouth of Jesus? We know that although *kyrios* and *christos* were all-important titles in the early church, they have left scarcely a trace in the tradition of the sayings of Jesus. This is in direct contrast with the Son of man

62. Although the one like a son of man in Daniel is "not explicitly said to be given the task of judging, this is implicit in the rule committed to him." Joyce G. Baldwin, *Daniel: An Introduction and Commentary*, Tyndale Old Testament Commentaries (Downers Grove, Ill.: Inter-Varsity Press, 1978), 150.
63. Michaelis, "Homologeō ktl.," 208 n. 27.
64. Pesch, "Über die Autorität Jesu," 47.

phenomenon. *Ho huios tou anthrōpou* occurs again and again in the Gospels, and the references to Daniel 7 are several. But the title is found in Acts only once and never in the epistles, and allusions to Daniel 7 are few and far between. This should spell caution for those who would solve the Son of man problem by continual recourse to the creative activities of the early church.

It remains to inquire how reference to Daniel 7 served Jesus. Three points are to be made. First, it is suggestive that while, on the one hand, T. W. Manson and others after him have suggested that the Son of man in the Gospels is a corporate figure,[65] Casey, on the other hand, has recently shown that first-century Judaism did in fact know a collective interpretation of Daniel 7.[66] The book of Daniel itself seemingly identifies the one like a son of man with the saints of the most high (7:17-18, 21-22, 26-27). It is altogether likely that when Jesus spoke of the Son of man he had in view a community at whose head he saw himself: a corporate personality embodied most fully in his own person. This would at least explain why, to quote Morna Hooker, "in all the sayings which predict suffering for the Son of man, Jesus is linked in the context with his followers, who are expected to share both his suffering and his glory."[67]

Second, Daniel's one like a son of man is a suffering figure—because the saints of the most high, who are apparently identified with the Son of man, suffer. "'As I looked, this horn made war with the saints, and prevailed over them'" (7:21; cf. 7:25). A pious Jew hearing Daniel 7 read, and finding himself persecuted or in a situation of suffering would no doubt have viewed the events involving the one like a son of man as a promise of passage through affliction to victory: if Daniel's figure had suffered difficulty only to be given the triumph, so too, the listener would hope, might he be delivered from a painful predicament into the state of salvation.[68] Further, the supposition that Jesus interpreted the Son of man in these terms is credible. Many of the Synoptic Son of man sayings have to do either with suffering (for example, Mark 14:21 and 41) or with vindication (for example, Mark 14:62 and 13:26) or with both (for example, Matt. 10:23 and the passion predictions). In both Daniel 7 and the Synoptics, the Son of man first suffers and then finds vindication.

Third, as we have argued throughout this chapter, Jesus interpreted his

---

65. T. W. Manson, "The Son of Man in Daniel, Enoch, and the Gospels," *BJRL* 32 (1950): 171-95.

66. Casey, *Son of Man: Interpretation*, 7-98.

67. Morna Hooker, *The Son of Man in Mark* (London: SPCK, 1967), 181-82.

68. Against Casey, for whom the one like a son of man "is a pure symbol with no experience at all, other than the symbolic ones in vss. 13-14," and for whom Daniel's figure is "separate ... dissociated from the sufferings of the saints," see Francis J. Moloney, "The End of the Son of Man?" *Downside Review* 98 (1980): 284.

mission and prospective destiny in eschatological categories; he entertained the prospect of death in the great tribulation and hoped to know vindication at the judgment. Is it coincidence that this prospect is the scenario of Daniel 7? The biblical text does not simply speak of suffering and vindication. It places these two concepts within an eschatological setting. The horn that prevails against the saints of the most high (Dan. 7:8, 11) is the last opponent. When he is defeated the kingdom comes. Later readers did not miss this (cf. Rev. 13:5, 7; 2 Apoc. Bar. 67—69; Barn. 4:5; Adv. haer. 5:25.1-5). Daniel 7 has to do with the final fling of evil. It tells of what will happen in the great tribulation, how at that time war will be made on the saints, who will suffer in the time of trouble such as has never been until then and will never be thereafter (12:1). When Jesus read or listened to Daniel 7, he could hardly have missed its fundamental character—a prophecy of the last times. Thus, if he appropriated its imagery to set forth his own life and fate, that could only be because he thought himself to be in the last times. And if, in foretelling the sufferings of himself and others, he drew upon the Danielic text, that could only be because he interpreted his own time as the birth pangs of the new age. By promising the vindication of himself and others with reference to Daniel 7, Jesus disclosed his hope that the near future would bring about the eschatological judgment. In sum, Jesus' probable use of Daniel 7 supports the direction of our work, for it strongly implies that he thought of his coming death and resurrection as defined by the eschatological sequence of tribulation—vindication.

## Passion Predictions

Many critical scholars have not hesitated to write off the three formal passion predictions (Mark 8:31; 9:31; 10:33-34) as formulations of the community. Bultmann was capable of disposing of them with the simple rhetorical question,"Can there be any doubt that they are all *vaticinia ex eventu?*"[69] This judgment, especially in view of the particulars in Mark 10:33-34, cannot be dismissed as cavalier. In their present form at least the passion predictions seem to be after the event. And although, as we have argued, Jesus did anticipate an untimely death, the passion predictions not only look forward to Jesus' end but also to his resurrection. Is it at all credible that a foundation for such two-membered predictions is to be discovered in the pre-Easter period?

One may confidently hold that Jesus did not simply predict his own death and the dissolution of his movement. He surely must have assumed that God would vindicate his cause notwithstanding the coming time of trouble. It would have been altogether natural for one who had faith in God's justice and

69. Bultmann, *Theology of the New Testament*, 1:29.

power to look beyond present and expected troubles and hope for the Lord's favorable verdict. Such faith and hope in fact together mark the heart of Jewish eschatology, and we can scarcely err in supposing that Jesus shared them. Just as the visionary group that spoke of its sufferings in Isa. 61:1-3; 63:17; and 65:13-14 also boldly declared its confidence in a swift victory (Isa. 57:13; 66:5-16), so Jesus will have believed in God as the one who would speedily rescue him from coming calamity. Moreover, if Jesus had sought to express the idea of vindication despite and subsequent to death, the category of resurrection would naturally have suggested itself, especially as (1) resurrection was closely tied to the thought of martyrdom; (2) it was hoped that the kingdom of God was at hand; and (3) Jesus, with the Pharisees and against the Sadducees, accepted the doctrine of the resurrection. On this last point, one may refer to Mark 12:18-27 and to Matt. 12:41-42 = Luke 11:31-32, and an observation of Walter Schmithals may be recalled: "The primary and fundamental utterance of the community that looked back upon Jesus' activity"— that is, the confession, He is risen—"shows with sufficient clarity that the expectation of the resurrection of the dead as a *now* imminent eschatological act must have been an essential object of hope of the disciples who followed Jesus during his time on earth."[70] Further, it is surely significant that the tradition not only predicts suffering and death for Jesus' closest followers but implicitly pledges them a glorious resurrection: Matt. 19:28 = Luke 22:29-30. There is, admittedly, debate over the authenticity of this saying, but elsewhere Jesus clearly presupposes the vindication or resurrection of those in his circle; see, for instance, Mark 10:28-31, 35-45; and Luke 18:6-8. One could hardly be surprised to learn that Jesus spoke of his own resurrection. And for those still persuaded that Jesus hoped to share in the destiny of the one like a son of man, the issue would seem to admit of little doubt; for as Jesus expected to die, any sharing in the Son of man's destiny could only come by way of resurrection.[71] Finally, it is to be noted that Mark 14:25—"'Truly, I say to you, I shall not drink again of the fruit of the vine until that day when I drink it new in the kingdom of God'"—must have sprung from hope in an impending resurrection: notwithstanding death, Jesus announces that he will feast at the messianic banquet. So there are good reasons for the verdict of C. K. Barrett: "That Jesus should ... predict that, after dying in fulfillment of the commis-

---

70. Walter Schmithals, *The Apocalyptic Movement: Introduction and Interpretation*, trans. J. E. Steely (Nashville: Abingdon Press, 1975), 153.
71. "It is noteworthy that there is no saying which predicts both resurrection and second coming. It is therefore at least possible that the two are alternatives." So Dodd, *Parables of the Kingdom*, 76 n. 2. Cf. C. J. Cadoux, *The Historic Mission of Jesus* (New York: Harper & Brothers, n.d.), 286-94. This position, which we find unavoidable, goes back at least as far as Wilhelm Weiffenbach's work (1873); see Schweitzer, *Quest*, 233-34.

sion laid upon him by God, he would be vindicated, and that he should give his vindication the form of resurrection . . . is in no way surprising."[72] Any prediction of death followed by resurrection would originally have been tied into the eschatological sequence. After the onset of Easter faith, forecasts of suffering and resurrection would, one suspects, have been reinterpreted as realized in the exaltation of one man and filled out in the light of his historical passion. But resurrection was primarily a collective category, and for Jesus himself, talk of resurrection would almost certainly have been talk about eschatological matters, about the vindication of all the saints[73]—just as the prospect of suffering was, in Jesus' proclamation, a collective category and part of the latter days. To be sure, Jesus is the focal figure of the passion predictions as we now know them. But the original horizon must have been wider. The structure of the passion predictions, death—resurrection, coincides with the eschatological scheme, tribulation—salvation. Just as the great tribulation precedes the coming of the kingdom, so Jesus is to die and then know resurrection. The parallel is not fortuitous. The passion predictions will have had their origin in dominical prophecies about the final affliction and ultimate vindication. The picture originally painted was of Jesus and the community around him facing the great tribulation, yet confident in the hope that glory lies on the other side of suffering.[74]

Perhaps the passion predictions go back to a saying that looked something like this: *mtmsr br 'nš' lydy bny 'nš wlbtr tlth ywmyn yqwm*: "the Son of man will be delivered up to the sons of men but after three days he will rise up." The note of time could well be original. "Three days" seems to have been equivalent to "a little while" or "a few days."[75] It is also possible that Hos. 6:12,

---

72. C. K. Barrett, *Jesus and the Gospel Tradition* (Philadelphia: Fortress Press, 1968), 78.

73. According to Ulrich Kellermann, *Auferstehung in den Himmel: 2 Makkabäer 7 und die Auferstehung der Martyrer*, SB 95 (Stuttgart: Katholisches Bibelwerk, 1978), some Jews believed that the resurrection of a martyr would follow immediately upon his death. Kellermann finds the most persuasive evidence for this in 2 Maccabees 7 and proposes that Jesus expected such a resurrection. But even if belief in the resurrection of martyrs immediately after death is attested (and the indications are meager), the words of Jesus readily fit collective categories and, because they contain a *Naherwartung*, presuppose the nearness of the general resurrection.

74. Schweitzer's portrait of Jesus fell out from two different sets of data. On the one hand, certain traditions seem to place Jesus' fate within the final tribulation; yet others focus entirely on Jesus and his solitary passion. Schweitzer eliminated the tension between these two traditions by positing a change within Jesus' thought. At an early time Jesus expected the tribulation to encompass all; later he anticipated taking up in himself alone the coming affliction. If, however, one takes account of the post-Easter reinterpretation of the Jesus tradition, there is no need to postulate any development in Jesus' thinking, at least on this matter. Jesus expected to die in the final drama (which accounts for the first set of data) and the church interpreted and modified his words in the light of what actually happened (which accounts for the second set of data).

75. See J. B. Bauer, "Drei Tage," *Bib* 39 (1958): 354–58.

which the targum and the rabbis took to refer to the general resurrection, stands in the background.[76] As for *br 'nš'*, there are reasons to suppose that, for Jesus, the phrase would have had a collective dimension. This means that a passion prediction such as the one we have reconstructed envisions more than the fate of Jesus; it also encompasses the fate of those around him. Thus, just as in Daniel 7 the saints of the most high, who are identified with the one like a son of man, are delivered into the hands of their enemy, only to receive the kingdom after a time, two times, and half a time, so Jesus promises that the Son of man, the faithful community whose representative he is, will be delivered into the hands of men, only to be resurrected after three days.

## The Lord's Prayer

The essential authenticity of the Lord's Prayer (Matt. 6:9–13 = Luke 11:2–4) is widely regarded as firmly established, and we find no good cause to question this nearly unanimous opinion. As to its integrity, most would concur with Jeremias that "the Lukan version has preserved the oldest form with respect to length, but the Matthean text is more original with regard to wording."[77] The debate concerning the original language—Aramaic or Hebrew?—continues.

A number of scholars have argued that the Lord's Prayer was, originally, thoroughly eschatological. "Hallowed be thy name" and "thy kingdom come" entreat God to reveal his glory and usher in his absolute reign. In the petition, "Give us this day our bread for the morrow" (RSV alternate), "our bread" may refer to the heavenly manna, the bread of life, and "the morrow" may be the great tomorrow, the consummation.[78] "Forgive us our debts, as we also have forgiven our debtors" is prayed in view of the coming judgment. Finally, "And do not bring us to the test" (NEB) alludes to the coming time of trouble. "The test" (*peirasmon*) does not so much envision the trials or temptations of everyday life but, as in Rev. 3:10, stands for the final time of trouble which precedes the renewal. One prays for preservation from evil or apostasy in the coming tribulation.

This interpretation of the Lord's Prayer has gained a good following.[79] There are, however, criticisms to be brought against it; for although it is

76. Texts and discussion in Harvey K. McArthur, "On the Third Day," *NTS* 18 (1971): 81–86.
77. Joachim Jeremias, "The Lord's Prayer in the Light of Modern Research," in *The Prayers of Jesus*, SBT 2/6, trans. J. Bowden, et al. (Philadelphia: Fortress Press, 1978; London: SCM Press, 1967), 93.
78. For a brief review of the discussion, see I. H. Marshall, *Commentary on Luke*, NIGTC (Grand Rapids: Wm. B. Eerdmans, 1978), 458–60.
79. Typical is Raymond E. Brown, "The Pater Noster as an Eschatological Prayer," in *New Testament Essays* (Garden City, N.Y.: Doubleday & Co., 1968), 275–320.

difficult to dispute that the first two petitions refer to the still outstanding consummation, this is not so obvious with regard to the last three, especially the request for bread and the prayer for deliverance from trial.[80] Now, it is beyond the scope of the present work to assess whether or not the objections raised against the eschatological interpretation should carry the day—especially as we are persuaded that a verdict on this issue is exceedingly difficult to render.

Nevertheless, one may observe that *if* that approach be accepted, then certain results relevant for our thesis follow; for although one may rightly speak of a giving of the Lord's Prayer to the disciples by Jesus, with the intent of characterizing the new community gathered around him (cf. Luke 11:1), such a judgment does not entail the supposition that, in the act of giving, Jesus somehow shows himself to be above praying the prayer. There is no reason to believe that the Lord's Prayer was any less Jesus' prayer than that of his disciples. On the contrary, its inspiraton must have come out of his own religious experience. But if so, and if *peirasmon* alludes to the eschatological affliction (a question we must leave open), then Jesus entertained the possibility of finding himself alive during the final tribulation, for as the Lord's Prayer implies, he asked to be preserved during the *peirasmon*.

## Conclusion

The pertinent results of this chapter may be summarized as follows. For Jesus, not only was the eschatological redemption near, but he expected (1) to suffer and die in the time of eschatological distress, which he thought of as already present and (2) to experience vindication at the general resurrection of the dead. The pattern of suffering—vindication that runs throughout the Gospels had its origins with Jesus and arose out of the conviction that before salvation came there would be tribulation for the saints. As with the harvest, so with eschatology: death must come before the bearing of fruit (cf. John 12:34). The road to the new world passes through the land of suffering and death (cf. Mark 8:35 and Matt. 10:39 = Luke 17:33).

---

80. See Schweizer, *Good News According to Matthew*, 154–56; and Anton Vögtle, "Der 'eschatologische' Bezug der Wir-Bitten des Vaterunser," in *Jesus und Paulus*, 344–62.

# Twelve

# CORRELATIONS: FROM
# EXPECTATION TO INTERPRETATION

It has been argued that Jesus foresaw for himself suffering, death, and vindication in the eschatological drama, which he took to be already unfolding. Assuming this conclusion, is it mere coincidence that members of the early church interpreted the death and resurrection of Jesus in eschatological categories? That is, is there any relevant connection between Jesus' interpretation of his prospective fate and the post-Easter traditions examined in chapters 3—9 of this book? The evidence, as we shall see, impels an affirmative answer whose explication supplies the key to understanding the so-called "realized eschatology" of the primitive community.

## Sociological Considerations

Social psychology abundantly demonstrates that people strongly tend to interpret their experiences in terms of previously established categories and prior expectations, even when those categories and expectations have seemingly proven false or inadequate. Although applicable to almost every sphere of human behavior, some of the most striking illustrations of this generalization are to be found in religion. For example, the members of messianic movements, when faced with the clear refutation of prophetic expectations, have again and again shown themselves capable of maintaining faith. By means of rationalizations, such as the reinterpretation of prophecy, believers have refused to face the obvious and have instead chosen to justify and thereby continue commitment to their cause. Although documentation from ancient times is relatively scanty, more recent examples of the phenomenon are abundant.

(1) The messianic movement associated with Sabbatai Şevi may be referred to first.[1] Sabbatai Şevi, a self-declared Jewish Messiah of the seventeenth century, committed anti-Halakhic acts and eventually apostatized to Islam.

---

1. For what follows see, above all, Scholem, *Sabbatai Şevi*.

But neither his antinomian behavior nor his abandonment of Judaism led (as one would expect) to the dissolution of the movement which he called forth or to the conclusion that he was not the Messiah. On the contrary, his followers, partly through their interpretation of the Scriptures, were able to incorporate every offense—including Sabbatai Şevi's conversion to Islam, the most serious offense imaginable—into messianic doctrine. Accordingly, the conviction that Sabbatai Şevi was the Messiah, once established, endured despite everything. Sabbatianism, then, offers a clear example of the ability of a messianic movement to maintain, against the witness of history, its belief structure.

(2) When, in 1666, the Russian church council anathematized the Rascolniks (the so-called "Old Believers" who rejected the liturgical reforms of the Patriarch Nikon, 1605–81), these latter declared that the reign of antichrist had begun.[2] Several popular theologians then took the next step: after three-and-one-half years—this being the prophesied duration of antichrist's rule—the world would come to its end. Despite the calculation, 1669 came and went, and the world continued as ever. But there were Rascolniks who claimed—and many peasants believed them—that the prophecy should be interpreted spiritually. Although antichrist had not come in the flesh, he governed, so it was held, in the Russian church. In this way, the eschatological prophecy was reinterpreted and thus, despite every appearance of invalidation, its truth maintained.

(3) Joanna Southcott (1750–1814) and her followers believed that, before her death, the virgin prophetess of England would bear a child who would rule the nations, Shiloh (cf. Gen. 49:10, KJV). Although she did in fact manifest in her body every symptom of pregnancy at the age of more than sixty, thereby causing a number of reputable physicians to declare that she was, indeed, with child, Joanna died without giving birth. Further, a post-mortem examination revealed no appearance of her ever having been pregnant. While this disconcerting news wrecked the faith of many, some Southcottians could not lay their beliefs to rest. Encouraged by the satiric words of the doctor who performed the autopsy—"Darn me if the child is not gone!"—they came up with the idea that, in accordance with a prophecy in Revelation, the child had been "caught up to God and to his throne" (12:5). There are still a few people who believe that Joanna's child, Shiloh, whom no one has ever seen, waits in heaven until the appointed hour.[3]

2. See Wilson D. Wallis, *Messiahs: Their Role in Civilization* (Washington, D.C.: American Council on Public Affairs, 1943), 177–78; and Frederick C. Conybeare, *Russian Dissenters*, HTS 10 (Cambridge: Harvard Univ. Press, 1921), 65–68, 94–99.

3. George R. Belleine, *Past Finding Out: The Tragic Story of Joanna Southcott and Her Successors* (London: SPCK, 1956); Jack Gratus, *The False Messiahs* (New York: Taplinger, 1975), 171–78; Ronald Matthews, *English Messiahs: Studies of Six English Religious Pretenders,*

(4) The millennial prophecy of the Millerite movement (mid-1800s) and its reinterpretation also provides a telling illustration. When Jesus did not come back at the expected date, 2 October 1844, some Millerites (a minority) proceeded to maintain that the second coming had in fact occurred—but spiritually, in heaven, not on earth. For these people, 2 October 1884 became the date on which Jesus entered his heavenly sanctuary and inaugurated a new phase of salvation history. The Seventh-day Adventists, an off-shoot of the Millerites, still believe this.[4]

(5) The Jehovah's Witnesses, known also as "Watch Tower Bible and Tract Society," believe that Jesus Christ returned to earth in 1874. This tenet derives from a prophecy that the second advent would occur at that time. When Christ did not return as anticipated, the forecast was simply reinterpreted. According to the Witnesses, Christ came, but it was an invisible coming. Other misdirected prophecies of the same group have been handled similarly.[5]

(6) In the state of Bihar, India, in 1895, a Munda named Birsa announced that he was the father of the world.[6] He would, so he claimed, rescue his people and deliver them from British bondage. Birsa rapidly gained a large following. Early on he prophesied that a great deluge would flood the country, sparing only the spot where he and his sympathizers resided. Many Mundas, believing the prophecy, stopped all cultivation and turned livestock loose. When the appointed hour came, a vast number of people gathered around Birsa on a hilltop. When nothing happened, the prophet explained that the catastrophe had been postponed for a while. With this rationalization he saved face. Birsa's subsequent career took a more militant turn as he sought to stir up the people to open rebellion. Thus, the government had him arrested, and the resistance was dispelled. Yet faith in Birsa was far from extinguished. It was believed that he had been taken up to heaven, that the jailers only pretended to have their prisoner. Upon receiving pardon, Birsa once again began to make trouble for the government and, to avoid arrest, he had to go into hiding. But it was rumored that he had in fact left the earth for a time and would return soon. Finally, when the prophet died, many Mundas refused to accept the fact. They

*1656-1927* (London: Methuen & Co., 1936), 45-84.

4. John N. Loughborough, *The Great Second Advent Movement* (Washington, D.C.: Review & Herald, 1905), 185-97; Clara Endicott Sears, *Days of Delusion* (Boston: Houghton Mifflin, 1924).

5. See James A. Beckford, *The Trumpet of Prophecy: A Sociological Study of Jehovah's Witnesses* (New York: John Wiley & Sons, 1975), 1-21 108-10; Eric R. Chamberlin, *Antichrist and the Millennium* (New York: E. P. Dutton & Co., 1975), 167-95; Alan Rogerson, *Millions Now Living Will Never Die: A Study of Jehovah's Witnesses* (London: Constable & Co., 1969), 101-15, 191-92.

6. For this and what follows, see Stephen Fuchs, *Rebellious Prophets: A Study of Messianic Movements in Indian Religions* (London: Asia Pub. House, 1965), 27-34.

continued to believe that someday he would reappear and bring the final deliverance.

(7) Concerning the "cargo cults" of Melanesia, Peter Worsley has written:

Mere failure of a prophecy is no assurance that a cult will lose its hold on the people. Indeed, failures can be interpreted in such a manner that they contribute to the strengthening of the basic concepts involved. A particular failure could be admitted without undermining the belief that other movements and other rituals might hold the key to the Cargo. Moreover, failures could always be attributed to the malice of the Europeans who were preventing the ancestors from coming. And although failures were real enough and directly observable, the reasons for the failures could not be so easily shown. Since there *was* no existent reality to which they referred, they could not be verified or disproved. The non-arrival of the spirits did not prove that they did not exist, and to the natives the non-existence of unobserved phenomena could only be asserted, not proved.[7]

(8) In their well-known book, *When Prophecy Fails*, Leon Festinger, Henry W. Riecken, and Stanley Schachter argued that missionary activity has sometimes been a response to cognitive dissonance created by disappointed hopes.[8] Whatever be the merit of this, their central thesis, their work attests that the group studied—an American UFO cult that believed it would soon be delivered from a coming catastrophe by beings from another planet—at points claimed the fulfillment of obviously falsified expectations. For instance, when the sect was not taken from the world at the predicted time, it was suggested that the original prophecy had been misunderstood, and straightaway a reinterpretation, declaring the fulfillment of that prophecy, was offered.[9]

(9) On 4 July 1960, 29 American families, 135 men, women, and children—members of the Church of the True Word, a Pentecostal group—entered underground shelters in response to a prophecy that nuclear disaster was imminent. The prophecy had been delivered through their minister, a Mrs. Shepard. She had for several years preached that a great war was on the horizon and that the true believers would be saved to enter a new world, as happened to Noah. Finally, a specific prediction was delivered—"The Egyp-

7. Peter Worsley, *The Trumpet Shall Sound: A Study of "Cargo" Cults in Melanesia*, 2d ed. (New York: Schocken Books, 1968), 122.
8. Leon Festinger, Henry W. Riecken, and Stanley Schachter, *When Prophecy Fails: A Social and Psychological Study of a Modern Group that Predicted the Destruction of the World* (New York: Harper & Row, 1964). On the theory of cognitive dissonance, when two beliefs or items of knowledge are dissonant—that is, inconsistent with each other—and when this is accompanied by an awareness of the dissonance, there will arise discomfort and therefore pressures to reduce or eliminate the sources of discomfort. This can take one or more of three forms: a change in beliefs, opinions, or behavior involved in the dissonance; an increase in existing consonance, or in new cognitive elements, so that the individual's existing dissonance is lessened; a forgetting or reduction of the importance of the cognition constituting the dissonance.
9. Festinger, Riecken, and Schachter, *When Prophecy Fails*, 166–67; also 164, 165, 180–82.

tians are coming; get ye to the safe place"—and the believers descended into underground facilities for forty-two days. When they received the word to come out, the group was anything but distraught, despite the fact that no bombs had been dropped. They rather rejoiced that their experience had brought them closer to each other and to God. They felt that their stay in the shelters had only strengthened their beliefs. And what of the prophecy? It was not false. In going back over their messages, it was discovered that nothing clearly indicated that the attack was strictly imminent, only that it would surely come sometime in the not-too-distant future. That is, the prophetic messages had been misunderstood. Further, the retreat had not been without good result. God had tested their faith, and they had proven true, and they had become a warning to all the world of the disaster still coming.[10]

(10) Some rather odd religious doctrines have appeared in Rastafarianism, a contemporary movement of protest centered in Jamaica. Among these is the belief in the divinity of Haile Selassie I (Ras Tafari), the late Emperor of Ethiopia. Before 1975, Rastas were persuaded that Haile Selassie would destroy "Babylon" (the source of all the evil in the world) and bring the faithful out of Jamaica to the promised land, Ethiopia. Difficulties therefore arose when the Emperor was deposed and subsequently died (27 August 1975).[11] How could such things happen to the living god? The Rastas came up with a number of responses. Some said that Haile Selassie had not really died, that he would soon be resurrected. Many explained things by arguing that Ras Tafari had existed as a person during his life but existed now as a spirit; thus, his death was only apparent, not real. Still others affirmed that the emperor had been only an exteriorization or vehicle of God, not God himself. Today, most Rastas accept one of the latter two positions. But in terms of function, all are identical; they have permitted believers to keep their faith entrenched and their hopes alive. Incidentally, Rastafarianism, so far from being crushed by the death of Haile Selassie, has known its greatest growth since 1975.[12]

By citing, within a work on Christian origins, the contrived rationalizations of certain messianic movements, our intent is not to suggest that the followers

10. Jane A. Hardyck and Marcia Braden, "Prophecy Fails Again: A Report of a Failure to Replicate," *Journal of Abnormal Social Psychology* 65 (1962): 136–41.
11. See Ernest Cashmore, *Rastman: The Rastafarian Movement in England* (London: George Allen & Unwin, 1979), 13-37.
12. If we knew more about Elchasai and his followers, it is probable that study of them would also be instructive; for although Elchasai announced that a universal conflagration would blaze up three years after the Parthian War (114–16 A.D.).—something that did not, of course, happen—his movement survived. See Johannes Irmscher, "The Book of Elchasai," in *New Testament Apocrypha*, 2:747, 750. The lack of data in this instance is frustrating and unfortunately typifies the problems faced in any attempt to draw conclusions about ancient millenarian groups.

of Jesus were—like, let us say, the pitiful disciples of Joanna Southcott—hopelessly and insensibly alienated from the solid world. Our object is rather to offer evidence, by way of concrete instances, for two generalizations: (1) continuity and fixity—not change—typically characterize the religious beliefs of those committed to a messianic movement or sect; and (2) the declaration that eschatological promises have been fulfilled can, in the first place, function to vindicate the expectations of a messiah and those who believe in him; that is, the declaration can serve to maintain or legitimate a particular set of cherished religious convictions.

If one turns to the New Testament with these two conclusions in mind, it becomes possible, on sociological grounds, to suggest a plausible origin for "realized eschatology." The first followers of Jesus witnessed a disjunction between the course of events (Jesus died alone in the midst of history and appeared in visions to his disciples) and an eschatological expectation (Jesus and his supporters were to experience the eschatological denouement). This disjunction issued in two courses of action which in no way surprise, given the record of other messianic movements. On the one hand, the eschatological expectations of the pre-Easter period were not discarded but were interpreted in the light of Jesus' historical passion and faith in his victory over death. On the other hand, an attempt was made to comprehend the fate of Jesus in pre-Easter (and that means eschatological) categories. The disciples did not simply begin over again at Easter and forget their previous expectations. This they could not do, for they had given themselves over to the cause of Jesus of Nazareth; his words had become their life. Nor were they able to remain blissfully unawares and overlook the fact that what had happened was not exactly what had been anticipated. Indeed Jesus had, in accordance with his prophecies, suffered and died and—so his post-mortem appearances indicated —conquered death. Still, the kingdom of God had not yet been fully or manifestly revealed, and the Parousia of the Son of man had not occurred. Time seemingly marched on as before, and Jesus' fate was one which he met alone. What then could the disciples do but seek to reinterpret their expectations by construing faith and history in the light of each other?

At this point we must digress to state our conviction that much work on Christian origins can be criticized for imposing a yawning gulf between the pre- and post-Easter periods. Many scholars have, with too little reflection, permitted historical reconstruction to be determined by the New Testament's theological assertion of the centrality and revolutionary character of the death and resurrection of Jesus. They have thereby come to stress the discontinuities between the time of Jesus and the time of the church, and almost every facet of early Christian faith and practice has been explained without recourse to the pre-Paschal epoch. But sociological considerations make the drawing of a heavy line between the pre- and post-Easter periods questionable and encourage one to work with the presumption of strong forces favoring fundamental continuities. It is noteworthy that the collective appearance to the Twelve (1 Cor. 15:5) implies that the disciples remained together even before they gained Easter faith. This means that they were a sociological unit after the passion and before their belief in the resurrection of Jesus.

Returning now to the main line of our argument, the disciples' attempt to bring faith into harmony with history took at least three different turns, none of which can be regarded as exceptional, for each is well attested for other messianic movements. First, expectation and outcome were, despite the tension between the two, made out to be promise and fulfillment. The church believed that, although the Son of man had not come with the clouds of heaven, Jesus had suffered tribulation and been vindicated by God. The church could therefore argue that his prophecies had met partial fulfillment in his own destiny, that the great tribulation and the general resurrection had begun, that the Day of the Lord had dawned. *This is the genesis of so-called "realized eschatology."* Second, it was asserted that expectation and outcome did not exactly match because the prophecies of the master had been partially misunderstood. Thus, as we shall see, several sayings about eschatological events were subjected to a process of reinterpretation by which their scope was narrowed, the result being that they found their immediate realization in the fate of one individual, Jesus. This process was justified by an appeal to misunderstanding. Third, Christians claimed that the eschatological goal had not been reached because certain preconditions—for example, the repentance of the people of Israel—had not been met. Hence, one finds that the early church picked up on traditional Jewish beliefs about the contingency of prophecy. It now remains to document the three courses of action just indicated.

### The Origin of "Realized Eschatology"

But rather than turn immediately to the New Testament, it will prove profitable first to return once again to *Jubilees* 23. Elsewhere herein (17–19) we have seen that this chapter contains an "inaugurated eschatology." Its author believed that the time of trouble and tribulation was past and that the kingdom of God was dawning in his time. What explains this? *Jubilees* was composed not long after the critical events that saw the rise of the Maccabees, events which also witnessed a sudden rise in fervent eschatological expectation. The dream visions of Daniel, the first edition of the *Assumption of Moses,* and portions of *1 Enoch* (83—90) come from this period. Many Jews were then convinced that their sufferings marked the presence of the eschatological tribulation and that the final redemption was nigh (note, for instance, Dan. 12:1-4). What happened, then, when Antiochus was defeated and Judea established itself as an independent state under the Maccabees? Were the prophecies simply forgotten? The answer is no. Events could be read so as to allow the claim that eschatological expectations had been and now were being fulfilled. Had not tribulation come and gone, and had not an era of peace and prosperity set in (cf. 1 Maccabees 14)? That is, had not the eschatological affliction been experienced, and was not the promised age already entering history? Expectation and outcome were sufficiently close to allow pious Jews of a pro-Maccabean persuasion to suppose the one to be the fulfillment of the other. Thus it is that *Jubilees* 23 identifies the great tribulation with a past set of occurrences and asserts that the eschatological kingdom is already establishing itself. The chapter offers an example of how, within ancient Judaism, an "inaugurated eschatology" could originate in circumstances that permitted history to be read as the fulfillment of eschatological expectations.

It is our conviction that something similar occurred in early Christianity. The disciples of Jesus came to the passion and to the events of Easter with definite expectations, and although their expectations were not precisely met, there was a clear note of harmony between the predictions of Jesus and the actual course of events. It was this note of harmony which nourished the belief that eschatological promises had begun to be fulfilled. In the pre-Easter period, the eschatological tribulation and the general resurrection were impending prospects. Subsequently, when Jesus died and was seen alive, his fate was readily interpreted in pre-Easter categories: the great tribulation and the general resurrection had begun. The death of Jesus and its sequel, the appearances of the risen Lord, were not in themselves the sufficient cause of the interpretation that made them into eschatological events. That interpretation had its primary source in the pre-Paschal period. In other words, the disciples brought to the passion and to the appearances their previously formed expectations, and these moved them to interpret the end of Jesus as the onset of the end of the age.

We are now equipped to understand the genesis of the traditions examined in chapters 3—9 of this book. The declaration that eschatological expectations had been and were being fulfilled was not first of all an interpretation of Christian cultic experience. It arose instead as a sociological response to a pressing issue of belief. How could the prophecies of Jesus, the eschatological expectations of the disciples, be related to the sphere of history, to what had happened? The proclamation of fulfillment, of "realized eschatology," was the solution. It legitimized the commitment of faith. It meant that Jesus was right, that his disciples had not misplaced their trust. If, as was claimed, the sun went dark when Jesus died, then, in agreement with expectation, he had suffered in the great tribulation. And if, as was reported, saints arose from their tombs after Jesus breathed his last, then, as prophesied, the end of Jesus belonged to the end of the age. Similarly, the conviction that the passion and resurrection fulfilled Zechariah 9—14 served the same function, as did the account of the rending of the veil, the parallels between the eschatological discourse (Mark 13) and the passion narrative (Mark 14—16) and the other traditions that use eschatological colors to paint the fortune of Jesus. In sum, "realized eschatology" came to birth in the early church as an interpretation of past events, an interpretation which was dictated by the eschatological expectations of Jesus and his disciples.

If our conclusions are so far correct, a comment on terminology is perhaps in order. The disciples of Jesus did not initially proclaim eschatology as an accomplished fact—"The age to come has come." They rather thought of eschatology as in process: the final sequence had been set in motion. Thus, "inaugurated eschatology" is seemingly a more accurate term with reference to primitive Christianity than "realized eschatology," as this last implies fulfillment without remainder. On our reconstruction, the earliest Christian preaching contained an "already" that by no means excluded a "not yet." In fact, the two went hand in hand. The inbreaking of the new age was thought to be entering by steps or stages, some of which had already occurred, some of which were present, and some of which remained outstanding.

This conclusion applies not only to the primitive community but furthermore to Pauline theology and to Mark and Matthew. "Inaugurated eschatology," not "realized eschatology," better describes each of these. Paul understood his present experience to partake of the messianic woes because he thought this period to have been launched with the sufferings of Jesus; and he spoke of the resurrection of his Lord as the first in a series because he conceived of it as belonging to an eschatological process already begun and about to be completed. It was the same with Mark and Matthew. These two evangelists, when they presented the end of Jesus in eschatological terms, thought of that end as the beginning of a new time. The period marked on the one side by the passion of Jesus and on the other by the Parousia constituted for them the time of the eschatological woes, in which the kingdom of God was coming to birth.

John's Gospel offers something different. Here we find process displaced by stasis. John does not clearly present Jesus as setting in motion an eschatological sequence that will be completed at the last day. The span between the first and second advents does not often draw to itself language descriptive of the eschatological transition; and when it does, that is due to the remnants of pre-Johannine tradition. For the evangelist himself, such language is properly reserved to describe the fate of Jesus alone. It is as if eschatology has become so concentrated in the person of Jesus that it is thereby removed from the surrounding history. Although there is, technically, a last day coming, eschatology has all but come to an end in Jesus. This almost certainly represents a later development, no doubt fostered in large part by the passing of much time since the death and resurrection of Jesus.

At this point, that which has been dubbed "over-realized eschatology" must be reconsidered. It has already been argued that Luke may have polemicized against people who held that the Parousia had come to pass at Pentecost or before, and notice has been taken of those scholars who have found an "over-realized eschatology" at Corinth. The view of Hymenaeus and Philetus, who thought the resurrection already past (2 Tim. 2:17–18), was evidently not entirely their own idiosyncrasy. Perhaps 2 Thess. 2:2 should also be mentioned. Paul, or whoever penned the passage, tells us that his readers had been informed of a strange belief, namely that "the Day of the Lord has come" (*enestēken*). This can hardly mean that, according to some, eschatological troubles had already become manifest, for Paul himself believed this, and our author affirms that "the mystery of lawlessness is already at work" (2:7). Something more is indicated, perhaps the presence of eschatological salvation. If so, 2 Thess 2:2 provides further evidence for the existence of Christians who held to an "over-realized eschatology."

What accounts for their conviction? The eschatological interpretation of the passion and resurrection of Jesus originally meant that the last day had dawned. But the longer that history ran its usual course, the more awkward it would have become thus to interpret the end of Jesus. For the original conception of a process begun and soon to be finished was scarcely constructed to endure the passing of much time. Given this, we suggest that certain members of the early church, not long after Pentecost, came to see the eschatological promises of Jesus as wholly fulfilled in their master's fate. In order to avoid dissonance created by the failure of the eschatological process to come quickly to its conclusion, they argued that the Day of the Lord had come (2 Thess. 2:2), that the resurrection was past (2 Tim. 2:17–18), and so on. This course of action is quite conceivable in view of the typical responses to unfulfilled prophecy documented herein. It is our proposal that the type of thinking evidenced in 1 Corinthians and elsewhere developed as an extension of an early, less extreme belief which held that Easter fulfilled some of Jesus' expectations but not others.

To sum up the results of this section in a sentence: it was the pre-Easter expectations of Jesus and his followers which occasioned first the "inaugurated eschatology" of the early Christian communities and second, at a slightly later period, led to a more extreme "realized eschatology."

## The Motif of Misunderstanding

Instead of or in addition to affirming that their eschatological expectations had been partially fulfilled in the passion of Jesus and its sequel, the disciples also concluded that they had originally misunderstood to some extent the prophecies they had heard before Easter. The inference naturally suggested itself. If outcome and expectation were not in complete concord, the cause could never lie with Jesus, for his word was unquestionably true. If, then, expectations had been disappointed, those expectations could not have been legitimately founded upon the teaching of Jesus—and if anyone so thought, that could only be because he had misapprehended Jesus. This line of reasoning is reflected in several texts.

(1) John's version of the cleansing of the temple (2:13–22) concludes with a prophecy: "'Destroy this temple, and in three days I will raise it up'" (v. 19). After a note recording the response of Jesus' hearers (v. 20: "The Jews then said, 'It has taken forty-six years to build this temple, and will you raise it up in three days?'"), John appends the following comment: "But he spoke of the temple of his body" (v. 21). With this remark, the object of the prophecy ("this temple") is clearly not a building in Jerusalem but Jesus' own body. The saying is thus read so that it finds its fulfillment in the person of Jesus. If the saying, as is altogether probable, originally referred to an eschatological event, to the destruction of the temple and to the setting up of a new temple, then here is an obvious instance of the constriction, from the post-Easter perspective, of an eschatological forecast. The temple of Jerusalem was not taken down until 70 A.D., and no new temple was established—unless one wishes to count the community itself as such. In any event, for early Christians, God has raised Jesus from the dead; hence, Jesus must have been speaking of what did in fact come to pass: his death and resurrection. John 2:22 ("When therefore he was raised from the dead, his disciples remembered that he had said this; and they believed the scripture and the word which Jesus had spoken") all but proves that the followers of Jesus wrestled, in the time after Easter, with the saying preserved in John 2:19.

The synoptic treatments of the same tradition are also instructive. There is no problem with the simple announcement of the destruction of the temple: Mark 13:2 is taken over without significant alteration into Matt. 24:2 and Luke 21:6 (cf. Acts 6:14). But the prophecy of destruction *and renewal* (Mark 14:58 = Matt. 26:61; Mark 15:29 = Matt. 27:40) is another matter. Luke drops it altogether. Matthew makes it plain that the witnesses against Jesus heard him say only "*I am able* to destroy the temple of God, and to build it in three days." Mark asserts that the saying came from the mouths of false witnesses, and the prediction is not, as in John, found on the lips of Jesus himself. Obviously, the prophecy of destruction and renewal was cause for stumbling. The reason is not far to seek. The old temple had not been taken down, and the messianic temple had not been raised. In addition, it appears that the prophecy was remembered outside the church and used polemically against the Christians. It is surely no coincidence that it is always linked with the opponents of Jesus. In Mark and Matthew it is first the accusers at the trial (Mark 14:58 = Matt. 26:61) and second the mockers at the cross (Mark 15:29 = Matt. 27:40) who quote the saying. In John, Jesus' declaration brings an incredulous response from "the Jews:" "'It has taken forty-six years to build this temple, and will you raise it up in three days?'" (2:20).

It is highly probable that the prophecy concerning the temple was dealt with in the earliest period as it is in John—namely, in terms of Jesus' death and resurrection, which means that John has only made explicit what was implicit in his tradition. The prophecy of destruction and renewal always carries with it the chronological note of three days. Certainly, this would have encouraged a reading with reference to Jesus' fate. So the church could affirm that, with Jesus' death and resurrection, the prophecy of the eschatological destruction and renewal of the temple had been fulfilled.

The tradition history of the prophecy in John 2:19 and Mark 14:58 supports the direction of our work. It offers a transparent instance of an eschatological prophecy whose fulfillment was found in the passion and resurrection of Jesus. It also serves to illustrate that the process of interpretation was accompanied by recourse to the claim of misunderstanding. Jesus had spoken, so it was held, not of the temple but of his own body, and those who thought otherwise were mistaken; they had misunderstood.

(2) According to Mark 9:31–32, Jesus "was teaching his disciples, saying to them, 'The Son of man will be delivered into the hands of men, and they will kill him; and when he is killed, after three days he will rise.' But they did not understand the saying, and they were afraid to ask him." Some commentators have argued that the misunderstanding of the disciples, which is particularly prevalent in Mark, has some historical basis. According to others, it should be explained as a (Markan) theological construct. These two opinions do not, however, exhaust the alternatives. Recalling our previous discussion of the passion predictions, another possibility suggests itself. As observed earlier, the passion predictions probably had their origin in dominical prophecies about the eschatological turning point: the great tribulation and general resurrection

are just around the corner. If this explanation be accepted, Mark 9:32 may be judged as warrant for the post-Easter interpretation of the passion predictions. When the original scope of the prophecies concerning tribulation and vindication was narrowed so as to find fulfillment in the fate of Jesus alone, the process was at least partially justified by the motif of misunderstanding. Jesus had predicted tribulation and resurrection for all. But it was Jesus alone who suffered and rose from the dead. The disciples could only conclude that they had somehow misunderstood, and the passion predictions were therewith reinterpreted. Mark 9:9–10 also readily lends itself to such an analysis.

(3) Attached to the Johannine version of Jesus' entry into Jerusalem (12:12–15) is the following verse: "His disciples did not understand this at first; but when Jesus was glorified, then they remembered that this had been written of him and had been done to him" (John 12:16). This is preceded by a citation of Zech. 9:9 (= John 12:15), whence the reference to the things written. In 12:16 the evangelist presumably intends to say not only that the disciples failed initially to understand that the entry fulfilled a prophetic scripture but also, as many commentators recognize, that they held a mistaken notion of Jesus' kingship: the disciples, before Jesus was glorified, did not grasp that the kingdom of Jesus is not of this world (cf. 18:36). In other words, the fourth evangelist here tells us that there was a difference in the messianic doctrines of the pre- and post-Easter periods. One was focused first on Israel, the other was for all peoples. In accounting for this difference, he writes, "His disciples did not understand this at first" (12:16). It is our suggestion that John or his tradition well knew about the tension between expectations of the pre-Easter period and convictions of the post-Easter period, and John or his tradition explained this tension by recourse to the proposal that the intent of Jesus had not been rightly comprehended (note also the problem implicit in 21:20–23). Only after the resurrection did the aim of Jesus become evident.

(4) Before his entry into Jerusalem in the Gospel of Luke, Jesus tells his followers the parable of the pounds (19:12–27) because they are wrongly persuaded that the kingdom of God is about to appear (19:11). Later, while standing on the Mount of Olives before the ascension, the apostles inquire of their Lord, "'Will you at this time restore the kingdom to Israel?'" (Acts 1:6). According to the answer which Jesus gives, it is not for men to know the times or the seasons that the Father has fixed by his own authority; and that which now faces them is not the restoration of the kingdom to Israel but mission in the power of the Spirit to Judea and to Samaria and to the end of the earth (1:7–8). Luke 19:11 and Acts 1:6 clearly attribute to the disciples of Jesus a false eschatological doctrine. In chapter 8 we argued, following Talbert, for interpreting these two verses as Luke's refutation of a "realized eschatology"

that identified the resurrection and subsequent events with the coming of the kingdom of God. By rejecting the view of the disciples, Luke rejects his heretical opponents. But there is another feasible reading. Perhaps Luke 19:11 and Acts 1:6 are Luke's way of making plain that Jesus did not erroneously anticipate the time of the kingdom's coming, and that if his disciples understood him to announce an impending Parousia, then they had misunderstood him. That is to say, one might detect behind these two verses, first, an awareness that the Twelve, before Easter, expected the kingdom to come immediately and, second, a desire to avoid implicating Jesus as the source of the mistaken supposition. Such a conclusion conforms well with what we have discovered elsewhere in the tradition, namely, the affirmation that the disciples originally failed to understand the pronouncements of Jesus pertaining to the future. Great weight, however, cannot be assigned to this interpretation of Luke 19:11 and Acts 1:6, for we have already offered another one which we regard as no less probable.

## Contingent Eschatology as an Apologetic

Despite the historical determinism which undoubtedly characterizes much ancient Jewish apocalyptic literature, there are nevertheless a good many apocalyptic texts in which it is undoubtedly taught that the eschatological climax is contingent upon, or at least will be hastened by, the repentance of Israel. That the juxtaposition of these two convictions involves a real contradiction we need not doubt. This difficulty, however, is scarcely extraordinary. Paradoxes and antinomies run throughout—indeed, especially mark—all religious traditions, including the biblical. But with this fact we are not here concerned. For our purposes, what matters is this: despite neglect of the theme by many historians of ancient Judaism and early Christianity, the contingent nature of God's eschatological promises and judgments is a well-attested belief, appearing in quite a few Jewish documents composed before and after the turn of our era.[13] For example, according to T. Dan 6:4 (first or second century B.C.), Satan knows "that upon the day on which Israel shall repent, the kingdom of the enemy shall be brought to an end."[14] And in T. Sim. 6:2–7 (first or second century B.C.), the vision of the end is introduced by "if ye remove from you your envy and all stiff-neckedness." Again, T. Jud. 23:5 (first or second century B.C.) affirms that the great redemption will be preceded by Israel's repentance: the people will be held captive "until the Lord visit, when

---

13. For the Old Testament background see Jörg Jeremias, *Die Ruhe Gottes: Aspekte alttestamentlicher Gottesvorstellung*, BS 65 (Neukirchen-Vluyn: Neukirchener Verlag, 1975).
14. This and the following quotations are, unless otherwise noted, from vol. 2 of *APOT*.

with perfect heart ye repent and walk in all His commandments, and He bring you up from captivity among the Gentiles." The same idea probably lies behind *As. Mos.* 1:18 (second century B.C. or first century A.D.), where we read of "the day of repentance in the visitation wherewith the Lord will visit them in the consummation of the end of days." In *2 Apoc. Bar.* 78:6–7 (late first century or early second century A.D.) we find this: *if* the Babylonian exiles remove themselves from error, God will gather them together (into the land) at the last times (cf. 84:2–6). Similarly, the *Apocalypse of Abraham* (late first century A.D. or early second century A.D.?) recounts a vision in which righteous men "hasten" the glory of God's name.[15] Moreover, Jacob Licht has persuasively argued that it is the death of Taxo and his seven sons—a death which is actively sought—which "forces" the end in the *Testament* (or *Assumption*) *of Moses;*[16] and Sigmund Mowinckel has correctly observed that *Psalms of Solomon* 17 (first century B.C.) places the promise of the consummation within a context of moral exhortation and thus implicitly contains the idea that national penitence can hasten that consummation.[17] Finally, *4 Ezra* (4:38–43) (late first century A.D.) rebuts the thought that the kingdom has been delayed on account of the sins of those who dwell on the earth and thereby evidently discounts somebody's claim that righteousness might hasten the end. *Fourth Ezra* 4:39 reads: "It is perhaps on account of us that the time of threshing is delayed for the righteous—on account of the sins of those who dwell on earth." Clearly, if the Pseudepigrapha are reliable testimony, the expectation that the Day of the Lord would be heralded by Israel returning with a whole heart to her God was widespread.

Rabbinic literature is also familiar with this belief in the contingency of eschatology. The following passages are typical: (1) R. Eliezar b. Hyrcanus (ca. 80–120 A.D.) is purported to have said, *If* Israel does not repent she will not be delivered; but *if* she does repent she will be delivered (*b. Sanh.* 97b). (2) According to R. Simeon b. Yohai (ca. 140–160 A.D.), *if* the nation were to keep only two Sabbaths, the Lord would immediately usher in salvation (*b. Šabb.* 118b). (3) In *b. Sanh.* 98a we read that Ze'iri (middle Amoraic) declared in the name of R. Ḥanina b. Ḥama (early Amoraic) that the Son of David will not come until no conceited men remain in Israel. (4) *Sipre Deut.* 4 (79b, Tannaitic) announces that *if* Israel were to keep the Law, God would therewith send Elijah. Similar sentiments are expressed in, among other places, *b.*

---

15. *Apocalypse of Abraham,* 31: "And then shall righteous men of thy seed be left in the number which is kept secret by me, hastening in the glory of My Name to the place prepared beforehand for them. . . ." Cf. the *speudontas* of 2 Pet. 3:12.
16. Licht, "Taxo," 95–103; cf. Carlson, "Vengeance and Angelic Mediation," 85–95.
17. S. Mowinckel, *He That Cometh* (Oxford: Basil Blackwell & Mott, 1956), 297.

*B. Bat.* 10a (R. Judah, ca. 170–200 A.D.); *b. Sanh.* 97b (R. Samuel b. Nahmani [middle Amoraic] in the name of R. Jonathan [early Amoraic]); *b. Sanh.* 98a (R. Alexandri, early Amoraic); *b. Yoma* 86b (R. Jonathan, early Amoraic); and *y. Ta'an.* 63d (R. Joshua b. Levi, early Amoraic).

Reference may likewise be made to the Synoptics. Elsewhere we have argued in detail that Matt. 23:39 = Luke 13:35b ("I tell you, you will not see me again, until you say, 'Blessed be he who comes in the name of the Lord'") is a conditional prophecy which exhibits a standard form found in declarations attributed in *b. Sanh.* 98a to Ze'iri, R. Ḥama b. Ḥanina, R. Simlai, and R. Ḥanina, in *b. 'Abod. Zar.* 51a to R. Jose, and in *b. Sanh.* 98b to *Rab.*:

(a) statement about the messianic advent with adverbial particle of negation attached;
(b) conditional particle;
(c) condition to be met (in Israel) for fulfillment of the messianic advent.[18]

On our reading, Jerusalem can, if she will, bless in the name of the Lord the one who will come, and her doing so—that is, her repentance—will lead to deliverance. Even more patent is the implication of Luke 18:1–8, the parable of the unjust judge, in which the eschatological act of salvation is represented as an *answer* to the cry for justice: for the sake of his elect who cry out to him day and night, God will act speedily, will hasten the day of salvation.[19] One should compare Mark 13:20, a verse which may or may not go back to Jesus. Here God "shortens"—again for the sake of his elect—the days of tribulation. One could not wish for a more explicit statement on God's freedom to abandon an eschatological timetable. Another telling text is Matt. 6:10 = Luke 11:2 ("Thy Kingdom come"), the ramifications of which have been seldom grasped. Every other petition in the Lord's Prayer is uttered in the hope that God hears and answers the requests of his people. Does not the instruction to pray "Thy kingdom come" presuppose that the coming of God's kingdom is—like bread, forgiveness, and deliverance—a proper object of petition? Should not those who utter the words hope that God will indeed incline his ear and hasten salvation? In short, does not Luke 11:2 = Matt. 6:10 imply that the supplication of the saints can reach God and move him to act and bring the kingdom? Cf. *b. B. Meṣ* 85b (prayer can bring the Messiah).

If the Pseudepigrapha, rabbinic literature, and the Synoptics are all familiar with the notion of a contingent eschatology, what of the early church? 2 Peter

---

18. Dale C. Allison, Jr., "Matt. 23:39 = Luke 13:35b as a Conditional Prophecy," *JSNT* 18 (1983): 75–84.
19. Cf. Jörg Jeremias, *Die Ruhe Gottes*, 121; and Joachim Jeremias, *New Testament Theology*, 140.

3:11–12[20] and *2 Clement* 12[21] are much too late to tell us anything about primitive Christianity. Acts 3:19–21 is a different matter. In this passage, the apostle Peter appeals to the people of Jerusalem, "'Repent . . . and turn again, that your sins may be blotted out, that the times of refreshing may come from the presence of the Lord, and that he may send the Christ appointed for you, Jesus. . . .'" These words, which surely derive from a pre-Lukan source,[22] contain quite plainly a contingent eschatology. If only Israel would repent and turn from her sins, God would send times of refreshing—that is, he would send Jesus the Messiah—and all that the prophets spoke of concerning the redemption would come to pass. This is exactly the conception we have encountered in the Pseudepigrapha, in rabbinic literature, and in the Synoptics. Acts 3:19–21 is thus evidence that this Jewish conviction was shared by someone or some group within early Christianity and probably within very early Christianity, in view of the presumably primitive Christology embedded in the third chapter of Acts.[23]

Two other texts point in the same direction. In Mark 13:10 Jesus is represented as saying, "'The gospel must first be preached to all nations.'" This verse—which, with its absolute use of *to euaggelion* and the reference to a Gentile mission, we cannot trace back to Jesus—makes the completion of the eschatological prophecies wait upon a human activity: God will not bring the kingdom until his people have completely discharged their divinely appointed task. Also of interest for our theme is Mark 13:20—if it does not go back to Jesus (an uncertain issue). "'And if the Lord had not shortened the days, no human being would be saved; but for the sake of the elect, whom he chose, he shortened the days.'" Here, as already remarked, the time of the eschatological crisis is thought of as lasting for a fixed period of time, yet it is also a period of time God can—indeed, will—shorten. For the sake of the elect, God in his mercy is capable of altering the course ordained for the events of the latter days.

To judge from the three texts just cited, the concept of a contingent eschatology seemingly found a home in the church very early on. What factor or factors encouraged this? It was possible for the followers of Jesus, picking up on their pre-Easter expectations, to interpret their master's death and resurrec-

---

20. New English Bible: "Look eagerly for the coming of the Day of God and work to hasten it on."

21. Lightfoot: "These things, if ye do, saith He, the kingdom of my Father shall come."

22. See Ferdinand Hahn, "Das Problem alter christologischer Überlieferungen in der Apostelgeschichte unter besonderer Berücksichtigung von Act 3, 19—21," in *Les Actes des Apôtres: Traditions, rédaction, théology,* BETL 48, ed. J. Kremer (Louvain: Louvain Univ. Press, 1979), 129–54.

23. See Richard F. Zehnle, *Peter's Pentecost Discourse,* SBLMS 15 (Nashville: Abingdon Press, 1971), 44–60, 71–94, 131–35.

tion as the beginning of the eschatological process: the great tribulation and the general resurrection of the dead had begun. But this interpretation left a few loose ends, for the eschatological words of Jesus did not have to do with the fate of one man. Their orientation was towards a collectivity, the faithful community. Jesus had spoken not of his own death and resurrection as isolated events but of the great tribulation and the general resurrection of the dead. When, therefore, he passed through death and entered into vindication alone, this was not perfectly in harmony with the prophecies. One could in spite of this proclaim that, with the passion and victory of Jesus, the eschatological drama had opened, and this the disciples did proclaim. But there remained an inconsistency between the communal dimension of the promises and their initial realization in a solitary figure. Jesus had never intimated that he would rise first or by himself, or that the general resurrection would take place in stages over a stretch of time. But how could this be? How could the course of events not correspond exactly to the expectations of the Lord? Why had only one man achieved the final destiny? Why had God gathered the first sheaf of the great and last harvest and then left the rest of the field untouched? These are questions which almost certainly arose not after the Lord had tarried for fifteen or twenty years but questions which posed themselves as soon as Jesus was believed to have risen from the dead.[24] They were inevitable given the tension between the communal orientation of the pre-Easter prophecies and their fulfillment in one person.

We suggest that, at this point, the idea of the contingency of prophecy entered the church and served its purpose. Remembering the words of Jesus that taught the necessity of repentance before the redemption, his disciples judged that the program half-begun waited upon the repentance of the people. For this reason they preached, Repent and turn, that times of refreshing might come from the Lord, and that he might send the Messiah (cf. Acts 3:19–20). To prepare for the Day of the Lord, the gospel had to be preached (cf. Mark

---

24. Contra Paul J. Achtemeier, "An Apocalyptic Shift in Early Christian Tradition: Reflections on Some Canonical Evidence," *CBQ* 45 (1983): 231–48; he considers only the delay of the Parousia over the decades of the first century to be the decisive factor which led to a revision of eschatological doctrine. Achtemeier is also to be faulted for eliminating all traces of "realized eschatology" from Q and Mark, and for downplaying the note of fulfillment in the authentic Paulines—all of which leads to a one-sided view of the development of early Christian eschatology. A similar complaint is to be lodged against C. L. Mearns, "Early Eschatological Development in Paul: The Evidence of I and II Thessalonians," *NTS* 27 (1981): 137–57. But he, in attempting to prove that Paul and his earliest converts believed in an almost entirely "realized eschatology," puts things exactly the other way around: the "already" of the first churches became less and less distinct as the "not yet" came into prominence. In our judgment, surely the fact that Achtemeier and Mearns can come to such conflicting conclusions signals the need for a higher synthesis, one which can account for the early community's "realized eschatology" as well as for its forward-looking glance.

13:10). The missionary impulse was thus given with the resurrection itself, for this last created a note of discord between expectation and outcome and accordingly led to reflection on the contingency of prophecy, which in turn led to missionary activity. It is telling that the accounts of the appearances to the Twelve all contain a command to carry on missionary work (Matt. 28:19; Mark 16:15; Luke 24:47; John 19:21).

There is another point to be considered. Not only was belief in a coming resurrection bound up with a communal dimension but, in the eyes of Jesus, resurrection and Parousia were functionally equivalent: both referred to the coming vindication of the saints after tribulation. That is, Jesus (and we should add, his followers, at least at first) did not distinguish between the resurrection and the Parousia of the Son of man. But the events of Easter made such a distinction necessary; for although Jesus had risen from the dead, the Son of man had not, obviously, come on the clouds of heaven. Here then was one more difficulty facing those who felt compelled to maintain the integrity of Jesus. This moves us to reiterate a point made previously. Consciousness of a delay in the eschatological proceedings first appeared in the earliest community. It is an error to think that a contingent eschatology could arise only at a later time because only at a later time were Christians forced to face a *Parusieverzögerung.*

## The Origin of the Second Advent

Before we close this chapter, it may be observed that our results bear on— indeed, resolve—the origin of the doctrine of the second advent. The New Testament contains two strands of eschatology that stand in tension. One stresses the "already," the other the "not yet." These two strands correspond to the first and second advents. Now, according to Glasson and Robinson, the doctrine of the second advent was no original part of the most primitive Christian preaching but arose later, in part out of hesitation as to whether the history already accomplished (the history of Jesus) could fully be the eschatological event.[25] With this we agree. The idea of two advents cannot be found in the authentic words of Jesus, if by that it is meant that Jesus looked forward to two separate acts of vindication—namely, resurrection and the Parousia of the Son of man. Yet another explanation for the origin of belief in a second coming must be offered.

The pre-Easter hope was corporate, but Jesus passed through tribulation alone, and his followers obviously did not share in his resurrection. Further, although Jesus was proclaimed as raised from the dead, the church could not

25. Glasson, *Second Advent;* Robinson, *Jesus and His Coming.*

announce that the Son of man had come upon the clouds in judgment, for that hope was bound up with too many things that had clearly not taken place. Thus, Easter marked the fulfillment of certain pre-Easter expectations but left others unfulfilled, with the result that these last were naturally moved to another advent, the Parousia of the Son of man. It is hardly surprising, then, that the New Testament contains an "already" and a "not yet." Easter, interpreted within the context of pre-Easter prophecies, split the predictions of Jesus and thereby inevitably implied a doctrine of two advents.

This solution is not wholly novel. Many years ago Kirsopp Lake wrote that the prophecies of Jesus were interpreted by his followers in two ways. "Some they regarded as prophecies of the Resurrection. . . . But the resurrection did not seem completely to satisfy their expectation, and thus they regarded other sayings as prophecies of the second coming."[26] Although not buttressed by the kind of reasoning we have given, this statement offers an accurate insight. The confrontation between the words of Jesus and the actualities of history compelled the disciples to see the dominical utterances as referring to two different occasions: resurrection at the first advent, Parousia at the second.

The differences between our own position and that of Glasson and Robinson derive from dissimilar interpretations of Jesus' eschatological announcements. According to Glasson and Robinson, the passion and resurrection (and the later downfall of Jerusalem) truly fulfilled—without remainder—the expectations Jesus held for the near future. On our view, Jesus looked for much more. His words predict much that has never come to pass, and this was as obvious to his disciples as it is to us. For example, the coming of the Son of Man on the clouds of heaven, however symbolically understood, was for Jesus part and parcel of the final judgment; it was tied in with the general resurrection of the dead, with the gathering of all peoples before the throne of almighty God. How could Easter have fulfilled this expectation? Again, many of the words of Jesus have, as we have seen, a collective dimension, but the passion and resurrection of one man did not. Jesus met his fate alone. So how could the followers of Jesus see their eschatological hopes completely realized in the end of their master? In the last analysis, it is the pre-Easter eschatological expectations, as reconstructed herein, which prohibit the postulation that a fully "realized eschatology" accompanied the birth of Christianity. The

---

26. Kirsopp Lake, *The Historical Evidence for the Resurrection of Jesus Christ* (New York: G. P. Putnam's Sons, n.d.), 258. See further 255-59, and note Brown, *Gospel According to John*, 2:730: "A distinction between seeing Jesus at the time of his post-resurrectional appearances and seeing him at the time of his parousia may well have been a distinction formulated by the early Church precisely when it came to realize that all Jesus' promises had not been fulfilled in his appearances after the resurrection. Such a distinction would not be original in sayings stemming from the ministry."

early preaching held both an "already" and a "not yet." It proclaimed two acts of vindication. If Jesus' expectations were, as contended in this essay, the starting point, then after Easter there must have existed a twofold proclamation: the Christ has come and has been raised from the dead, and the Christ will come again in glory on the clouds of heaven.

## Conclusion

The chief contribution of this work lies in delineating the original connection between two items, the first being the early church's use of eschatological language to interpret the passion and resurrection of Jesus, the second being the eschatological expectations of Jesus and his disciples, as far as these can be reconstructed. The evidence compels us to conclude that the former is a reinterpretation of the latter; it represents an attempt to bring history into concord with prophecy. Moreover, the attempt to achieve such concord evidently encouraged both the appearance of a contingent eschatology within the primitive community and belief that the eschatological prophecies of Jesus had in part been misunderstood.

The frequent attempts to discuss the history of early Christian theology without repeated recourse to the teachings of Jesus of Nazareth are, on sociological grounds, highly suspect; and the present work has demonstrated at least one point at which it is necessary first to understand words of Jesus before one can understand certain beliefs of the early church. The Christian community was not God's creation *ex nihilo* after Easter. Its nucleus was established before the resurrection. Too much critical work proceeds as if the disciples had been whisked off to heaven with Jesus, as if the church at Pentecost were like to Melchizedek—without father or mother or genealogy. But the post-Easter community was heir to the pre-Easter Jesus movement, and the life and teachings of Jesus were constitutive for the first believers. In fact, if our argument is sound, the "inaugurated eschatology" that is on so many pages of the New Testament reveals the continuity between the pre- and post-Easter periods, for it is to be explained by the fact that the early church was compelled to come to terms with the eschatological prophecies of Jesus. These last, indeed, constituted the framework within which the members of the Way thought.

# EXCURSUS: BELIEF IN
# THE RESURRECTION OF JESUS

By arguing that beliefs of the pre-Easter period decisively influenced post-Easter formulations of faith, and by claiming that the resurrection of Jesus (as part of the general resurrection) was already an object of hope in the days of the earthly ministry, have we not supplied an explanation for the onset of Easter faith? Is it not possible to regard the affirmation "God has raised Jesus from the dead" as arising not so much out of post-Paschal experiences as out of pre-Easter eschatological expectations? Certainly, other messianic movements have declared the fulfillment of prophecy in the face of the hostile verities of history. Why see anything different in early Christianity? Ernest Renan wrote long ago: "Enthusiasm and love do not know of the impossible, and, rather than renounce all hope, they do violence to reality.... The faith of the disciples would have been sufficient to have invented it [the resurrection] in all its parts."[1]

An application of the theory of cognitive dissonance to faith in the resurrection of Jesus might take the following form. The disciples believed that Jesus would pass through the eschatological drama, that he would suffer, die, and be vindicated. When, after Good Friday, they were confronted by his suffering and death, they were able to take a step of faith and come forward with the proclamation that Jesus had not only suffered and died but, in accordance with expectation, been raised from the dead. On this account of things, the preaching of the resurrection was the product of pre-Easter hopes, an attempt to maintain previously established convictions. One could compare the story of Joanna Southcott and her followers' belief in Shilo (see 143 herein). Expecting their prophetess to bring forth from her womb the coming world deliverer, they postulated after her death that she had indeed been with child but that God had taken the infant into the heavenly places. Another parallel could be drawn from the Millerite movement (see 144). When the date

1. Ernest Renan, *The Apostles* (New York: Carleton, 1871), 54.

163

set for the coming of Jesus Christ transpired without incident, faith declared that the Lord had in fact come—but it was an invisible coming, in the heavens, not on earth. The lesson is evident: eschatological expectations can dictate their own fulfillment without the cooperation of history.

Of the many attempts to account for Easter faith on purely naturalistic grounds, this, in our estimation, is one of the most plausible. A closer look at the data, however, prohibits us from embracing it. A comparison of pre-Easter eschatological expectations with post-Easter proclamation and several other considerations disallow resolution by sociological analysis.

(1) The theory of cognitive dissonance requires as its point of departure the existence of some tension between two cognitions or beliefs. But before the appearances of the risen Lord, no cause for dissonance existed. The disciples had, it appears, suffered a moral collapse, for they scattered when their master was arrested (Mark 14:50; John 16:32); and Peter, although he had dared to follow the crowd that had taken Jesus, did not have the courage to confess his allegiance to the Nazarene (Mark 14:54–72; John 18:15–18, 25–27). Nevertheless, the passion of Jesus had done nothing to confute the disciples' eschatological expectations. Jesus had taught the presence of the eschatological tribulation. Thus, when he met his end, it would have been natural and in accord with the expectations of social psychology for his followers (1) to interpret his death as part of the final chaos; (2) to anticipate for themselves suffering and violent ends in the near future; and (3) to keep their eyes firmly fixed upon the coming resurrection, in which they and their master would share vindication. Despite the assumption of many and of Luke 24:20–21,[2] there was nothing in the crucifixion itself—however much of a stumbling block it was because of Deut. 21:23—that contradicted the eschatological expectations of Jesus or of his disciples; there was nothing to extinguish hope. A martyr's fate agreed perfectly with what Jesus had predicted. Thus, the teacher's end could only have confirmed his followers' outlook. Where can one find in this the opportunity for dissonance?

The resurrection, on the other hand, did not conform so nicely to what was expected in the pre-Easter period, for with Easter faith "a piece of eschatology was split off from the end of the world and planted in the midst of history."[3] As we have already seen, the resurrection stood in tension with the collective character of Jesus' prophecies. So Schweitzer was correct: given their hopes, it was "almost unintelligible that His disciples were not involved in His fate."[4]

---

2. "Our chief priests and rulers delivered him up to be condemned to death, and crucified him. But we had hoped that he was the one to redeem Israel." This is probably redactional.

3. George Eldon Ladd, "Apocalyptic and New Testament Eschatology," in *Reconciliation and Hope*, ed. R. Banks (Grand Rapids: Wm. B. Eerdmans, 1974), 295.

4. Schweitzer, *Quest*, 392.

Moreover, the good news of the resurrection implied two acts of vindication—the resurrection of Jesus and the coming of the Son of man—and thereby split asunder what Jesus' words had held together. Hence, however surprising the result, it seems that belief in the resurrection of Jesus, but not knowledge of the crucifixion, would have forced the disciples to reinterpret their expectations. Far from being the straightfoward product of dissonance, Easter faith appears to have been, if anything, the cause of dissonance. We are not surprised that the accounts of the appearances of the risen Lord portray the disciples as full of doubt and disbelief (Matt. 28:17; Mark 16:14; Luke 24:38; John 20:24–25; see further below).

(2) Even if, contrary to our conclusion, conditions after the passion and before Easter were favorable for creating dissonance, one would still perhaps hesitate to explain the resurrection as the result of a refusal to abandon prophetic dreams. For while we have documented cases in which the falsification of prophecy did not wreck belief, it is even easier to cite cases where it did. Jewish messianism supplies numerous instances of unfulfilled promises, and Jews have usually had the good sense to confess their delusions when they have been unmasked as such (see further below). On the Christian side, when the English messiah Richard Brothers (1752–1824), "God Almighty's nephew," was imprisoned, his followers disbanded, and his support dissipated. No life remained in the movement.[5] The same thing happened upon the death of "the Peasants' Saviour," John Nicholas Tom (1799–1838). When he was killed in a revolt that he had instigated in the English countryside, faith faded. The death of the leader was the death of his movement.[6] Examples could be multiplied. It is not always the case that "faith procures for herself all the illusions she needs for the conservation of her present possessions and for her advance to further conquests."[7] One must also recognize that, even when a movement survives misdirected prophecy, it frequently falls into a crisis and loses many members. Most of the Millerites abandoned their adventist faith; only a few were able to believe that Jesus Christ had in fact returned. Most of the followers of Joanna Southcott gave up the cause when she died. Those who continued were a minority. Again, the apostasy of Sabbatai Şevi, while it did not destroy Sabbatianism, was certainly the occasion for considerable defection.[8]

5. See Matthews, *English Messiahs*, 87–125; and Chamberlin, *Antichrist and the Millennium*, 110–30.
6. See Matthews, *English Messiahs*, 129–59.
7. Thus, Alfred Loisy, *The Birth of the Christian Religion*, trans. L. P. Jack (London: George Allen & Unwin, 1948), 98.
8. See Scholem, *Sabbatai Şevi*, 687–820.

It is difficult to determine why some individuals or groups are able to persist in illusion despite the shocks of external reality and why others cannot do so. But without resolving the issue, it is clear, in view of the preceding remarks, that faith is not always capable of upholding itself against the verdict of history, and "we cannot ... generalize in advance with respect to the possible dislocative or transforming character of events and causes."[9] One therefore cannot assume, as a matter of course, that the disciples of Jesus would have proclaimed, against all reason, his resurrection. This judgment is reinforced by Martin Hengel's observation that for a whole row of messianic movements around the first and second centuries A.D. the violent death of the leader meant the end of the movement. So was it with the Samaritan prophet executed by Pilate, with Theudas, with the one-time slave Simon, with the shepherd Athronges, with Andreas Lukuas, and with Simon bar Kokba. The failure of the leader was, one guesses, understood by his followers to be God's judgment.[10]

(3) Additional support for the direction of our argument can be inferred from a motif found in the postresurrectional narratives of the Gospels. These report that news of the empty tomb and of a vision of angels by women met with disbelief on the disciples' part (Luke 24:11, 22–24) and that confrontation with the risen Lord was the cause of doubt and confusion (Matt. 28:17; Mark 16:14; Luke 24:37–38; John 20:24–25). It is possible that these notes of unbelief served an apologetic function: the evidences for Jesus' resurrection were so compelling that they even convinced doubters. But it is more likely that an historical memory has here been preserved: the disciples were not completely credulous; they had difficulties coming to faith. If so, this is an important datum. The ability to violate reality and to create fictions does not long abide in company with doubt and skepticism; for such ability comes from "an historical consciousness" that can "absorb the shocks of external reality," from an "emotional reality which nothing in the realm of 'outward' events ... can shake."[11] The exhibition of doubt is the first step in recognizing the "tension between inner and outer truth"[12] for what it is—namely, the child of vain illusion. Thus, one may reasonably hold, in conformity with the picture everywhere met with in the New Testament, that without the encouragement of certain post-Easter experiences there would have been no proclamation of the resurrection of Jesus. The cause of Jesus, like that of John the Baptist,

9. Thus, Robert A. Nisbet and Robert G. Perrin, *The Social Bond,* 2d ed. (New York: Alfred A. Knopf, 1977), 291.

10. Martin Hengel, "Is der Osterglaube noch zu retten?," *TQ* 153 (1973): 262.

11. Scholem, *Sabbatai Şevi,* 689.

12. Ibid., 691.

might have continued, but its contours would not much resemble those of the faith that produced the New Testament.

(4) If belief in the resurrection of Jesus had been chiefly the consequence of pre-Paschal faith, one would expect a much closer correspondence between expectation and fulfillment than actually obtains. For example, one of the fundamental focuses of the eschatological words of Jesus was, on our reading, the coming of the Danielic Son of man. But this focus does not reappear in 1 Cor. 15:3-8 or in the postresurrectional stories in the Gospels. Why are the accounts of resurrection appearances not filled with the imagery of eschatological expectation? Why does the resurrected Lord not come on the clouds of heaven? And why is it that the appearance narratives find their closest parallels neither in the prophetic teachings of Jesus nor in the apocalyptic literature but in the anthropomorphic theophany narratives of the Old Testament? In sum, why is it, if the words of Jesus were the primary source from which the Easter faith sprang, that the appearance narratives and 1 Cor. 15:3-8 mirror those words so poorly? Supposing that our primary sources have reliable testimony to contribute, it is difficult altogether to reduce the reports of encounters with the risen Lord to projections of eschatological expectations formed at the feet of Jesus. (And it should perhaps be observed in passing that pre-Easter expectation can in any case have had nothing to do with Paul's visionary experience and conversion; and presumably James, the brother of Jesus, was not a believer before Easter [Mark 3:21, 31-34; John 7:5] but only after he had an encounter with the risen Lord [1 Cor. 15:7]).

As we have argued throughout this book, the primitive community interpreted the resurrection of Jesus as the beginning of the general resurrection. But this does not entail that expectation of the general resurrection was the sufficient cause of faith in the resurrection of the one man, Jesus of Nazareth. We are persuaded that, at this point, we are dealing with an interpretation of events, not with an interpretation that postulated events.[13]

(5) The most profitable parallels with which to approach the resurrection appearances are, we suggest, not to be found in the study of messianic movements faced by the failure of prophecy but in the extensive literature on apparitions.[14] Whatever one makes of the fact, it cannot be disputed that

13. Matt. 27:51b-53, although a projection of faith, is not evidence to the contrary. It *presupposes* the sole resurrection of Jesus and seeks despite this to justify the collective dimension of the disciples' expectations. In other words, the text offers a secondary reflection and is not comparable with the fundamental declaration of Jesus' resurrection.

14. Particularly noteworthy are Edmund Gurney, F. W. A. Myers, and Frank Podmore, *Phantasms of the Living,* 2 vols. (London: Rooms of the Society for Psychical Research, 1886); and George N. M. Tyrrell, *Apparitions,* rev. ed. (New York: Collier Books, 1963).

visions of the recently deceased are rather commonplace. Even collective perceptions of the departed are well attested. This can hardly be irrelevant for the quest to understand belief in the resurrection of Jesus—even if the canonical narratives do present us with certain details seemingly without analogy. There is no good reason to doubt the united voice of our sources: the disciples of Jesus had visionary experiences, and these were the chief catalyst towards Easter faith (cf. 1 Cor. 15:3–8).[15] Thus, any satisfactory account of Easter should come to terms with the serious studies of apparitions. This is not to say that the appearances of Jesus must be seen as nothing more than typical instances of a common class (an inference we reject). Nevertheless, before one explains away the visions of the disciples of Jesus, one must explain away the similar visions others have had—a task which, it seems, has yet to be convincingly accomplished. And even if this were not so, the New Testament's claim that several groups and many individuals, not all of them believers, over a period of time and in diverse places, had visions of the risen Jesus, has no point of contact with the messianic movements and sects that we have investigated. The study of groups confronted by their own false prophecies does not much help us to explain the phenomenon of the appearances.

In our estimation, Easter faith came into the world by way of the interplay of three independent factors: visions ostensibly of Jesus, belief in his empty tomb, and pre-Easter eschatological expectations. Whether in this we are correct or not must be left for another time. Here, however, we can at least conclude that belief in the resurrection of Jesus is not likely to be explained away by the sociological fact that faith can, despite everything, declare the fulfillment of its hopes. The mystery of the resurrection is not dissolved so easily.

---

15. Against those who have denied that the *ōphthē* of 1 Cor. 15:3–8 refers to true visionary experiences and have rather affirmed that the verb is to be understood solely as part of a legitimation formula, see Eduard Schweizer's review of Klaus Berger's *Auferstehung des Propheten*, *TLZ* 103 (1978): 878.

# Thirteen

# SUMMARY AND CONCLUSION

The early church attached no single meaning to the death of Jesus. His death was understood in a variety of ways—as, for example, a sacrifice for sins (Rom. 3:25), an act of obedience (Phil. 2:5-11), or the death of representative man (2 Cor. 5:14) The resurrection likewise received no one interpretation. It was proclaimed to be the vindication of Jesus of Nazareth (Acts 2:22-36), the pledge of the coming resurrection of Christians (1 Cor. 15:12-28), and the basis of justification (Rom. 4:25). The history of Christian theology is largely responsible for determining to which of the various canonical interpretations of the death and resurrection of Jesus critical scholars have directed their attention. It is for this reason that the doctrine of Jesus' death as atoning sacrifice has received its fair share of attention. The same reason accounts for the insufficient notice paid to the primitive interpretation reviewed in these pages, an interpretation which employed eschatological categories; for Christian theology has rarely grappled seriously with the eschatological presuppositions that permeate the New Testament, and although the twentieth century is the century of Albert Schweitzer, contemporary students of the New Testament have yet to explore fully the importance of eschatological language for the early followers of Jesus. It has not, however, been our purpose to evaluate the tendencies of critical biblical scholarship but to explore some problems pertaining to early Christian eschatology.

In at least some early Christian circles, language that Judaism typically reserved for discourse about eschatological expectations came to be associated with the end of Jesus. Jesus' resurrection was interpreted not as an isolated event but as part of the general resurrection, and his death was understood as though it were a death in the great tribulation of the latter days. Perhaps the most persuasive evidences for this assertion are to be found in Matthew and Mark, in which the passion of Jesus is associated with eschatological motifs— such as the darkening of the sun (Mark 15:33) and a resurrection of saints (Matt. 27:51b-53)—as well as with eschatological scriptures, especially Zechariah 9—14. But the first two books of the New Testament are not the only sources for the tradition to which we have called attention. In the Pauline epistles, the sufferings of the apostle and those of his Lord belong to the "messianic woes," and the resurrection of Jesus is seen as part and parcel of the eschatological resurrection of the dead. The Fourth Gospel is also a witness to the eschatological interpretation of the end of Jesus; for John's fully developed "realized eschatology" seems to have had its point of departure in pre-Johannine traditions that portrayed the passion and resurrection as inaugurating the prophetic denouement.

Why did the first Christians associate the end of Jesus with motifs otherwise connected with the end of the age? The closest parallels to the phenomenon in question occur in Jewish texts for which past occurrences and present experiences belong to the eschatological time of trouble. The explanation of such texts is this: events of history were thought sufficiently close to eschatological expectations so as to encourage some Jews to believe that certain of those expectations had come and were coming to pass. Something similar happened in the early church. Jesus had proclaimed that the kingdom of God was at hand, that eschatological suffering and resurrection were near. Hence, when he suffered and died and subsequently appeared alive to his followers, they concluded that the eschatological drama had opened, that the final tribulation had begun with the suffering and death of the Messiah, that the general resurrection had begun with his resurrection. In brief, the eschatological expectations of the pre-Easter period were drawn upon in the attempt to understand the crucifixion and Jesus' conquest of death.

This was almost inevitable. People strongly tend to interpret their experiences in terms of previously established categories and prior expectations. This remains the case even when those categories and expectations have been revealed as less than perfectly adequate. In fact, messianic movements have, again and again, and against the cold facts of history, interpreted prophecies in such a way that their "fulfillment" could be announced as realized. Scrutiny of such groups as the Seventh-day Adventists, Jehovah's Witnesses, and the Church of the True Word clearly demonstrates that expectation has frequently dictated fulfillment. Thus, the distinctiveness of primitive Christianity can hardly lie in its claim that eschatological promises had been fulfilled.

By way of conclusion, two final points should be made. First, our thesis is, in essence, quite simple. The followers of Jesus—whose religious expectations and outlook had been largely shaped by the days of the earthly ministry—interpreted the passion and the events of Easter in terms of the pre-Easter expectations. This should surprise no one. Jesus was among other things a teacher, a commanding authority. One might have anticipated that, if he had preached the imminence of tribulation and resurrection, and if he had suffered and died and been seen again alive, his friends would have concluded that his end belonged to the end of the age.

Second, if our thesis is simple, it also has utility. It accounts for the signs and wonders at the cross, for the systematic employment of Zechariah 9—14 in the passion narratives, and for the parallels between Mark 13 and Mark 14—16. It explains why Paul was convinced that the great tribulation had entered the present with the passion of Jesus and why he spoke of the resurrection of Jesus as the "first fruits," as the beginning of the resurrection of all the saints. It makes sense of the fact that, as we have seen, a contingent eschatology appeared quite early on within the church. It reveals the original function of the several Gospel texts that tell how the disciples of Jesus misunderstood prophecies of their master. It elucidates the origins of "over-realized eschatology," of the claim that the Day of the Lord had fully come (cf. 2 Thess. 2:2) and that the resurrection was already past (cf. 2 Tim. 2:18). It resolves the debate over whether Christianity began with a "realized eschatology" or with an intense, forward-looking expectation—by showing how it could, and indeed did, begin with both, that is, with an "inaugurated eschatology." And in general, it explains those facts that led Dodd to speak of "realized eschatology." The eschatological prophecies of Jesus were believed to have met their initial fulfillment in the Messiah's death and resurrection. Thus had dawned the great Day of the Lord.

# EPILOGUE:
# THEOLOGICAL REFLECTIONS

It is not out of place to observe, however briefly, that the results of our historical investigation are relevant to the concerns of Christian theology.

(1) A paradox runs throughout the teaching of Jesus and much of the New Testament. On the one hand, language descriptive of the eschatological tribulation is used to describe the present. There is not peace but a sword (Matt. 10:34). The kingdom of God is suffering violence (Matt. 11:12). That which is lacking in the sufferings of Christ is even now being filled up (Col. 1:24). On the other hand, Jesus and the first Christians speak as though the blessings of the messianic age or the age to come had already appeared. Satan has fallen like lightning from heaven (Luke 10:18). Those in Christ know a new creation (2 Cor. 5:17). The hour is coming *and now is* when the dead will hear the voice of the Son of God and live (John 5:25). It is difficult to imagine any greater paradox than that created by the juxtaposition of such statements as these. Of the latter days of affliction we read in Daniel that "'there shall be a time of trouble, such as never has been since there was a nation till that time'" (12:1). Mark puts it similarly: "'In those days there will be such tribulation as has not been from the beginning of the creation which God created until now, and never will be'" (13:19; cf. *As. Mos.* 8:1 and Rev. 16:18). A glance at *4 Ezra, 2 Baruch,* the Apocalypse (Book of Revelation) and other pertinent sources gives substance to these prophecies: the seers use the blackest shades to portray the terrors of the end. By way of contrast, the descriptions of the coming salvation lack for nothing. According to Rev. 21:1–8, for example, all things will be made new; God will dwell with men, and they will be his people; death and pain and tears will be no more; the former things will pass away. What then do we make of the people who could interpret their experience as partaking simultaneously of the unsurpassed evils of the latter times and of the unsurpassed blessings of the eschatological redemption?

At least three things may be said. First, any satisfactory religious interpretation of human existence must take account of the extreme polarities or contradictions that run throughout life. Ours is a world of malevolence and madness, of sin and shame, of fear and folly, of innumerable lessons never learned. Ours is a world of death and pain, of disease and pestilence. Indeed, such is our world that in it dwell people who find it impossible to acknowledge their creator. And yet ours is also a world in which one may know love and friendship, experience delight and ecstasy, acquire knowledge and wisdom. Moreover, if we accept the testimony of the saints, it is possible, even in this world, to gain the vision of God and achieve holiness. Thus, human experience in general and religious experience in particular are marked by intense paradoxes. It is not difficult to understand what Pascal meant when he wrote, "It is incomprehensible that God exists, and it is incomprehensible that he does not exist."[1]

Jesus and the early Christians, using the language of eschatology, gave fitting expression to the contradictions of life when they proclaimed the presence of both eschatological tribulation and eschatological salvation. The extremes of human experience are such that they are effectively represented by the extremes of eschatological expectation. If Jesus and his followers had discovered in their midst only the terrors of the end, then their faith would have been too weak, their hope too small, and the distance between them and God too great. If they had spoken only of the realization of the blessings of the future age, then their religion would stand exposed as an illusory flight from the inescapable contradictions of life. By recognizing the realities of both tribulation and salvation, Jesus and his followers show us that their eyes were wide open.

Second, the declaration that tribulation and salvation were present was, for the early Christians, largely a christological statement. The messianic woes had shown themselves above all in the passion and death of Jesus, and the general resurrection had been inaugurated with Jesus' resurrection. Hence, the eschatological pattern of suffering—vindication had found its focus in one person. This implies that the polarities of human existence were most evident in Jesus, that faith saw in him, as nowhere else, life's contradictions. That which men both feared and hoped for when they spoke of the end of the age— the ultimate terrors and the ultimate blessings—had appeared in Jesus of Nazareth. Jesus was a man of sorrows, one acquainted with grief. He was rejected by his own. He had nowhere to lay his head. He lived with the knowledge that a cruel end awaited him. Others called him names—blasphemer, drunkard, glutton. He was tortured and crucified; and his life ended with a question, "My God, my God, why hast thou forsaken me?" But if Jesus

---

1. Blaise Pascal, *Pensées*, intro. and notes by Ch.-Marc des Granges (Paris: Gernier Freres, 1964), 134.

had known the depths of tribulation and despair, he had also passed through them to the other side; he had attained the eschatological glory. Crucifixion was followed by resurrection. "God has highly exalted him and bestowed on him the name which is above every name, that at the name of Jesus every knee should bow, in heaven and on earth and under the earth, and every tongue confess that Jesus Christ is Lord, to the glory of God the Father" (Phil. 2:9–11). Thus, Jesus stood—and stands—as the paradigm of our paradoxical existence, his story demonstrating the inextricable bond between suffering and salvation, his life exhibiting the extremes of terror and beatitude. Moreover, his vindication after his passion is the pledge to Christians that, ultimately, those who trust in God will overcome the ambiguities of this life and enter into a better world.

Third, the first Christians thought of eschatology as in process. They proclaimed that events of the latter days had begun to occur, and on this assumption they interpreted Jesus' work. It is not easy for us today to think that in this they are correct; for quite simply, nearly 2,000 years have come and gone, and the messianic age has not appeared. Nevertheless, the eschatological interpretation of Jesus' fate should not be completely abandoned. If the first advent did not, for whatever reason, inaugurate the eschatological process, it did, so Christians affirm, mark the fulfillment of many promises that Judaism held to be outstanding—which is why Jesus is confessed to be the Christ. Above all, the life for which the best and most religious of us have longed—the life of the world to come—has appeared in Jesus, and those who are joined to him can share that life. "In him was life, and the life was the light of men" (John 1:4). "If any one is in Christ, he is a new creation; the old has passed away, behold, the new has come" (2 Cor. 5:17). It is therefore inevitable that the church use eschatological language to describe the significance of Jesus. And insofar as the traditions studied in this book express the truth that the Christ-event brought into the world things otherwise only hoped for, their meaning should be maintained.

(2) "Is there anything more ludicrous in the history of Christianity than the stream of apocalyptic prophets and publicists whose announcements of the proximity of the end of history have long since been overtaken by its course?"[2] The answer to this question is probably no. Thus, one is hardly edified by the knowledge that a *Naherwartung* runs throughout much of the New Testament. Matters are even more difficult because Jesus himself, according to our sources, spoke of the eschatological transition as impending. Is this not cause for stumbling?

2. Bernard McGinn, Introduction to *Apocalyptic Spirituality*, trans. B. McGinn (London: SPCK, 1971), 1.

Joachim Jeremias has faced the problem we are concerned with and has proposed that the answer lies in the *Selbstaufhebung* of the will of God.[3] He also claims that Jesus' unfulfilled hopes were an expression of his being very man: they belonged to the incarnation. But he finds the significant fact to be that the God of the Bible can rescind his declared will. From the Old Testament he cites Jer. 18:7–10:

"If at any time I decree concerning a nation or kingdom that I will pluck up and break down and destroy it, and if that nation, concerning which I have spoken, turns from its evil, I will repent of the evil that I planned to do to it. And if at any time I decree concerning a nation or kingdom that I will build and plant it, and if it does evil, then I will repent of the good that I had planned to do to it." (RSV revised)

From the New Testament he calls attention to Mark 13:19–20; Luke 13:6–9; and Luke 18:7–8, in which Jesus teaches or implies that God can alter his holy will. Above the holiness of God, Jesus places the grace of God, who can shorten the time of affliction or lengthen the season of grace.

Jeremias has offered a valid insight. The standard generalizations about the determinism of the apocalypses and their distance from the prophetic perspective have obscured an evident fact—namely, that there stands beside the eschatological hopes of the New Testament the awareness that prophecies are to some degree contingent. If Jesus and his followers announced that the kingdom of God was near, and if they hoped for that above all, they believed at the same time that God might have mercy upon his people and thus put off the judgment (Luke 13:6–9); and they called upon the people in Jerusalem to repent so that God might send the Messiah from heaven (Acts 3:18–22); and they encouraged people to live righteous lives in order to hasten the coming of the Day of the Lord (2 Pet. 3:12). There is, then, a tension in the New Testament. There is a *Naherwartung*. But there is also belief that any particular prophecy isolates only one of the possible course of events that appears in the mind of God, a course that can be communicated either as a warning that may or may not be heeded or as a promise whose conditions may or may not be met.

It is our suggestion that this idea of the conditional nature of prophecy might help us to formulate an interpretation of biblical eschatology. Before developing our argument, however, we must stop to consider the problem of the meaning of eschatology in general.

W. D. Davies has written that intense eschatological expectation,

---

3. Joachim Jeremias, *New Testament Theology*, 139–41.

emerging and re-emerging again and again in time of extreme suffering and despair, is the expression, in the light of the divine purpose, of a legitimate critical response to the iniquities, corruptions, and distortions of this world, to which, alas, most of us are at least half-blind. It is the element of divine discontent, of the desire for something afar, of the aim which exceeds our grasp. Without this discontent, the dead hand of custom, stagnation, and insensitivity throttles life, and even ancient good becomes uncouth. From this point of view, apocalyptic is the leaven of history. Its societal and cosmic imagery, symbols and hopes, which turn human longings to vivid expectations, are always necessary as a spur to sensitivity and a corrective against a false, irresponsible, individualistic piety....  A literature produced when man is at the end of his tether has its own stark, unblinded, and penetrating insight, even though its actual practical counsels, born of despair, are often dubious.[4]

This is a sensitive attempt to come to grips with what Davies calls the "positive side" of "apocalyptic"—as far as it goes. But it does not go far enough. The discontent of those looking for the end may, at times, become the leaven of history. But eschatology tends to look beyond history, or at least sees history in the light of a future that differs radically from the present. Thus, it is not to be interpreted primarily as a cry directed towards human beings. It is not chiefly a plea to the established to repent and give themselves to the disenfranchised. Eschatology is first of all hope in God: it knows the divinity as the only power which can bring about eschatological reversal and redemption. To be sure, God acts through his people, and the persistence of messianic and millenarian movements should awaken us from self-contented slumber. But eschatological hope believes that justice and meaning will not be finally established by or through any force in this world, that these things can only come to our world from without, to history from outside of history. Only the transcendent God can justify himself, vindicate his people, cast out all evil, overcome meaninglessness. It is with faith in such a God that eschatology looks expectantly into the future. In the following sentences from *The Brothers Karamazov*, Dostoevski gave expression to this faith:

> I trust that the wounds will heal, the scars will vanish, that the sorry and ridiculous spectacle of Man's disagreements and clashes will disappear like a pitiful mirage, like the sordid invention of a puny, microscopic Euclidean, human brain, and that, in the end, in the universal finale, at the moment universal harmony is achieved, something so magnificent will take place that it will satisfy every human heart, allay all indignation, pay for all human crimes, for all the blood shed by men, and enable everyone not only to forgive everything but also to justify everything that has happened to men.[5]

4. W. D. Davies, "From Schweitzer to Scholem: Reflections on Sabbatai Svi," *JBL* 95 (1976): 529–58.

5. Feodor Dostoevski, *The Brothers Karamazov*, trans. A. R. MacAndrew (New York:

Embedded in these words is, I submit, the heart of eschatological hope. What then do we make of it?

If God is the god of the Scriptures, it is difficult to deny that, sometime and somewhere, Dostoevski's vision must be realized. Only when God satisfies every human heart, allays all indignation, pays for every crime, and justifies his ways with humanity will he be revealed and known in his fullness. Thus, it is legitimate, even necessary, for us to think that beyond this world, in the transcendent order, the foolishness of God will be revealed as wisdom and every wrong made right. We might leave matters at that, except for one thing. Jesus and his disciples were more than Platonists. They hoped that the eschatological promises would be realized not only beyond history but within it, that the transcendent order would merge with the mundane order—and soon. This is the difficulty.

Dostoevski also treated of the last things in "The Dream of a Ridiculous Man," a short story which recounts what the title states. The dream itself concerns an unfallen world, a planet far away. Having told us of this wonderful world, Dostoevski writes that our world could be like that one, and that "in one day, *in one hour,* everything could be arranged at once! The main thing is to love your neighbor as yourself—that is the main thing, and that is everything, for nothing else matters.... If only we all wanted it, everything could be arranged immediately."[6] In other words, heaven on earth would come about if we would only obey the commandment to love. In this our author shares something with certain traditions in the New Testament, traditions that speak of repentance as the precondition for the coming of the kingdom of God on earth. He is, admittedly, less confident than the New Testament that men will repent, and thus the fulfillment of the vision within history is precarious. Dostoevski nevertheless writes that he will fight for the truth of his dream: he will seek to persuade men to love their neighbor.

It is our conviction that, if the hope of eschatological fulfillment within history is to retain any sense, it must follow Dostoevski's lead. We may, perhaps, be assured that, beyond history, all will be well. But within history there is no certainty, and humanity bears a terrible responsibility. We cannot, to be sure, build God's kingdom, and thus, no human institution can ever be legitimately identified with that kingdom. And yet God waits upon humanity. Just as the salvation of the individual is God's work but at the same time requires a believing response (grace not being effective unless the object of its bestowal responds as grace demands), so the arrival of the kingdom of God on

Bantam Books, 1970), 283.

6. Feodor Dostoevski, "The Dream of a Ridiculous Man," in *Great Short Stories of Fyodor Dostoevsky,* trans. D. Magarshack, et al. (New York: Harper & Row, 1978), 738.

earth can only be conceived of as a work of God that will not be established unless humanity participates. This is why the gospel must first be preached to all peoples (Mark 13:10). The kingdom does not come to unbelief. Hence, the church, professing a faith that can move mountains (Mark 11:23), must undertake the task of preparing for the redemption—and do so believing that "salvation history is not a fixed scheme but rather a living occurrence between God and men."[7]

Eschatology, then, has two points of realization, one certain, the other uncertain. The victory of God on the arena of eternity is assured. But his victory within the limits of the finite is not. The millennium is the goal of history, the great lodestone, the ever-beckoning ideal towards which we strive, but its achievement is not certain. So although comforted by her confidence in God's ultimate triumph beyond this world and hopeful of participation in that triumph, the church's comfort should be tempered, for humanity is answerable for the course of history; and if the kingdom is no longer at hand but afar off, the people of God must acknowledge their failure. When human beings do not repent and love their neighbors, we must in some measure blame ourselves.

(3) The sociologist would have few misgivings in affirming that Christianity began as a messianic movement. And as we have seen, much that went on in the early church can profitably be compared to much that has gone on elsewhere in groups looking for an imminent redemption. Theology cannot ignore this fact. It will not go away. So what does one say?

First, most messianic movements uphold important truths. They invariably recognize the full magnitude of evil in our world and serve to call our otherwise distracted attention to it. (One is inclined to think that their exaggerated mythological depictions of wickedness are often more useful and valid than more accurate but mundane analyses.) Furthermore, evil is, for messianic movements, a religious problem with nothing but a religious solution. In this their instincts are sound. Our world is not sufficient of itself to establish its own meaning, and it certainly holds no solution for its own evils. Hence, it is right and necessary to look outside the normal course of history for answers. One should not, therefore, dismiss the hopes of messianic movements as nothing more than the pipe dreams of alienated peoples. Vital issues are here at stake.

Second, if Christianity began as a messianic movement, it soon became much more. Indeed, the New Testament contains documents in which the meaning of Jesus Christ is already separated from the idea of an inaugurated eschatological process. We have in mind primarily the Gospel and epistles of

---

7. M. Künzi, *Das Naherwartungslogion Markus 9,1,* Beiträge zur Geschichte der biblischen Exegese 21 (Tübingen: J. C. B. Mohr [Paul Siebeck], 1977), 208.

John. In these the new life brought into the world by Jesus is presented in all its fullness, even though the original eschatological framework has been modified. For John, the application of eschatological language to Jesus and to the time of the church does not entail that the last drama has opened and is about to close. A process of reinterpretation has gone on here. The theologian may regard it as precedent for contemporary attempts to maintain the significance of the eschatological interpretation of Jesus. Thus, for example, the Johannine literature supplies some justification for Pannenberg's argument that God has already made known the meaning of history because in Jesus he has revealed history's end: Jesus is the proleptic revelation of the consummation.[8] It seems to us that this idea opens one promising path theology might take in reinterpreting primitive Christianity's eschatological understanding of Jesus Christ.

Finally, one must never forget the fundamental role that the person of Jesus played in early Christianity. His words and story, even character, were decisive in shaping the Christian movement. They left an indelible stamp. It is telling that the New Testament opens with four books which purport to tell us about Jesus of Nazareth—and that no gospels were written about apocalyptic seers or rabbis. At the heart of Christianity is a person. He is the one treasure of the Christian religion, its pearl of great price. Whatever one's conclusions about eschatological doctrine or millenarian movements, Jesus Christ remains to be reckoned with, embodying in his own person the word with which he commands us—from heights we know not of—to love the Lord our God with all our heart, soul, strength, and mind, and our neighbor as ourself.

---

8. Wolfhart Pannenberg, "Dogmatic Theses on the Doctrine of Revelation," in *Revelation as History*, ed. Wolfhart Pannenberg, trans. D. Granskou (London: Macmillan & Co., 1968), 125–28.

# INDEX OF PASSAGES

# INDEX OF NAMES

# INDEX OF SUBJECTS